International Political Economy Series

Series Editor: **Timothy M. Shaw**, Visiting Professor, University of Massachusetts, Boston, USA and Emeritus Professor, University of London, UK

Titles include:
Morten Bøås, Marianne H. Marchand and Timothy Shaw (*editors*)
THE POLITICAL ECONOMY OF REGIONS AND REGIONALISM

Paul Bowles and John Harriss (*editors*)
GLOBALIZATION AND LABOUR IN CHINA AND INDIA
Impacts and Responses

James Busumtwi-Sam and Laurent Dobuzinskis
TURBULENCE AND NEW DIRECTION IN GLOBAL POLITICAL ECONOMY

Bill Dunn
GLOBAL RESTRUCTURING AND THE POWER OF LABOUR

Myron J. Frankman
WORLD DEMOCRATIC FEDERALISM
Peace and Justice Indivisible

Fred Gale and Marcus Haward
GLOBAL COMMODITY GOVERNANCE
State Responses to Sustainable Forest and Fisheries Certification

Richard Grant and John Rennie Short (*editors*)
GLOBALIZATION AND THE MARGINS

Graham Harrison (*editor*)
GLOBAL ENCOUNTERS
International Political Economy, Development and Globalization

Adrian Kay and Owain David Williams (*editors*)
GLOBAL HEALTH GOVERNANCE
Crisis, Institutions and Political Economy

Dominic Kelly and Wyn Grant (*editors*)
THE POLITICS OF INTERNATIONAL TRADE IN THE 21st CENTURY
Actors, Issues and Regional Dynamics

Sandra J. MacLean, Sherri A. Brown and Pieter Fourie (*editors*)
HEALTH FOR SOME
The Political Economy of Global Health Governance

Craig N. Murphy (*editor*)
EGALITARIAN POLITICS IN THE AGE OF GLOBALIZATION

Morten Ougaard
THE GLOBALIZATION OF POLITICS
Power, Social Forces and Governance

Henk Overbeek and Bastiaan van Apeldoorn (*editors*)
NEOLIBERALISM IN CRISIS

Jørgen Dige Pedersen
GLOBALIZATION, DEVELOPMENT AND THE STATE
The Performance of India and Brazil since 1990

K. Ravi Raman and Ronnie D. Lipschutz (*editors*)
CORPORATE SOCIAL RESPONSIBILITY
Comparative Critiques

Ben Richardson
SUGAR: REFINED POWER IN A GLOBAL REGIME

Simon Rushton and Owain David Williams (*editors*)
PARTNERSHIPS AND FOUNDATIONS IN GLOBAL HEALTH GOVERNANCE

Marc Schelhase
GLOBALIZATION, REGIONALIZATION AND BUSINESS
Conflict, Convergence and Influence

Herman M. Schwartz and Leonard Seabrooke (*editors*)
THE POLITICS OF HOUSING BOOMS AND BUSTS

Leonard Seabrooke
US POWER IN INTERNATIONAL FINANCE
The Victory of Dividends

Stuart Shields, Ian Bruff and Huw Macartney (*editors*)
CRITICAL INTERNATIONAL POLITICAL ECONOMY
Dialogue, Debate and Dissensus

Timothy J. Sinclair and Kenneth P. Thomas (*editors*)
STRUCTURE AND AGENCY IN INTERNATIONAL CAPITAL MOBILITY

J.P. Singh (*editor*)
INTERNATIONAL CULTURAL POLICIES AND POWER

Susanne Soederberg, Georg Menz and Philip G. Cerny (*editors*)
INTERNALIZING GLOBALIZATION
The Rise of Neoliberalism and the Decline of National Varieties of Capitalism

Kenneth P. Thomas
INVESTMENT INCENTIVES AND THE GLOBAL COMPETITION FOR CAPITAL

Helen Thompson
CHINA AND THE MORTGAGING OF AMERICA
Economic Interdependence and Domestic Politics

Ritu Vij (*editor*)
GLOBALIZATION AND WELFARE
A Critical Reader

Matthew Watson
THE POLITICAL ECONOMY OF INTERNATIONAL CAPITAL MOBILITY

Owen Worth and Phoebe Moore
GLOBALIZATION AND THE 'NEW' SEMI-PERIPHERIES

Xu Yi-chong and Gawdat Bahgat (*editors*)
THE POLITICAL ECONOMY OF SOVEREIGN WEALTH FUNDS

International Political Economy Series
Series Standing Order ISBN 978–0–333–71708–0 hardcover
Series Standing Order ISBN 978–0–333–71110–1 paperback

You can receive future titles in this series as they are published by placing a standing order.
Please contact your bookseller or, in case of difficulty, write to us at the address below with
your name and address, the title of the series and one of the ISBNs quoted above.

Customer Services Department, Macmillan Distribution Ltd, Houndmills, Basingstoke,
Hampshire RG21 6XS, England

Neoliberalism in Crisis

Edited by

Henk Overbeek
*Professor of International Relations, VU University
Amsterdam, The Netherlands*

and

Bastiaan van Apeldoorn
*Reader in International Relations, VU University
Amsterdam, The Netherlands*

First published 2012 by
PALGRAVE MACMILLAN

Palgrave Macmillan in the UK is an imprint of Macmillan Publishers Limited, registered in England, company number 785998, of Houndmills, Basingstoke, Hampshire RG21 6XS.

Palgrave Macmillan in the US is a division of St Martin's Press LLC, 175 Fifth Avenue, New York, NY 10010.

Palgrave Macmillan is the global academic imprint of the above companies and has companies and representatives throughout the world.

Palgrave® and Macmillan® are registered trademarks in the United States, the United Kingdom, Europe and other countries

ISBN: 978–0–230–30163–4

This book is printed on paper suitable for recycling and made from fully managed and sustained forest sources. Logging, pulping and manufacturing processes are expected to conform to the environmental regulations of the country of origin.

A catalogue record for this book is available from the British Library.

A catalog record for this book is available from the Library of Congress.

10 9 8 7 6 5 4 3 2 1
21 20 19 18 17 16 15 14 13 12

Printed and bound in Great Britain by

CPI Antony Rowe, Chippenham and Eastbourne

Contents

Tables and Figures

Tables

Figures

Abbreviations

ALBA	Alianza Bolivariana para los Pueblos de Nuestra América (Bolivarian Alliance for the Peoples of Our America)
BNDES	Banco Nacional de Desenvolvimento Econômico e Social (Brazilian National Development Bank)
BRIC	Brazil, Russia, India and China
CAPM	Capital Asset Pricing Model
CasP	Capital as power
CC	Comparative Capitalism
CCP	Chinese Communist Party
CEEP	European Centre of Employers and Enterprises providing Public Services
CEE	Central and Eastern Europe
CEO	Chief Executive Officer
CIC	China Investment Corporation
CME	Co-ordinated Market Economy
CNOOC	China National Offshore Oil Company
CSR	corporate social responsibility
CUT	Central Única dos Trabalhadores (United Workers' Centre, Brazil)
DME	Dependent Market Economy
EC	European Community
ECB	European Central Bank
ECJ	European Court of Justice
EP	European Parliament
ERT	European Round Table of Industrialists
ETUC	European Trade Union Confederation
ETUI	European Trade Union Institute
EU	European Union
FDI	foreign direct investment
FIH	financial instability hypothesis
FIRE	finance, insurance and real estate
FTAA	Free Trade Area of the Americas
G-20	Group of Twenty
G-7	Group of Seven
GATT	General Agreement on Tariffs and Trade
GDP	gross domestic product

GNI	gross national income
IASB	International Accounting Standards Board
IMF	International Monetary Fund
IOCs	International Oil Companies
LME	Liberal Market Economy
LTV	Labour Theory of Value
MAS	Movimiento Al Socialismo (Movement towards Socialism, Bolivian political party)
MC	monopoly capital
MDIs	multilateral development institutions
MNCs	multinational corporations
MoF	Ministry of Finance
MPT	marginal productivity theory
MST	Movimiento Sin Tierra (Brazilian Landless Workers Movement)
MVR	Movimiento Quinta República (Fifth Republican Movement, Venezuelan Socialist Party)
NDRC	National Development and Reform Commission
NOCs	National Oil Companies
NSS	National Security Strategy
OECD	Organisation for Economic Co-operation and Development
OPEC	Organization of Petroleum Exporting Countries
PBoC	People's Bank of China
PIW	Petroleum Intelligence Weekly
PNAC	Project for the New American Century
PSUV	Partido Socialista Unido de Venezuela (United Socialist Party of Venezuela)
PT	Partido dos Trabalhadores (Brazilian Workers' Party)
RMB	Renminbi (national currency of China)
ROCE	return on capital employed
ROE	return on equity
SAFE	State Administration of Foreign Exchange
SEC	Securities and Exchange Commission
SIA	Securities Industry Association
SME	state-permeated market economies
SNA	social network analysis
SOEs	state-owned enterprises
SWFs	sovereign wealth funds
TNCs	transnational corporations
TUAC	Trade Union Advisory Committee to the OECD

UK   United Kingdom
UNICE   Union des Industries de la Communauté Européenne
          (Union of Industrial and Employers' Confederations of
          Europe)
US   United States
USAID   United States Agency for International Development
WB   World Bank
WEF   World Economic Forum
WTO   World Trade Organization

Preface

The idea for this volume was conceived during several discussions among the core members – Bastiaan van Apeldoorn, Laura Horn, Andreas Nölke, Henk Overbeek, James Perry, Arjan Vliegenthart and Angela Wigger – of the erstwhile Amsterdam Research Centre on Corporate Governance Regulation (ARCCGOR, 2004–2009). Having completed what was our core business, that is, the four doctoral dissertations by Angela, Laura, James and Arjan, we originally intended to produce a volume centred on our collective work on the political economy of corporate governance regulation in order to present a coherent summary of our results. But the dynamics of our respective careers made it impossible to fulfil this project. As such things go, our group was quickly dispersed over universities in different European countries (Arjan even left academic life altogether), and each of us was facing new and demanding tasks in teaching and administration. In addition, each of us started a new phase in our research, often collaborating with new colleagues on issues that followed up on, but simultaneously had a different focus than, our collective work of the years before. However, we all felt there was enough overlap in our interests to maintain some sort of permanent affiliation: this was done through the creation of a virtual research network, the Amsterdam Research Center for International Political Economy (www.arcipe.eu), which our newest recruit, Naná de Graaff, also joined. During the founding meeting in the summer of 2010, we found that our new research interests had one common issue of overlap: the crisis that the neoliberal global order was thrust into by the still deepening disorder in the world's financial markets. And thus it happened that we decided to abandon the idea of writing a book summarizing our past research, resolving instead to produce a book on this overlap in our current research. By including in these plans some of the new colleagues with whom we had started to collaborate in other projects, we expanded our original group. The result is a collection of papers that, although coming from a variety of theoretical and methodological traditions, cohere through the fact that they address the same set of historical developments: the impact on the contemporary capitalist order (both and simultaneously in the key capitalist economies and globally) of the global crisis.

We wish to thank the editors at Palgrave Macmillan, in particular Series Editor Tim Shaw, for their enthusiastic support and for enabling us to get to the finish line in a relatively short period of time.

Contributors

Bastiaan van Apeldoorn, Reader in International Relations, Department of Political Science, VU University Amsterdam, The Netherlands.

Hubert Buch-Hansen, Assistant Professor, Department of Intercultural Communication and Management, Copenhagen Business School, Denmark.

Naná de Graaff, Doctoral Researcher, Department of Political Science, VU University Amsterdam, The Netherlands.

Sandy Brian Hager, Doctoral Researcher, Department of Political Science, York University, Toronto, Canada.

Laura Horn, Associate Professor, Department of Society and Globalisation, University of Roskilde, Denmark.

Paul Lewis, Lecturer in Comparative Employment Systems, Birmingham Business School, University of Birmingham, United Kingdom.

Andreas Nölke, Professor of International Political Economy, Department of Political Science, Goethe University, Frankfurt, Germany.

Henk Overbeek, Professor of International Relations, Department of Political Science, VU University Amsterdam, The Netherlands.

James Perry, Assistant Professor, International Center for Business and Politics, Copenhagen Business School, Denmark.

Andreas Tsolakis, Post-Doctoral Fellow in the Institute of Advanced Study at the University of Warwick, United Kingdom, and analyst at the Fundación Secretariado Gitano in Madrid, Spain.

Angela Wigger, Assistant Professor of International Relations and Global Political Economy, Department of Political Science, Radboud University Nijmegen, The Netherlands.

1
Introduction: The Life Course of the Neoliberal Project and the Global Crisis

Bastiaan van Apeldoorn and Henk Overbeek

In the wake of the fall of Lehman Brothers on 15 September 2008 and the subsequent near-total collapse of the global financial system, many predicted the end of the world of liberal capitalism or at least announced the death of the neoliberal ideology that had helped to constitute the global order over the past decades. The people making these predictions were those who had been leaders in espousing that ideology in the first place. Thus Francis Fukuyama, in October of 2008, declared that the 'American model' borne out of the Reagan revolution was 'the culprit' that had caused the crisis and worried that it would take many years to restore the damage to the 'American Brand' (Fukuyama 2008), while *Financial Times* columnist Martin Wolf (2009) argued that the 'era of liberalization contained the seeds of its own destruction'. Former Chairman of the Federal Reserve Alan Greenspan in a congressional hearing even famously admitted that his free market ideology was apparently 'not working', that there was 'a flaw in the model' that he had been working with for 40 years.[1] *The Economist* (2008), not quite buying the latter argument, did warn that 'economic liberty is [now] under attack and capitalism...is at bay'. In addition, the apparent failings of financial deregulation and liberalization as premised on the Washington consensus combined with worries about the rise of East Asian 'authoritarian state capitalism', producing concerns within Western elite circles regarding the survival of liberal capitalism itself (Bremmer 2010; Rachman 2011).

For some on the other side of the political spectrum, the 'crisis in the heartland' (Gowan 2009) not only spelled the end of neoliberalism, but also offered prospects for a more equitable and sustainable world.

Thus many shared the hope contained in Joseph Stiglitz's line that 'the fall of Wall Street is for market fundamentalism what the fall of the Berlin Wall was for communism' (Gardels 2008; Klein 2008; cf. Bond 2009; Albo et al. 2010; Peck et al. 2010). The moment of euphoria (like in 1989), however, did not last very long, and generally gave way to a much more sober mood, reflecting dismay about what is seen as the resilience of neoliberal practices if not an outright restoration, and in some respects even acceleration and further deepening, of the neoliberal project (cf. Peck et al. 2010; see also the contributions by Wigger and Buch-Hansen as well as Horn in this volume).

So the question must be raised whether, although the global financial and economic crisis from 2008 has obviously shaken the neoliberal consensus, this is a crisis *in* neoliberalism or a crisis *of* neoliberalism (cf. Saad-Filho 2010). In short, we tend to the view that the crisis is a crisis *of* neoliberalism, but not necessarily a terminal one: there is still life left for a phase of neoliberal dominance, but one wrought with deepening contradictions and increasingly unstable. Our arguments, which are borne out in the subsequent chapters in this book, can be summarized as follows.

First, although 'global finance' nearly derailed the global economy in 2007–2009, genuine reform of the financial sector throughout the Organisation for Economic Co-operation and Development (OECD) area has thus far been rather limited. Although many banks and other financial institutions have been (partially) nationalized or otherwise salvaged by capitalist states coming to the rescue of 'the system' in a global multi-trillion dollar bailout, government officials everywhere have been adamant in proclaiming that this is only a temporary measure, and that these institutions will be 'returned to the market' as soon as conditions allow.[2] Meanwhile many of the financial giants that survived the onslaught and escaped nationalization have restored much of their profitability (even if the outlook remains uncertain) and are again paying out big bonuses in spite of the public outcry (Murphy and Guerrera 2011; see also Henwood 2010). As the new CEO of Barclays Bank, Bob Diamond declared to the House of Commons Select Committee for the Treasury, 'the time for remorse is over!' (*The Guardian* 11 January 2011).[3]

Furthermore, in terms of government policy, most OECD governments are now hitting the brakes by going into full austerity mode. This return to neoclassical orthodoxy is particularly strong in the Eurozone, where the European Central Bank (ECB) and the German government are relentless in their imposition of the doctrine of balanced budgets and austerity programs on the Eurozone periphery (e.g., Bellofiore et al. 2010). In the US too, the brief and partial revival of Keynesianism (cf. Hay 2011) has given way to a return to austerity. The new austerity seems to be above all an excuse to make yet deeper cuts in social expenditure and public services and to pursue with renewed vigour the kind of 'reforms' (privatization and marketization) that neoliberals have advocated since the 1970s but were able to carry out with only partial, though not insubstantial, success until now. It thus appears as if neoliberalism, rather than having forever perished in the flames of the global financial crisis, is arising from its ashes like a phoenix (cf. Peck 2010: 275). As Alex Callinicos (2010: x) wrote in a recent book on the crisis of the liberal world, 'the illusions have survived the bonfire'.[4]

Third, the resilience of neoliberalism is also a reflection of the political weakness of any possible alternatives: there appears to be no 'counter-hegemonic project' in the making. This then seems to ensure what Bob Jessop (2010) calls the 'continuing ecological dominance of neoliberalism'. However, with Gramsci (1971: 276) we may argue that '[t]he crisis precisely consists in the fact that the old is dying and the new cannot be born'. That the new is not yet born, and that we are unable to perceive its shape, however, does not mean that in fact the potential for transformation is not there. Although processes of neoliberalization may still continue, neoliberalism as a hegemonic project resting upon wide societal consent does appear to be unravelling. Indeed, if nothing else, the crisis has further eroded what was an already weakening legitimacy of neoliberalism, possibly beyond repair. As such, the crisis may also be viewed as above all a crisis of the global hegemonic project of neoliberalism, or what Gramsci would call an 'organic crisis' of the neoliberal world order (cf. Gill 2010).

Actually, as in any historical rupture, the current crisis is a multilayered phenomenon. Yes, as argued above, the crisis is first of all simultaneously a crisis of the dominant accumulation model of the past decades, a crisis of the hegemonic ideology underpinned by that model, and consequently also a crisis of the political and social order in the heartland of global capitalism. In this book the emphasis will be predominantly on these aspects of the crisis of neoliberalism (see in particular Part I of this volume, dealing with the impact of the crisis on the nature of capitalist regulation in the heartland of global capitalism).

However, underneath this organic political and economic crisis lie two deeper layers that affect not only the appearance but also the shape of any possible future resolution of the current crisis. First, there is the crisis of the Anglo-American hegemony that has shaped the global capitalist order since its early days (cf. Van der Pijl 2006), expressing itself in the shift of the centre of gravity of global manufacturing towards East Asia, in the weakened position of the US dollar which has for so long underpinned US supremacy globally and indeed in a fundamental crisis of the ability of the US to impose its strategic supremacy world-wide. Second, there is the deep crisis of the ecosphere which has over the past decades been all but completely exhausted through the intense exploitation by capital, manifesting itself in the dual crises of climate change and fossil energy depletion, necessitating the creation of a new techno-industrial paradigm which will need to inform any potentially successful future accumulation model. These deeper layers of the crisis, while not the prime object of our attention in this introduction, do inform our understanding of the present and possible future trajectory of global neoliberalism (many aspects of these deeper layers of the global crisis are addressed in Part II of this volume).

In order to address these broad questions regarding crisis and continuity, we step back in this volume from the immediately apparent aspects of the crisis and focus on those contradictions revealing the limits of neoliberalism that were already visible before the crisis erupted. In this sense we go beyond recent literature addressing the theme of after/beyond neoliberalism, which displays a rather exclusive focus on the factors precipitating the (financial) crisis and its consequences (e.g., Albo et al. 2010; Panitch et al. 2010; McNally 2009 Duménil and Lévy 2011; Brand and Sekler 2009). However, before outlining in more detail the contents of this book, let us first elucidate its central *problématique* by (1) briefly outlining our understanding of neoliberalism and what we regard to be its central contradictions, and (2) indicating what might arise out of these contradictions in terms of possible trajectories of the post-crisis world.

The life course of the neoliberal project

We define neoliberalism as a political project aimed to restore capitalist class power in the aftermath of the economic and social crises of the 1970s and the challenge posed to the rule of capital globally by the call for a New International Economic Order (Overbeek and Van der Pijl 1993; also Harvey 2005; Plehwe et al. 2006). Such a project, or *comprehensive concept of control*, is characterized by (1) a specific and relatively coherent set of *ideas* on how to organize the accumulation of capital and the maintenance of the social order, and (2) a specific configuration of *social forces* that succeed in presenting their fractional interests as the *general interest*:[5]

> The capacity of a concept of control to become comprehensive, that is, to be effectively applied as a policy expressing the general interest by governments or international institutions, is based on its objective comprehensiveness (i.e., coverage of labour process, circulation relations, profit distribution, and state and international power relations) and on the particular balance between the 'systemic' requirements of capital accumulation and its concrete, momentary needs. The former tend to reflect the money capital perspective (economic liberalism), and will be most easily and eagerly propounded by those familiar to it by trade or tradition; the latter will tend to the productive capital viewpoint, reflecting the particularities of non–market, non–value aspects of the productive process and its immediate social setting. (Overbeek and Van der Pijl 1993: 3)

The *neoliberal project* is characterized by a mix of liberal pro-market and supply-side discourses (laissez-faire, privatization, liberalization, deregulation, competitiveness) and of monetarist orthodoxy (price stability, balanced budgets, austerity). These discourses express a prototypical *money capital perspective*: in the overall circuit of the expanded reproduction of capital, money capital is the form assumed by capital in general, the most abstract and mobile form of capital. Money capital strives to circumvent or eliminate all obstacles to its circulation, pursuing short-term profit and the abolition of capital controls and other state-imposed limitations on the free circulation of capital. Under neoliberalism the money capital perspective is not limited to the financial sector: in the guise of 'shareholder value' the same short-term monetary profit motive equally dominates what is sometimes called the 'real economy'.[6] The coalition of social forces whose fractional interests are articulated through these discourses is configured around the hegemonic fraction of transnational finance capital; it comprises not only the leading sections of the financial sector and a large segment of the leading transnational corporations, but also key segments of the 'new middle classes' and of organized labour.

Any hegemonic project needs not only a more or less coherent accumulation strategy serving the interests of the leading capital fractions and their immediate allies, but it also needs the political ability to mobilize majorities in parliamentary democracies, and a sufficient measure of at least passive consent. This is what Andrew Gamble has called a 'politics of support' (Gamble 1988: 208–241; see also ibid. 2009: 84–89). The result has been a two-thirds/one-third society character-ized by the rise of various forms of authoritarian and nondemocratic politics. In such societies, as Harvey reminds us, the neoliberal project seeks to disembed capital from its societal context and to insulate key market institutions from democratic accountability (Harvey 2005: 66; see also Gill 1995).

At the level of the global economy as a whole, the pursuit and pri-oritization of the free flow of capital has produced what we might call *really existing global governance*, i.e., the global governance of globaliza-tion through increasing informalization and various forms of private authority (see Overbeek 2010). Where the neoliberal project is not fully successful in establishing its hegemony or at least in enforcing compli-ance with the 'rules of the game', oppositional forces become the targets of destabilization and ultimately of some form of 'humanitarian inter-vention' (Van der Pijl 2006; see also Duffield 2001).

No hegemonic project is, or ever becomes, the direct and unmediated realization of the objectives and plans of its key 'authors'. Neoliberalism is no exception. The really existing neoliberalism of today is a far cry from what intellectual forebears like Hayek or Friedman would have considered as the realization of their dreams. Like any hegemonic project (see Figure 1.1), neoliberalism is a *project in motion*, continuously contested, a process of countless rounds of struggles and negotiations with oppositional forces, and of confrontations with what Gramsci called the 'limits of the possible'. A comprehensive concept of control is not a coherent and consistent set of ideas, policies and institutions put in place by an all-powerful group of actors, but it is what Drainville called an unending 'series of negotiated settlements' (Drainville 1994). This conceptualization of the neoliberal hegemonic project implies that neoliberalism does not have just one face, either in time or in space. The idea of neoliberalism as process requires us to understand and theorize diachronic and synchronic variations in the appearance of neoliberalism.

Let us first take a look at the *phases* that a hegemonic project goes through during its existence, its life course so to speak (see Figure 1.1).[7] A hegemonic project typically emerges during a crisis of the previously hegemonic project, which is delegitimized as a consequence of mount-ing contradictions and rising contestation by popular forces and by rival elite projects (as during the late 1960s and early 1970s in Britain with the crisis of the Keynesian compromise and the rise to power in the

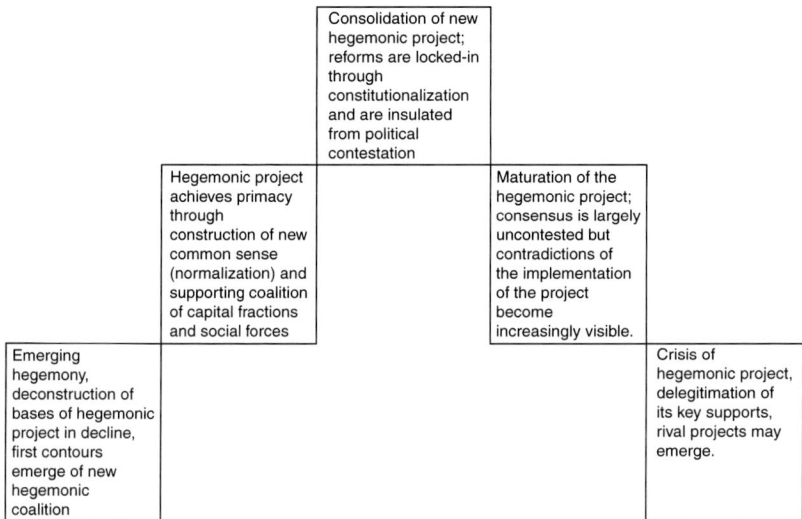

Figure 1.1   The life course of hegemonic projects

Conservative Party of the Thatcherites; Overbeek 1990). The first task, once the groups initially supporting such a new project come to power, is *deconstruction*: to destroy the coherence and remaining legitimacy of the previous hegemonic project. In these early phases in the emergence of a new hegemonic project, key roles are played by the organic intellectuals of the emerging new fractional configuration (for an excellent recent study of the rise of neoliberalism see Peck 2010; see also several contributions in Overbeek 1993). The hegemonic project then achieves primacy through the *construction* of a new common sense, or through the normalization of the new hegemonic discourse, and through the configuration of a supporting coalition of capital fractions and social forces that redefine their particular interests in the terms of the newly constructed and normalized 'general interest'.

It is during the *consolidation* phase of constitutionalization that certain crucial path dependencies are created. Interests become entrenched, ideologies become internalized, and in this manner institutional and ideological blockages arise that prevent an adequate response to emerging contradictions in later phases (as illustrated by the aforementioned confession of Alan Greenspan, who was at a loss to explain what happened with the crisis as it contradicted the model he had held on to for 40 years).

Consolidation in turn is followed by *maturation*. The new concept of control has become fully 'normalized', but contradictions begin to show in the practical implementation of policies (e.g., privatization of public utilities, which is derailed or produces unexpected and contrarian results). Maturation marks the transition from virtuous to vicious circle dynamics: hegemony begins to wear thin and show the first cracks. Finally, *delegitimation* marks the demise of the hegemonic project and the gradual emergence of a new one: contradictions in the implementation of the project mount, reproduction of hegemony in the heartland leans increasingly on authoritarian imposition rather than hegemonic consensus (something usually true of the periphery at all times) and germs of alternative projects and orders may slowly be taking root even if not yet very visible.

The transition from one hegemonic project to another, however, never entails a total rupture of previous structures at once, but is shaped by 'the paradoxical simultaneity of continuity/discontinuity in the flow of historical time' (Jessop and Sum 2006: 324). Such transitions are 'moments of disjunction and relative openness' in which different socio-economic forces search for new patterns of structural coherence in an experimental way (ibid.: 326). In such open and unstable conjunctures two types of outcome are possible: there can be a prolonged period of stalemate between conflicting social forces which may give rise to the emergence of Caesarism of some sort attempting to reproduce the existing social order in a non-hegemonic situation through the freezing of unresolved contradictions (cf. Cox 1987: 273, 285, 446 n. 30); or it may eventually usher in a new hegemonic era, with the ideas of those forces most in tune with the exigencies of capital accumulation most likely to succeed in elevating their particular fractional programme to the status of the new common sense (cf. ibid.: 273; Overbeek and Van der Pijl 1993: 4–5).

A final important point in the conceptualization of neoliberalism is its variegated appearance in different countries or regions (see also Brenner et al. 2010a). Neoliberalism does not have and cannot have the same features everywhere. A range of (interrelated and mutually constitutive) factors are responsible for the synchronic variation of *really existing neoliberalisms*. Among these are:

– the effects of the lack of synchronization between system time and local time; national neoliberalisms may be in different phases of the life course of neoliberalism, and may be out of synch with the life phase of neoliberalism in the transnationally hegemonic formations

- variation in the mode of insertion into world market structures; this may be explained by differences in economic structure or geographic factors
- path dependencies and historical legacies in terms of institutional structures; this is the main contention of the Varieties of Capitalism literature (e.g., Hall and Soskice 2001a)
- variation in the balance of class forces within countries, producing a relative autonomy of national politics
- variation in the composition of the hegemonic bloc as a result of the above (different configurations of hegemonic fractions of the bourgeoisie).

On this basis, it is possible, at any particular moment in time, to distinguish between various forms or versions of neoliberalism in different countries (e.g., Overbeek 1993; also Jessop 2010).

After neoliberalism? Possible trajectories of world order

As indicated, current developments suggest that we have not witnessed the final demise of neoliberalism. In several respects, and in different places and at different scales of governance, neoliberal practices continue unabated. On the other hand, few would dispute that the neoliberal project as such is in crisis and that this crisis does at least bring closer the prospect of various 'post-neoliberalisms'. Below we will first make the case for continuity, that is, the scenario that we will in fact be having more of the same in the years, if not decades, to come. We will then identify three dimensions of possible change to the neoliberal world order that would enable us to assess the potential for a transformation beyond neoliberalism. We will not make any definite predictions; we are dealing with a moving target and the instruments of social science are simply not up to the task of predicting with any degree of certainty what outcome these contradictory forces and tendencies will ultimately produce. The aim of these pages, and of the chapters to follow, is to give the reader a set of insights with which to read and interpret events as they unfold, and to determine which of the following trajectories seem to be supported or contradicted by them.

The case for continuity: the resurgence of neoliberalism

One early dissenter regarding the thesis that the current crisis heralds the end of neoliberalism has been David Harvey (2009, 2010; see also Bond 2009; Jessop 2010). Arguing that it must be seen as a 'class project, masked by a lot of neoliberal rhetoric about individual freedom, liberty, personal responsibility, privatization and the free market' (ibid.; see also Harvey 2005), he made the point that in restoring capitalist class power neoliberalism has been pretty successful and with current state responses to the crisis may very well continue that success. Thus, Harvey sees the bailout as fitting in a pattern of 'state power protecting financial institutions at all costs', and hence solving the crisis (only) for the capitalist class (ibid. 2009).

Understood as a global marketization and commodification project, ultimately serving the ongoing private accumulation of capital, the neoliberal project from his perspective might not only be set to continue for years to come, but may even get a new impulse from the global financial crisis on the one hand, and from structural developments in the world economy, in particular the way China has been brought into the capitalist world market, on the other. On the one hand, then, we can notice how throughout much of advanced capitalism a neoliberal policy framework remains rather firmly in place. For instance in the European Union, where the European Commission has launched a successor to the Lisbon strategy (called *Europe 2020*) that offers the same neoliberal recipes of labour market flexibilization and welfare state retrenchment (Van Apeldoorn and Hager 2010), and, as indicated, throughout the OECD area through a new austerity currently being imposed and likely to deepen neoliberal restructuring.

On the other hand, the rise of China as a state-led capitalist power, and less spectacularly, the rise of such capitalist powers as Brazil and India, can in itself be seen as an important step in the further development of global capitalism as a project of creating a system of global circuits of capital accumulation replacing the old national circuits (Robinson 2004), and with that in further pushing for marketization and commodification on a world scale. First, the integration of 1.3 billion Chinese into the circuits of global capital accumulation as both consumers and workers over the past decades since the gradual economic liberalization started under Deng Xiaoping in 1979 has been a giant step in the historical process of capitalist globalization. David Harvey, for instance, has included the Chinese market reforms in his brief history of neoliberalism, referring to it as 'neoliberalism with Chinese characteristics' (Harvey 2005: 120–151). Second, the global expansion, whether partly state-led or not, on the part of Chinese banking and industrial capital, buying up firms, setting up plants, engaging in transnational joint ventures, and so forth around the world, furthermore continues to contribute to and to deepen the global commodification process (see Arrighi 2008).

In sum, in light of these developments, and in spite of the ideological crisis of neoliberalism, neoliberalism as embedded in 'state structures, policy instruments and the political field of social forces' (Albo 2009: 121) may as yet continue its life. Peck et al. (2010: 105) came to a similar conclusion:

> Neoliberalism's intellectual project may be practically dead, but, as a mode of crisis-driven governance, it could be entering its zombie phase..., animated by technocratic forms of muscle memory, deep instincts of self-preservation, and spasmodic bursts of social violence.

In this scenario we are likely to witness a transnational restoration of neoliberalism as a globally dominant project and practice. This would then also imply the restoration of some semblance of a liberal order under rejuvenated US tutelage. However, even if we thus might see neoliberalism surviving another round, the question is for how long, and whether the contradictions engendered by a replay of the financial expansion of the past two decades would not in the end prove too sharp to resolve within the boundaries defining the neoliberal order. Thus, more speculatively, we now examine some possible pathways towards post-neoliberalism.

Pathways beyond neoliberalism

Within the trajectory of capitalist modernity we may identify many different capitalist class projects or, at a somewhat higher level of abstraction, concepts of control coalescing around particular fractional viewpoints. Although it is true that we should not take all the 'free market' rhetoric of neoliberalism at face value, part of this does reflect a genuine interest bound up with particular class fractions. In this sense we should not lose sight of the specificity of neoliberalism as a *particular* class project as we have outlined in the previous section. It may well be that the state's rescue (of the global financial elite), even if seemingly contradicting neoliberal ideology, will allow the continuation of this particular class project, but only in as far as transnational capital in general and financial capital in particular will see its nearly unlimited freedom of movement restored. On this the jury is still out.

It seems at least as likely that here we will observe some changes, that is, in the balance between different capital fractions, and within the overall constellation of social forces, and how this crystallizes into state power and the way the latter regulates the capitalist economy. In as far as significant changes would take place in this respect, this then would mean that we move beyond neoliberalism; possibly leading to the rise, nationally and transnationally, of a new hegemonic project or projects, articulating a political and socio-economic programme with what could also develop into a new accumulation strategy. But the succession of one hegemonic project by a next one is not a given. If the history of the Great Depression is anything to go by, it will require more than the near collapse of global finance alone to bring about such a pendulum swing. Conditions for such a transition in the 20 years after the Great Crash of 1929 included sharp repression of and much lower living standards for the working class in the core capitalist countries (fascism and national socialism), a large scale devaluation of existing capital stock and the political defeat of the previously dominant capital fractions (iron and steel, heavy machinery) in the War, the gradual application and spread of new production techniques (assembly line production) and new key sectors (petrol, motor cars), the gradual construction (New Deal, Keynesianism, liberal corporatism) of institutional structures supportive of a new phase of rapid capital accumulation and the elimination of barriers to the international expansion of capital (Bretton Woods, GATT).

Another possibility would be a prolonged period in which no new transnational hegemonic order emerges. Robert Cox (1987) referred to the era following the decline of British hegemony in the 1870s as a non-hegemonic world order with, in many societies, a stalemate between rival concepts and configurations of social forces, and with geopolitical confrontations between contending blocks internationally.

The outcome of the current crisis of the neoliberal order will be decided in and through struggles between contending social forces in relation to the state, and will thus depend precisely upon how and to what extent the overall balance of social forces is reconfigured, new class and state strategies are adopted and new projects articulated. Although theoretically the outcome of such struggles might move us not just beyond neoliberalism but also beyond capitalism, for now all the signs are clearly that there might be a crisis *of* neoliberalism, but this takes place *within* capitalism (Alvater 2009; cf. also Brenner et al. 2010b). Furthermore, *within* the limits of the capitalist mode of production we must distinguish between more progressive and more reactionary post-crisis forms.

In seeking to assess whether, and if so, how, a post-neoliberal order is arising, we can analyse change along different dimensions. Here we distinguish three such dimensions that we deem to be critical aspects of the neoliberal world order as it has been constructed over the past decades and that also relate to the main themes addressed in this volume: the dominant accumulation strategy, the issue of the legitimacy of the status quo, and finally the geopolitical dimension of the global order.

Financial regime change

The first dimension relates to the finance-led accumulation strategy that was central to the neoliberal project, and with that the hegemony of financial capital (see above). This raises the question of what Robert Wade (2008) has aptly called 'financial regime change', that is, whether we are now moving beyond the financialized capitalism that had nearly brought us to the brink of a total collapse of global capitalism. A resurgence of productive capital, especially if in alliance with labour, would be progressive inasmuch as this would imply a return to the era when, as Eric Helleiner (1993) so forcefully put it, finance was the servant (rather than the master) of the real economy, and hence allowing for more 'embedded' (Polanyi 1957) capitalist markets. For now, the quick restoration of the profits of at least a significant part of the financial sector, as well as the continuing disarray in which organized labour finds itself, does not point in the direction of such an alliance. At this point in time we may well see another round, albeit possibly quite short lived, of finance-led growth in the leading capitalist centres (see Germain 2010 for a different view).

The legitimacy crisis of neoliberalism and contending responses

The second dimension concerns what we could call the Gramscian dimension of neoliberal hegemony. As a project clearly driven by the interests of particular capital fractions (transnational capital generally, and financial capital in particular), to what extent and how was neoliberalism ideologically articulated with the interests of subordinate classes and grounded in a measure of institutionalized consent? Although there has been considerable debate on the extent to which this has been the case (a debate that we cannot go further into here), what is clear is that inasmuch as such consent existed it is currently eroding (Albo et al. 2010; Panitch et al. 2010; Callinicos 2010; also see Gamble 2009). This then raises the question to what extent any alternative (counter-) hegemonic project might emerge to take its place. This again is crucially linked to the questions of the overall configuration of class forces (transnationally and within the key capitalist formations) and of how (partly contingent) politico-ideological struggles will play out.

On the one hand, the economic crisis has clearly deepened the political and social crisis of neoliberal capitalism; indeed, it has deepened the legitimacy crisis of states throughout the OECD (for analysis of the EU in this respect see Van Apeldoorn et al. 2008). On the other hand, the fear that this initially instilled in the ruling classes, a fear, most palpable in the immediate aftermath of the September 2008 fall of Lehman Brothers, that the crisis might spell the death of liberal capitalism, seems to have receded by now. Still, given the contestation of neoliberalism that we have already witnessed in the past decade or so, a resurrection of neoliberal orthodoxy is unlikely to go unopposed. Whether in the context of these struggles neoliberalism will morph into something else or will be replaced by a genuinely more progressive mode of socio-economic regulation remains an open question. The outcome here is of course very much interdependent with that regarding the first dimension.

The power shift in the world economy and geopolitical implications for neoliberal world order

Crucially, neoliberal globalization has thus far been built on the foundations of US hegemony, conceived as the outward projection of the hegemony of the leading fractions of US capital (Cox 1987; Van der Pijl 1984). US hegemony thus understood has been crucially dependent on the territorial power of the US state (e.g., Gowan 1999; Wood 2003; Panitch and Gindin 2005). From this perspective, neoliberalism has been bound up with the need for the continuing subordination of any potential rival and thus the financial, economic, political and military supremacy of the US in every region (e.g., Van der Pijl 2006; Cafruny and Ryner 2007). At the same time, as a project restructuring the world economy, neoliberalism has been bound up not only with financialization but also with the shift of manufacturing, in particular to East Asia, which thus has become 'the centre of a new burst of world-accumulation' (McNally 2009: 50). The dialectics of neoliberal globalization have thus created a situation in which the hegemonic position of the US, one of the cornerstones of the neoliberal global order, may now very well be under threat from the rise of Asia, and in particular, China (Jacques 2009; Van der Pijl 2010; Arrighi 2009). Two aspects must be noted here. One is the fact that China in particular represents a different 'variety of capitalism' than that which has become hegemonic in the West. As Kees van der Pijl (2010) notes, the state class rather than capital is sovereign in China. Further, with the rise of China and the decline of the US, Western ruling classes are likely to feel less confident that their interests – which in spite of globalization (cf. Robinson 2004) can still be differentiated from the interests of ascending Chinese capital – will be looked after.

What some have conceived as the rise of a new Asian state or statist capitalism (cf. Bremmer 2010) may thus be viewed as a potential threat to neoliberal order, conceived as an order promoted and guaranteed by and primarily serving the interests of US capital, and the broader West (Van der Pijl 2006). What is above all new about this development is the outward-looking, economically expansionist (rather than protectionist) nature of this new 'statist' capitalism with often state-owned or state-controlled multinationals (such as national oil companies) or Sovereign Wealth Funds expanding on a global scale, integrating themselves into transnational circuits of capitalist production and finance, while still to some extent retaining their state-dependent nature. We are already witnessing some signs that these power shifts in the global economy, and in particular the rise of China, are causing renewed geopolitical rivalries which will, if intensified, surely undermine the current neoliberal global order.

By combining these trends and, by way of conclusion to this section, putting them together, we might speculate that the most plausible shape of a development beyond neoliberalism would, with Cox's notion of a non-hegemonic order in mind, be a global order in which the Anglo-American heartland, still organized around the internal hegemony of a neoliberal power bloc led by financial capital, is increasingly confronted by rival state capitalisms, first of all China, and possibly an intensified cooperation between a German-led Eurozone and Russia (building on existing interdependencies in energy and finance). This scenario would possibly lead to a semi-breakup of the world into three great currency zones, characterized by an uneasy balance between *tri-partite coordination* under the umbrella of the institutions of the old order (International Monetary Fund [IMF], World Trade Organization [WTO]) as well as of the new corridors of power (e.g., the G-20), and increasing *geoeconomic* rivalry primarily centred around access to strategic resources and around the struggle to achieve competitive advantages in new technologies. It cannot be completely ruled out (although at the time of writing it seems extremely unlikely) that the debt crisis in the Eurozone might spark a revival of the Euro-Keynesian tendency that was once powerful during the days of the Delors Commission, based on a revitalized trade union movement and the development of quasi-federal fiscal and economic policy-making institutions to complement the monetary union.

Plan of the book

The book is divided into two parts. The first part analyses developments in key areas of (transnational) socio-economic regulation, examining the nature and driving forces of the neoliberalization processes in these regulatory areas and assessing the extent to which the crisis of neoliberalism is now heralding important regulatory shifts possibly bringing us beyond neoliberalism. All four chapters in this part indicate that although neoliberal regulation has indeed entered into a serious crisis, no alternative regulatory model is in fact as yet emerging inasmuch as there is no constellation of social and political forces supporting such an alternative.

The first two chapters focus on the crisis of neoliberal regulation, and what might come after, in the European Union (EU). Angela Wigger and Hubert Buch-Hansen analyse the contradictions of the neoliberalization of EU competition policy that have taken place in the past decades. The authors argue that, driven by the interests and agency of transnational capital, competition has become the totalizing logic of the European neoliberal project – a logic that has been reflected in a competition regulation premised on narrow price competition in which there is no room for industrial or social policy considerations. Wigger and Buch-Hansen argue that this focus on price competition has only exacerbated what they see as the vicious cycle of over-competition and over-accumulation. The global financial and economic crisis is indeed testimony to this, but, the authors conclude, it has nevertheless failed to lead to a fundamental break with the neoliberal type of competition regulation, which is still strongly supported by the European transnational capitalist class while countervailing social forces have missed the opportunity to present an alternative. Laura Horn then focuses on the critical area of corporate governance regulation in which the EU, as a key element of its overall neoliberal project, has been consistently seeking to promote the marketization of corporate control and the related concept of shareholder value – reflecting the hegemony of financial capital. As the crisis has clearly revealed the pathologies of the shareholder value model, the question is now raised whether in fact we are moving beyond this model in the EU. According to Horn a key role in such a possible movement beyond neoliberalism here is to be played by organized labour. Her analysis, however, shows that despite growing contestation of the marketization of corporate control, the current regulatory responses to the crisis rather show the resilience of the shareholder value concept. Labour's role thus far has in fact been largely limited to defending existing concessions on the part of capital rather than establishing an alternative to neoliberal restructuring. Both chapters thus come to a similar conclusion: that prospects for moving beyond neoliberalism in the EU in the near future are dim, though in the longer run the struggle remains open.

The chapters by Sandy Hager and by Paul Lewis and James Perry both focus on financialization as a key aspect of the neoliberal project. Informed by a *capital as power* approach in which different capital groups are viewed as differentially accumulating on the basis of particular power relations, Hager offers a critique of at least one dominant version of the financialization thesis that simply sees it in terms of the wholesale rise of financial capital. Analysing the case of banking regulation in the US he argues that neoliberalism has been as much about growing competitive struggles within the financial sector, in particular, with investment banks having been empowered by US financial deregulation. Although obviously the crisis has seriously challenged their power, those investment banks that have survived the crisis are still thriving. In spite of the crisis, Hager concludes, the central pillar of neoliberal ideology, financial deregulation, has proven difficult to reverse. And with financial profits booming again, the opportunity for meaningful reform may have already passed.

The contribution by Paul Lewis and James Perry attempts to overcome the dichotomy found in the literature between two fundamentally different approaches to explaining the prices of assets. On one hand there is the financial perspective taking a 'top-down' view of assets as forward looking compressions of future cash flows; on the other hand, there is the production perspective taking a 'bottom-up' view of assets as input quantities. The authors argue that prior to the present financial crisis, financial asset prices were based entirely on risk discounted expectations of future cash flows. However, as was found to the cost of investors, those cash flows were ultimately dependent upon the incomes of productive input providers, specifically the lower half of earners in the US and other developed economies. Lewis and Perry examine the linkage between ideational rationalizations of price and the political limits of financialized accumulation, and demonstrate how the creation of financial assets as increasing claims on output can only expand so far before distributional tensions undermine the capacity to service these claims. In other words, restrained real wages and increased consumer debt have facilitated a distributive shift and a dominance of money over production that are now proving impossible to rationalize.

The second part of this volume addresses the question to what extent we may witness a shift beyond neoliberalism at the level of world order, taking into account important geoeconomic and geopolitical developments that have been coinciding with, and in some cases intensified by, the global financial and economic crisis.

Andreas Nölke develops the argument that the next phase of capitalism will not be a liberal, but an organized one, dominated by the variety of capitalism evolving in the BRIC (Brazil, Russia, India and China). The central coordination mechanism of this variety is the 'clan' mode of social coordination, linking state authorities with domestic capitalists. Based on an analysis of Brazil and India, Nölke concludes that this 'B(R)IC Variety of Capitalism' is based on specific economic institutions that are quite different from the neoliberal Anglo-Saxon type of capitalism, which he expects will give rise to increasing conflicts over global economic regulation. Such a post-neoliberal phase of capitalism, argues Nölke, does not necessarily spell a bright future: these economies are dominated by state institutions and rich autocrats with great internal inequalities.

Henk Overbeek and Naná De Graaff discuss two manifestations of the rise of state-owned capital in the global political economy, Sovereign Wealth Funds and State-owned Oil Companies, respectively. Henk Overbeek distinguishes between two ideal-typical accumulation strategies that emerging states may pursue: the rentier strategy based on the exploitation of natural resources, and the mercantilist-developmentalist strategy aimed at developing advanced industrial and technological capabilities as the basis for national development. China presents an example (though an atypical one in many respects) of such a mercantilist-developmentalist strategy. Overbeek argues that the creation of the Chinese Investment Corporation is related to the underlying dynamics of China's accumulation strategy. A closer look reveals that behind the facade of one-party rule, we may be able to distinguish two distinct competing accumulation strategies, each supported by a specific configuration of party factions, state institutions and societal interests. The outcome of the struggle between these two tendencies will determine in large measure what impact China will have on the governance of the global post-neoliberal order.

Naná De Graaff shows how state-owned oil majors, for example, from China, Russia and the Middle East, are rapidly expanding globally. However, they simultaneously *integrate* into the existing global energy order through increased cooperation with the major private oil companies. In spite of the growth of these 'statist' actors, world energy markets are hence getting increasingly interdependent, interconnected and *transnational*. This expansion/integration of the non-Western energy majors is, however, not yet paralleled by integration of the non-Western oil elites into typical Western elite and business circles. The chapter outlines and assesses three scenarios for the near future: a gradual co-optation of the rising non-Western powers and their companies into the neoliberal market regime; a growing dominance of the state-controlled regime; or a transition towards a more 'hybrid' regime.

Andreas Tsolakis explores, through a comparative analysis of Bolivia, Venezuela and Brazil, the regional dimension of the resurgence of state capitalism and anti-liberal discourses concurrent to the persistence of neoliberal principles such as monetary and fiscal stability, free trade and the promotion of foreign direct investment (FDI). Tsolakis suggests that incumbent governments, influenced by the historical trauma of the debt and inflationary crisis of the early 1980s, and in the face of recurrent capital strikes, have actively consolidated central neoliberal tenets. At the same time, pink governments have taken advantage of a favourable geoeconomic context, including the shifting centre of economic gravity towards East Asia and its insatiable demand for Latin America's primary commodities, European stagnation and US imperial overstretch, and at a deeper and less transparent level, the temporary frailty and reconsolidation of the transnational historic bloc and Multilateral Development Institutions (MDIs) to satisfy or rein in labour demands through the expansion of social welfare investment and the consolidation of polyarchy, to promote state capitalism through joint ventures with private transnational capital and to stimulate the formation of a Latin American power bloc. However, the revolutionary potential of all pink governments has been effectively contained by the disciplining forces of capital, and the Chávez government, while attempting to foster participatory forms of democracy at the grassroots level and to promote the socialization of production, has perpetuated Venezuela's rentier capitalism and the authoritarian tendencies of its preexisting governance model. In all three cases, incessant elite resistance and class struggles, including within state institutions, will most likely continue to imperil the transient hegemony achieved by pink governments.

In the last chapter, Bastiaan van Apeldoorn and Naná de Graaff focus on the neoliberal nature of US imperialism as it evolved in particular after the end of the Cold War, and assess to what extent America's current geopolitical strategy is likely to bring us beyond neoliberal order. Van Apeldoorn and de Graaff argue that even before the current crisis however, US *neoliberal* imperialism was increasingly beset by internal contradictions, which led to its reformulation into a *neoconservative imperialism*, which, however, continued to be premised on the same neoliberal accumulation strategy. Employing a social network analysis of the key foreign policy officials involved, the chapter shows how this continuity must be seen as linked to the hold that US transnational capital continues to have over the US state, a hold that continues with the current Obama administration.

Notes

1. In a congressional testimony (in response to questioning by Representative Henry Waxman) in front of the House Committee on Oversight and Government Reform, on 23 October 2008. Video and transcript available at: http://www.c-spanvideo.org/program/FederalRegula (accessed 24 January 2011).
2. In October 2008, the Dutch government legitimated its decision to nationalize two major banks to the public by claiming that the eventual return to the market will actually bring a profit to the taxpayer (e.g., *NRC Handelsblad* 4 October 2008). During the public debates throughout the OECD, frequent references were made to the Swedish experiences in the early 1990s (Jackson 2008; *New York Times* 22 September 2008), where the Swedish state nationalized banks in trouble in 1992 and privatized them again years later, making a profit in the process. The same profit motive has been used in both Germany and the Netherlands to justify support for the recent 'bailout' of Ireland.
3. For an excellent study predicting, contrarily, the eclipse of the hyper-liberal phase in global financial governance, see Germain 2010.
4. In seeking to explain this, Callinicos also quotes Marx (from the *Critique of Hegel's Philosophy of Right*): 'To call on them to give up their illusions about their condition is to call on them to give up a condition that requires illusions' (Marx quoted in Callinicos 2010: ix–x).
5. Van der Pijl 1984; see for early definitions of neoliberalism Overbeek 1990; Overbeek and Van der Pijl 1993; see also Jessop et al. 1988 for their early interpretation of Thatcherism as a hegemonic project. Also see Overbeek 2004.
6. See contributions to the extensive literature on 'financialization' for empirical illustration (e.g., Krippner 2005).
7. It is not uncommon to distinguish two basic phases in the life course of neoliberalism: the *deconstruction* of the Keynesian compromise and the *construction* of the new neoliberal alternative (cf. Overbeek 1990: 15). Peck and Tickell call this the roll-back and the roll-out phases (see Peck and Tickell 2002; also Birch and Mykhnenko 2010: 7). The notion of a distinct consolidation phase was first raised by Overbeek (2000a: 248–249).

Part I
Beyond Neoliberal Regulation?

2
The Unfolding Contradictions of Neoliberal Competition Regulation and the Global Economic Crisis: A Missed Opportunity for Change?

Angela Wigger and Hubert Buch-Hansen

Introduction

With the ascendancy of neoliberal 'free market' doctrines in the 1980s, competition has gradually become a totalising and all-pervasive logic within EU institutions and policies. It is argued that intensified competition boosts the overall competitiveness of European economies and increases social welfare, delivers sustainable economic growth, and more recently, even cures the root causes of the current economic crisis. The idea that the sheer exposure to global competition automatically leads to increased competitiveness was first endorsed in the European Commission's White Paper on Competitiveness, Growth and Employment in 1993. In the Lisbon Agenda of 2000, to outcompete the rest of the world by making the European Union the world's most competitive and knowledge-based economy in 2010 was even declared official EU policy. Notwithstanding the embarrassing failure of this over-ambitious headline goal, a failure that became apparent long before the current global economic crisis (see Kok 2004), the European Commission's successor strategy *Europe 2020* continues to be immersed in the same orthodox neoliberal spirit. The prioritization of the role of free market forces and the need for efficiency and unbridled economic growth live on. As a revamped clone of its ill-fated predecessor, *Europe 2020* once more seeks to reconcile the rigours of capitalist competition with 'high employment', 'social and territorial cohesion', as well as a 'greener' and 'more resource efficient' economy (European Commission

2010a: 3). It does so without a comprehensive discussion of the Lisbon Agenda's failure, however, and without acknowledging the need for structural change (EuroMemo Group 2010: 3, 6; see also Van Apeldoorn and Hager 2010).

The above programmes all placed centre-stage the 'resolute implementation of competition policy' (European Commission 1993: 69, 2010a; European Council 2000). Arguably, the concept of 'competition' has been one of the core constitutional principles since the Treaty of Rome in 1957, in which the promotion of 'a high degree of competitiveness' and the establishment of 'a system ensuring that competition in the internal market is not distorted' was stipulated in the opening articles (Articles 2 and 3). However, the actual competition rules and their application only gained prominence alongside the overall neoliberal restructuring of capitalism in the 1980s and 1990s (cf. Buch-Hansen and Wigger 2010, 2011).

This chapter argues that organized transnational capital has not only been the main beneficiary of, but also the main driving force behind the neoliberalization of EU policy-making, including competition regulation. In this process, it has acted in concert with the European Commission, which has been overtly responsive to corporate requests to establish 'a level playing field' as part of the completion of the common market in the course of the 1980s. Neoliberalism greatly advanced the deepening and extension of the market-mediated and competition-driven accumulation of capital to new social domains and geographical areas. This created a vast range of new profit opportunities, but it also intensified a range of capitalism's inherent social contradictions. After more than three decades of the neoliberal reign, however, growing political contestation increasingly points at the fault lines of the neoliberal economic order and the particular dynamics of competition. Most notably, the current economic crisis clearly showed that markets are far from self-organizing and efficient and that competition is not inherently good and benefitting everyone equally. Wealth has not been created for all. On the contrary, social inequality is on the rise. Radical corporate 'restructurings' in response to harsh price competition often went paired with redundancies, which left many people left in dire straits regarding their future careers and living standards.

So far, however, political contestation has mainly been articulated by industrial sectors that are afraid to branch out from the competitive race as a consequence of stagnating demand and falling rates of profits. A coordinated response of those bearing the largest part of the social costs has been missing so far. Most notably, trade unions and the vast range of social movements in Europe seem unable to formulate a coherent counter-hegemonic project to the neoliberal crisis management (for a more detailed analysis of this with regard to the related area of corporate governance see the chapter by Laura Horn in this volume). At the same time, the power of contenders from the less competitive and/or territorially restricted industries does not match that of the private-public alliance between organized transnational capital and the European Commission. The chapter argues that with the bailouts of transnational finance capital, and thereby the restoration of the social power configuration supporting the neoliberal project, an alternative type of competition regulation seems unlikely in the near future.

The chapter first theorizes the contradictions of capitalist competition against the backdrop of long-term structural problem of over-accumulation and over-competition, while also focusing on political agency in the articulation of competition regulation. Subsequently it explains the rise of neoliberalism more generally and the concomitant transnationalization of production, as well as processes of financialization. It then outlines the inherent contradictions that result from the neoliberalization in the fields of cartel prosecution, state aid, privatization, and mergers and acquisitions, and discusses the role of organized transnational capital in shaping these regulations. Finally the chapter explains why the neoliberal order fails to be successfully challenged despite the growing contestation in the wake of the global financial crisis.

Capitalist competition, over-accumulation and 'over-competition'

Capitalism as an economic system 'is defined by the fact that it makes structurally central and primary the endless accumulation of capital' (Wallerstein 2000: 147). The process of capital accumulation is premised on the ability of capitalists to realize surplus value by producing and selling goods and services with a profit. The consumption of labour power in the production, as the main source of real added value, ultimately makes possible a process in which capital expands through the successful reinvestment of past profits. This process is, however, neither stable nor unproblematic, nor is it linear nor infinite. Most evidently, capital accumulation is hampered by the limits of natural resources and energy, sweeping pollution and climate change. Moreover, it is also pervaded by a range of intrinsic contradictions and class antagonisms, which, once they intensify, can erupt in economic crises.

One of the main contradictions of capitalism relates to the problem of over-accumulation: the lack of attractive possibilities for capital owners to reinvest past profits at a particular historical juncture and location (Harvey 2006; Robinson 2010). If expected profits on investments are not considered satisfactory, capitalists can decide either to hold on to their surplus capital or invest it in another part of the system. There can be varying reasons for a lack of attractive reinvestment opportunities. For instance, rising real wages due to low unemployment levels or strong labour unions can result in a profit squeeze, leading to an investment slowdown. Moreover, over-accumulation can result from previous over-investment leading to over-capacity in certain sectors. Another, yet often overlooked, factor is excessive competition – here referred to as *over-competition*.[1] To be sure, competition is widely considered to be a desirable phenomenon as it compels capital owners to innovate and improve the quality of their products and services, while keeping down prices. As individual capitalists cannot afford to lag behind the price and quality standards set by competitors, competition exerts coercive pressures on 'every individual capitalist', irrespective of his 'good or ill will' (Marx 1965 [1887]: 270). Furthermore, as Marx (ibid.: 626) reminds us: 'The battle of competition is fought by cheapening of commodities. The cheapness of commodities depends... on the productivity of labour...'. Once an individual capitalist can no longer exploit labour input to undercut the prices of competitors (either through technological replacements or by keeping down wages), profit and profit expectations fall, leading to diminished levels of investments in real production capacities (see also McDonough et al. 2010: 3).

This is, however, not the only way in which over-competition is related to the phenomenon of over-accumulation. On one hand, reduced prices that result from competition may benefit the purchasing power of consumers and other industries. On the other hand, most consumers also happen to be employees, and in this position they feel the direct repercussions of excessive competition in the form of lower wages and redundancies. Over-competition can thus have a backlash in insufficient levels of consumption of produced goods and services. Low or insufficient consumption levels are further reinforced by the exclusion of a significant portion of humanity from production through un- or underemployment and the accompanying downward pressures on wages (Robinson 2004: 147–148; Foster and Magdoff 2009: 39). In the context of the transnationalization of production, and concomitantly also of competitive pressures, the presence of what Marx termed the 'industrial reserve army', creating chronic insecurity among labour about the preservation of employment, further adds to this. Geographically segmented, racialized and gendered labour markets (see Silver 2003) have rendered wage repression, unpaid overtime, degradation of working conditions and labour flexiblization a fact of life in many parts of the world, decreasing in many respects aggregate demand for goods and services. To recapitulate the argument, over-competition has the potential to bring about what Harvey (2010: 29) denotes a 'peculiar combination' of low profits and low wages, which reinforces the overall crisis tendency in the accumulation of capital.

Over-accumulation and over-competition can vary across economies, and so can temporary solutions. Surplus capital that is not invested in real means of production and labour can seek refuge in speculation with financial assets. 'Bubble markets' created by speculation may temporarily offer new outlets for absorbing liquid capital. Financial capital may in the short term be disassociated from the real economy and generate high yields, but ultimately it is deeply anchored in it (cf. Hager in this volume). As actual material wealth first needs to be produced before it can be redistributed, bubbles always burst at some point. Speculative attacks on the real economy trying to reap as much as possible of the produced surplus in the form of interest rates and rates of return on financial investments eventually push the real economy into a crisis. Even though bubble markets can camouflage the problem of over-accumulation, they can never solve the contradictions that lie at the heart of capitalism.

The nature of competition is highly contradictory; while it is the key engine of capitalism, it also restricts its expanded reproduction. This is because competition is in essence a self-undermining phenomenon: to secure profits and economic survival, many capitalists seek to evade the vicissitudes in the anarchy of competition. The conclusion of cartels and other forms of collusive arrangements, and demands for state aid or economic concentration through mergers and acquisitions are tangible examples thereof. Importantly, attempts to monopolize or oligopolize markets are thus irreversibly coupled to competition. In that sense, mergers and collusive agreements are responses to, and elements of, the concentration of capital.

Marx prophesied that ultimately all capital would be 'united in the hands of either a single capitalist or a single capitalist company', effectively putting an end to competition (and capitalism) (Marx 1965 [1887]: 627). He did not, however, take into account state-imposed competition rules in modern capitalist economies, which is understandable as such rules only emerged after his death. Rules on competition, defining the possibilities for market entry, the level of economic concentration and the scope of corporate freedom, can form part of the broader regulatory ensemble that seeks to stabilize the continued accumulation of capital. Due to the contradictory and inherently dynamic nature of the system, such a 'stabilization' is by definition fragile and only temporary. Moreover, competition regulation can serve different and opposing social purposes, thereby benefitting some groups and segments in society more than others. The social purpose of any given competition regulation at a particular juncture is likely to reflect, albeit imperfectly, the existing balance of power between the social forces engendered in the capitalist production process and the prevailing accumulation structures. Such accumulation structures are associated with the prevalence of particular capital fractions. Examples of such fractions are industrial (productive) capital versus financial or money capital and domestic versus regional, or transnational capital (see also Overbeek and Van der Pijl 1993: 3–5; Robinson 2004: 49–53). Thus, the redesign of competition rules at a particular juncture needs to be seen as embedded in the wider social power relations that follow from prevailing accumulation structures.

The Rise of Neoliberalism in Europe

Neoliberalism in Europe evolved as a counter project to the post-war socioeconomic order of 'embedded liberalism' in the 1970s (Ruggie 1982). The era of embedded liberalism, stretching roughly from the 1950s to the early 1970s, was characterized by Fordist production methods, selective pro-industrial mercantilist policies, the development of redistributive Keynesian welfare states, and the overall reliberalization in the international sphere (Overbeek 1990: 87; Jessop and Sum 2006: 124–125). This social order was politically underpinned by a class-based compromise between organized labour and national industrial capital and gave rise to 'the Golden Age of capitalism' – a time of an exceptional economic boom in the world of developed capitalism (see Hobsbawm 1994: 258–261). As part of the Fordist accumulation structures, the concomitant relatively high wages translated into expanding aggregate demand, while investment was generated mainly through internal funds. This provided the owners of industrial capital with a certain independence from the control of financial capital (Foster and Magdoff 2009: 72; Overbeek and Van der Pijl 1993: 6, 11–14).

Although neoliberal ideas had been around for quite some time (cf. Mirowski and Plewhe 2009), they only gained prominence in the course of the crisis of 'embedded liberalism' in the late 1970s (on the origins of neoliberalism see also the Introduction to the volume). This crisis was rooted in the fact that Fordist mass production led to over-production and over-investment in a number of industrial sectors. Increasing competitive pressures from technologically more advanced companies from the US and later also Japan, also referred to as the 'American Challenge' (Servan-Schreiber 1968), forced down prices and henceforth, returns on capital investment. The profit squeeze resulted not only from over-competition, but also from the power of organized labour to combat wage reductions (see also Robinson 2010). Ultimately, the overall decline in aggregate demand amounted to a crisis of the world economy. Especially after 1973, this culminated in sharp decreases in output, productivity and export growth, combined with increasing unemployment and inflation in the industrialized world (Glyn et al. 1990: 43–47). Attempts to restore profitability through investments in innovations and new technologies, as well as reduced employment and wages, only worsened the problem of over-accumulation. Against the backdrop of declining productivity rates and rising unemployment in Europe, the transnationalization of capitalist production caused the balance of power between social forces to change. Organized capital, notably its transnational fraction, was re-empowered vis-à-vis organized labour. This allowed it to advocate neoliberal policies, comprising different sets of regulation facilitating the expansion of free markets and free competition, including the rollback of welfare state, a monetarist focus on keeping inflation low, reduced taxes and fiscal austerity, as well as reduced labour costs in the form of wage repression and deregulation. Thus, the shift towards neoliberalism was premised on broader processes of deindustrialization and technological change, as well as the growing transnationalization of ownership structures and capitalist production circuits through subcontracting and outsourcing, thereby marking a gradual and partial transition towards 'post-Fordism' (cf. Jessop and Sum 2006).

Neoliberal ideas were not endorsed overnight. Initially, national governments opted for various protectionist measures to shield less competitive national industries from outside competition. Once the crisis endured, it was, however, increasingly framed as a crisis of the Fordist accumulation structures and the Keynesian-type welfare states. This increased the receptiveness of national governments to neoliberal crisis solutions. What initially was limited to the Conservative Thatcher government in the U.K. (and the Reagan administration in the US) was followed suit in the course of the 1980s by other governments on the European continent and most notably, the European Commission at EC level. The neoliberal political project was essentially promoted by an alliance of political elites and an emerging transnational capitalist class, which pushed for the realization of an 'ever-closer Union' – an attempt to create a homogeneous market situation for European companies to reap the benefits of economies of scale and scope. It gained particular political momentum with the creation of the Single European Act, removing 300 nontariff trade barriers, and was further consecrated by the Maastricht Treaty of 1991 establishing the European Union (EU) and the Economic and Monetary Union, which consolidated a more market-based regulatory architecture within the common market project.

Neoliberal ideas never became manifest in a pure fashion. Rather, 'in order to become hegemonic within the European arena, the neoliberal project had to be transformed by articulating itself with some elements of the contending projects' (Van Apeldoorn and Hager 2010: 215). Due to variations in the contestation by various social groups, regulatory experimentation and inherited institutional landscapes, important differences in the neoliberal organization of capitalist markets endured at different places and levels of regulation (Brenner et al. 2010; see also McCartney 2011). Overall though, the view that capital had to be disembedded from a great part of the web of social, political and regulatory constraints and that key market institutions had to be separated from the democratic processes came to prevail (Harvey 2005: 11, 66). Neoliberalism, in short, sustained a capitalist order in which the dynamics of competitive accumulation of capital could proceed largely unhindered and uncontained.

The rise of neoliberalism in Europe, and more generally, also unleashed unregulated finance-led accumulation structures. In response to increasingly liberalized markets, enhanced global competition, and falling returns on profit, financial markets burgeoned as sites of profit making in the course of the 1990s. This process has also been referred to as a financialization – a pattern of accumulation according to which profits accrue primarily through financial channels rather than trade and commodity production (Krippner 2005: 174; on financialization see also the chapters by Hager, and Lewis and Perry in this volume). With the growing influence of financial markets and the proliferation of new financial agents and financial instruments and practices (cf. Bryan and Rafferty 2006), financial capital became increasingly mobile, which significantly strengthened it vis-à-vis capital 'embedded in broader sets of social relations' (Jessop 2010: 176; see also Boyer 2000a: 301).

The neoliberalization of EC competition regulation and its contradictions

The broader shift towards the neoliberal order was also reflected in EC competition regulation, encompassing the prohibition of cartels and restrictive business practices (Article 101 since the Treaty of Lisbon), abuse of dominant positions (Article 102), state monopolies (Article 106) and state aid (Article 107). Although EC competition rules were market-making from the outset, aiming at opening up national markets to foreign competition, it was only in the early 1980s, as part of the broader neoliberal turn, that rigorous competition came to be seen as something genuinely desirable, not to be prevented, restricted or distorted by private and public market barriers. In the previous era of 'embedded liberalism', EC competition regulation was fine-tuned to a broad set of socioeconomic objectives, exhibiting strong Euro-mercantilist traits, streamlined with a proactive industrial policy stance, also leaving room for employment considerations in the decision making (see Buch-Hansen and Wigger 2010, 2011). With the advent of neoliberalism, competition and not the interventionist arm of the state or state-like organizations such as the EU was increasingly believed to pick the rightful winners and losers in the market place. Put on a par with a natural selection process and drawing on a particular notion of 'market justice', competition was believed to engender positive feedback loops in the form of higher competitiveness and better performance of entire economies, ultimately benefitting consumers in the form of lower prices. The efficacy of unbridled competition was intellectually legitimized by neoclassic equilibrium economics, most notably its Chicago-style version which identified competition as the chief catalysing force for the most efficient and most profitable allocation of production factors (Wigger 2007). This resulted in narrow definitions of price competition to benchmark anti-competitive conduct, supported by sophisticated econometric modelling and complex algorithms, all following the rationale that corporate efficiency ultimately enhances consumer welfare.

The neoliberal type of competition regulation gained particular momentum when the free market hardliners Peter Sutherland (1985–1989) and Leon Brittan (1989–1995) assumed leadership in the Directorate General responsible for the Commission's enforcement of EC competition rules. Ever since, consecutive competition commissioners were devoted to the neoliberal project. The changed course became manifest in the aggressive prosecution of cartels, state aid and public monopolies. Whereas the Commission tolerated crisis cartels and imposed no fines until the 1970s, it started to prosecute them with unparalleled vigour from the mid-1980s onwards. The imposition of ever higher fines testifies this: from 2005 to 2009, the total amount doubled that from 1990 to 2003 (European Commission 2010b). Likewise, the prohibition of state aid became one of the Commission's central targets. By further specifying the conditions for state aid, the Commission narrowed the leeway for member state market intervention through protectionist industrial policies, one of the central vestiges of the mixed economies of the embedded liberalism era. What started with a 'naming and shaming' strategy on the basis of periodic surveys on the size of state aid granted by each member state (Wilks 2005: 124), led to the State Aid Scoreboard in 2001 and the so-called State Aid Action Plan in 2005, obliging member states to recover illegal aid from past beneficiaries. This culminated in 608 retroactive decisions on unlawful aid for the period of 2000–2006 (European Commission 2007a).

The imperatives of unfettered competition were also expanded to state-owned public utility sectors and networked industries, such as telecommunications, energy, postal services, water, sewerage systems, and transport – all sectors that previously were exempted from the need to compete under EC competition regulation for reasons of national public interests. On the basis of Article 106(3), a previously unused provision entitling the Commission to issue privatization directives without the further approval of the Council or the European Parliament, public enterprises and monopolies were gradually privatized. In addition, the EC merger control regulation that was adopted in 1989, and revised in 2003, entailed a purely neoliberal text, giving primacy to undistorted competition in assessing anti-competitive mergers, leaving no room for industrial and social policy considerations. Moreover, the introduction of EC merger control ensured that the assessment of the largest and also most critical mergers was automatically channelled to the EC level, thereby eroding democratic control and accountability in this issue area. In 2004, the EC competition regime underwent a far-reaching reform, officially titled the 'modernization', which further institutionalized neoliberal practices, and consolidated a more market-based competition regime (see Wigger 2007).

At the very heart of competition and its regulation lie a few glaring contradictions. Competition does not (always) come naturally. Notably, human beings are capable both to compete and to cooperate. Competition therefore cannot be taken for granted, but effectively needs to be enforced upon capitalist markets and its agents. Most people intuitively understand that competition's centrifugal forces of sorting out the efficient and the innovative from the inefficient and unprofitable leaves not only winners. Competition as a panacea for almost everything seems difficult to sell to a broader public, which explains why policy-makers tend to link the imperative of competition to utterly positive connoted social phenomena. Romano Prodi, former President of the European Commission, for example, went as far as giving equal weighting to competition as to democracy and human rights when stating that the EU's ultimate goal was to guarantee European citizens 'prosperity and peaceful co-existence on the basis of democracy, competition, solidarity and unconditional respect for human rights' (Prodi 2001). As noted in the introduction, the Commission's political rhetoric employed in the 2000 Lisbon Agenda and the *Europe 2020 Strategy* is similarly striking. Competition is conceptually paired with 'high employment', 'social and territorial cohesion', as well as a 'greener' and 'more resource efficient' economy (European Commission 2010a: 3). The same rhetoric has been employed in the prohibition of state aid, which the Commission (2001) promoted under the guise 'growth, jobs and cohesion', or in the field of cartel prosecution, in which the Commission portrayed itself as capitalism's Robin Hood, stopping companies 'stealing money from customers' pockets' (Kroes 2005).

Another contradiction that comes into play is that while free competition is held to be a blessing, neoliberal competition regulation seeks to simultaneously augment corporate freedom by keeping state interferences in economic structures to a minimum. More concretely, this implied that since the inception of the EC merger control regulation, the Commission has unconditionally approved the vast majority of the notified mergers: only 20 out of 4,376, or 0.45 per cent of the mergers notified in the period of 1990 to the end of May 2010 were blocked (European Commission 2010c). Many of these mergers were so-called 'mega-mergers', that is, transactions exceeding US $1 billion, involving companies of equal size. Especially in the late 1990s, the number of such mega-mergers rose considerably (see Evenett 2003: 31).

With rare exceptions of plain monopolies, the Commission justified economic concentration on the basis of expected efficiency benefits from economies of scale and scope production. As argued by former competition commissioner Neelie Kroes (2007): '[The] merger tsunami is a good sign. It shows that the market itself is adapting to change, and that European companies are adapting to global competition'. Henceforth, such processes 'must be allowed to run their course without undue political interference'. EC competition regulation has without a doubt contributed to strengthen the global market position of transnational corporations by allowing for economic concentration and subsidiary ownership. Thus, while smaller and less competitive companies were prevented from engaging in cartels and receiving state aid to face growing competitive pressures, larger transnational corporations could grow even bigger. This is not to suggest that transnational corporations face no pressures to compete in comparison to smaller and less competitive companies. On the contrary, with the rise of what is generally referred to as 'emerging markets', competition (and in some cases over-competition) has in many respects become stronger than ever before. Increased competition, however, usually hits small and medium sized companies much harder due to, among other things, their more limited bargaining leverage vis-à-vis regulators, labour and other contractors along the production chain.

The blind faith in self-restoring markets under the reign of intensified price competition has exacerbated in many ways the vicious circle of over-accumulation. Sweeping worldwide liberalization of trade and capital, together with the accelerated pace of the relaunch of the common market project in Europe, was constitutive for corporations to grow in size, mobilize financial capital more easily and henceforth, to invest in new spheres of production on a global scale. Economic concentration often goes together with radical corporate 'restructurings' in the form of large-scale job losses, especially if companies from the same industry are involved. Rationalization and the elimination of duplicate job functions frequently constitute the downside of the much-praised synergy effects. This is even more pertinent considering that the number of mergers and acquisitions has grown exponentially over the past decades, while overall levels of Greenfield investments and the concomitant production of jobs have decelerated. Particularly, the emergence of a market of corporate control, of which mergers and acquisitions form an integral part, is illustrative in this regard (see also the chapter by Laura Horn in this volume). Although all mergers are driven by profit motives in one way or another, this is not necessarily linked to creating new productive capacities. Moreover, the relocation of industrial facilities and outsourcing to cheap labour areas intensified the pace of competition in many sectors, triggering a chain reaction of increased pressures on wages, and henceforth declining aggregate demand both in the advanced economies of the West and the developed world. Credit facilities temporarily sustained consumer spending in the Western world, as a result of which household debt as a percentage of disposable income increased significantly. This, however, merely led to a superficial boom in the US and Europe in the early years of the twenty-first century, after which the underlying crisis of over-accumulation soon surfaced in what has become the current global economic crisis (cf. Schwartz 2009; Bello 2006).

Finally, there is a strong contradiction between the *postulated* and the *actual* beneficiaries of neoliberal competition regulation. According to the line of reasoning of the Commission and other advocates of the neoliberal type of competition regulation, competition serves the inter-est of consumers, and thus the vast majority of citizens. Certainly, con-sumer welfare forms part of the rhetoric employed in the use of price theories and price modelling as a central reference point for determining anticompetitive conduct. Such an approach, however, quintessentially gives precedence to a microeconomic perspective and to short-termism, limiting the focus to single company behaviour in relation to consum-ers only, while disregarding macroeconomic issues like unemployment and economic concentration. Ultimately, neoliberal competition regu-lation safeguards harsh price competition, and its actual beneficiaries are those companies that are able to set the standards of competition for others. This also means that the protection of consumer interests is, at best, a by-product of the main social purpose of such regulation. Carchedi (2001: 126) captures this contradiction well when he observes that the 'protection of the interest of the tiny majority of the powerful is smuggled into the collective consciousness as being the protection of the overwhelming majority of the society'.

Social forces supporting and contesting neoliberal competition regulation

Organized transnational capital has been the key driving force behind the neoliberalization of EC competition regulation during the past 30 years. The role of the European Roundtable of Industrialists (ERT) (cf. Van Apeldoorn 2002), a highly influential network consisting of top executives from a range of Europe's largest transnational corporations, has been pivotal. Established in 1983, the ERT took an interest in EC competition regulation from the very start (Buch-Hansen and Wigger 2011: 79). As many ERT companies were involved in transnationaliza-tion processes through cross-border mergers and acquisitions in the late 1980s, the ERT strongly supported the introduction of the aforemen-tioned EC merger control regulation (see ERT 1988), particularly after the Commission assured taking a business-friendly stance and not to block mergers on social or industrial policy grounds. Moreover, the creation of supranational regulatory structures was very attractive for transnational capital. Notably, the introduction of a 'one-stop-shop' rule, which equipped the Commission with exclusive powers to vet mergers above a certain turnover threshold, provided an opportunity to circumvent the problem of having to comply simultaneously with multiple national regulatory systems. Apart from issuing position papers and having several meetings with Commission officials and national ministers, the ERT sought support from other business groups, such as UNICE (now BusinessEurope), the umbrella organization of national business federations. Once CEOs of transnational corporations assumed leadership in UNICE (Van Apeldoorn 2002: 102–103), UNICE turned from a fierce opponent (see UNICE 1974) to a genuine supporter of EC merger control (see ibid. 1987). In 1989, EC member state governments succumbed to the pressure and reached an agreement. Ever since, organized transnational capital has taken a keen interest in the development of EC competition regulation, with the ERT and UNICE being at the forefront of promoting further neoliberal reforms, such as the prosecution of state aid and cartels, and the privatization of state-owned companies.

Nonetheless, even though organized transnational capital has been the most important social force driving EC competition regulation, this does not imply that the specific regulatory details are also decided in boardrooms. This can be seen in the 2004 reform of EC competition regulation. Although it in many ways consolidated the neoliberal approach, some aspects did not resonate well with the preferences expressed by the ERT, UNICE and other business groups. Instead it reflected the position of the Commission, some member state governments and the legal profession (Buch-Hansen 2008: 212–213, 232–247; Wilks 2005; Wigger 2007). This indicates that it would be wrong to conceive of the emerging EU state apparatuses in an instrumental or functionalist fashion – that is, as mere conveyor belts for the interests of organized transnational capital. At the same time, to ascribe a fully autonomous role to a body like the Commission would be equally mistaken. Organized transnational capital in many respects informed and fostered the neoliberalization of EC competition regulation, but the overall control and detailed fleshing out of competition rules is anchored in the institutional ensemble of the EU, and thus remains beyond its grasp. The mediating role of the legal profession in this respect is particularly noteworthy. The growing Community law production triggered by the Single European Act in the mid-1980s and the creation of the European Union in the early 1990s on the one hand, and the growing number of cross-border mergers and acquisitions and intercompany agreements on the other, has increased the corporate demand for a broad range of legal counselling services. This stimulated the creation of EU-based 'mega-law firms and alliances that are socially well connected to Community institutions' (Schepel and Wesseling 1997: 182). Experts on competition regulation, both from the private commercial and public realm thus enjoy a quasi-autonomous role in influencing the discourses that eventually provide the broader interpretation framework of Commission officials (see also Wigger 2009).

The extensive disembedding of capital accumulation from social relations and democratic institutional orders has repeatedly led to social demands for their re-embedding and re-regulation to ensure structural coherence and social cohesion (Jessop 2010: 176). As part of this, contestation of the neoliberalization of EC competition regulation has regularly flared up. Notably, already prior to the current economic crisis, EC member state governments expressed the concerns of less competitive national industrial sectors and companies worried about the effects of over-competition. *The Financial Times* (2006a), for example, reported that Italy was 'almost literally cracking up under exposure to competition from Eurozone partners and from China in textiles and shoes', and that 'Paris' was 'reacting with even more fury than Rome' about the EU being a transmission belt for bringing in the forces of globalization. Although most concerns against extra-European competition did not specifically address the neoliberal type of competition regulation, but rather the overall trade liberalization fostered within the WTO, French President Sarkozy evolved as a prominent proponent of a Euromercantilist type of EC competition and industrial policy. He argued that 'neither France nor Europe can become industrial deserts [...]. It is not a right for the state to help industry. It is a duty' (in Murray 2004: 8). Next to various measures to block hostile foreign takeovers, the French government declared 11 sectors off-limits to foreign investment (*The Financial Times* 2006b). Likewise, the German, Italian, Spanish and Polish governments went against the neoliberal free competition stance taken by the Commission and sought to prevent foreign takeovers through direct government interventions. The Commission, together with commentators in the financial press and organized transnational capital, rather successfully suppressed this 'drift to mercantilism'. This demonstrates that rather than being a politically neutral supranational body, the Commission is a 'strategically selective' (see Jessop 2007) institution that systematically privileges certain ideas, strategies and actors over others. In this context, the Commission has actively privileged and promoted crude notions of free markets and free competition since the 1980s, and it continues to play a central role in maintaining the hegemony of the neoliberal discourse.

Organized labour and left wing parties also regularly contested the neoliberalization of EC competition regulation, pushing the Commission to take employment levels into account when judging upon the effects of a merger on competition, however, without success. The Commission's decision to approve the merger between ABB and Alstom in 2000 is illustrative in this regard. When a fifth of the workforce in the newly created entity faced redundancy, 2000 French, German, Belgian and Italian workers marched 'for a social Europe and against the Commission because they felt that they had no voice in its competition policy' (Erne 2008: 128, 154). The Commission did not reverse its decision, nor did it more generally give way to centre-left elements in the way competition is regulated. Moreover, the reduction of real-world complexity into microeconometric modelling in the analysis of anticompetitive conduct has as a consequence that excluded parameters, such as the welfare of employees and employment aspects, simply remain unnoticed in the decision making. This is very much in the vested interest of organized transnational capital. So is the undemocratic nature of the Commission, which enables it to turn a deaf ear to those groups who are critical of its neoliberal approach. Indeed, the ERT quite overtly argued that the greater involvement of groups like consumers and employees 'risks diverting the attention from the competition focus of the European Commission's analysis and increasing both uncertainty and delay' (ERT 2001: 4).

The global economic and financial crisis: the end of neoliberalism?

The global financial meltdown in 2008 was interpreted by some commentators to signal the beginning of the end of the existing form of capitalism. Altvater (2009: 75) even went as far as to suggest that '[t]he neoliberal era lasted until August 2008 when the liberalized system of global financial markets imploded'. Although this conclusion is rather premature, it is beyond doubt that the financial crisis, which quickly developed into a deep global economic crisis, represents a serious challenge to neoliberal accumulation structures and regulation. As a strategic project, neoliberalism has been highly successful in redistributing wealth from the majority of citizens to the privileged few, which can be seen from the fact that the employees' share of the economic pie all over the developed world shrank, while the already wealthy became even wealthier (see Cammack 2009). Neoliberalism has, however, been less successful in overcoming the slow economic growth in the advanced capitalist economies since the 1970s. That is, when correcting growth figures for economic bubbles, growth rates have been rather modest compared to those in post-war capitalism's 'Golden Age' (see Bello 2006: 1348). The same applies to investments, which slowed down significantly in the neoliberal era (Stanford 2008: 148–150).

Neoliberal policies have failed to generate the necessary aggregate demand and thus, high returns on investment. For one thing, employees receive a shrinking share of GDP while social welfare programs have become less generous. This has reduced the level of aggregate demand, a problem that was only exacerbated by over-competition. Despite 'an abundance of low-wage labour', global competition depressed profit rates in the real economy in the 1990s, with the result that 'more and more money went into speculation on asset values because that was where the profits were to be had' (Harvey 2010: 29). Also nonfinancial companies increasingly channelled capital to financial markets expecting comparatively higher returns on investment (Krippner 2005: 182). This strengthened competition for short-term profits in the financial markets, at the expense of productive reinvestment of past profits and the creation of employment. Increasing levels of household debt could only postpone the crisis of the system, but did not constitute a lasting solution to the inherent problem of insufficient demand.

In 2008, when the Bush administration decided not to save Lehman Brothers from bankruptcy, the financial bubble burst in the US. The crisis spread quickly to Europe, where banks and other financial institutions faced insolvency, while a number of stock markets found themselves on the edge of collapsing. The crisis led to large-scale state interventions. In the absence of concerted action at the EU level, member governments adopted national rescue packages, infusing massive loans in financial behemoths and in industries hit by the credit crunch. Moreover, they pursued other strategies, such as nationalizing banks or sponsoring defensive mergers. They did this without awaiting the Commission's approval (Da Silva and Sansom 2009: 28). According to the Commission's State Aid Scoreboard (2009a), the overall aid volume increased from € 66.5 billion or 0.52 per cent of the EU-27 GDP in 2007 to € 279.6 billion or 2.2 per cent of GDP in 2008 (with crisis measures excluded, the total aid was 0.54 per cent of GDP).

The overall tendency towards nationally-based crisis solutions went against the neoliberal type of EC competition regulation of the past decades. Eager to prevent a lasting break with the neoliberal path, the Commission, backed up by organized transnational capital reacted with a renewed commitment to rebalance neoliberal economic policies. In October of 2008, it allowed member states to rescue certain financial institutions on the basis of Article 87(2b), a legal waiver for aid remedying 'a serious disturbance in the economy of a Member State' (European Commission 2009b: 3–4). Two months later, it outlined general standards for recapitalizing banks and financial institutions, which had the purpose to ensure a sufficient volume of lending in the European economies. On this basis, the Commission approved bank state guarantees of more than € 2,900 billion and bank state recapitalizations of more than € 300 billion (Kroes 2009). Subsequently, in the so-called 'clean-up phase', the Commission set out to restructure the rescued financial sector in order to reverse the alleged damaging effects on competition and to warrant viable business plans for the future. Thus, although the Commission acknowledged the need for state aid, it sought to ensure 'a level playing field' and avoid 'subsidy races' among member states (European Commission 2009c). In a similar vein the Commission made it clear that cartels would not be tolerated as this would only drag down economic recovery. In other words, the Commission evolved as a neoliberal-type crisis manager, who effectively coordinated the national supports by simply temporarily enforcing state aid rules in a more flexible manner than was hitherto the case. The Commission's crisis management was supported once more by organized transnational capital. The ERT praised the Commission 'for swift and crucial action to stabilize the banking system', and expressed concern about 'the apparent rise in economic nationalism and protectionist sentiment' (ERT 2009: 1). Likewise the European Financial Services Round Table, whose members are chairmen and CEOs of leading European banks and insurance companies, stated the need for European oversight of national crisis management practices to monitor competitive distortions and externalities (EFR 2009: 3). In fact, organized transnational (financial) capital has persistently been pushing for even more stringent neoliberal crisis solutions, such as wage moderation, disciplined austerity programmes to tackle the current sovereign debt crisis, the transposition of the Stability and Growth Pact into national law and the imposition of fierce penalties, as well as a stricter surveillance of national economic policies for the stabilization of the euro (BusinessEurope 2010).

Paradoxically, even though over-competition was a contributing factor to over-accumulation in the real economy, which in turn resulted in the financial bubble, the Commission and organized transnational capital continue to seek salvation in even stronger competition. In other words, there is no break with the neoliberal type of competition regulation in sight in Europe. There are two main reasons for this. First, the crisis has not (yet) resulted in a serious disturbance of the balance of power between social forces. Indeed, national rescue packages have served to ensure that transnational financial capital continues to be the dominant social force. A similar relaxation or suspension of state aid rules for the real economy has not taken place. In fact, to the contrary, once more and more crisis-ridden industries from the real economy started queuing up for their share of state aid, the Commission fiercely intervened and demanded in 2010 the recovery of €530 million of the state aid granted by EU member states (European Commission 2011). Second, no comprehensive alternative project has emerged (yet) that can attract the support of a strong, new constellation of social forces. It seems that the disruptive and world-encompassing competitive pressures negatively impact on Europe's least privileged citizens, which substantially weakens political opposition. Notably, with the subjugation of ever more social domains and geographical regions to the logic of market-mediated and profit-driven capital accumulation, the imperative to compete has spread from private companies to individuals, local townships, cities, regions and even entire countries and regions. The continuous exposure to comparative evaluation through scoreboards and performance indexes are a tangible testimony of the fact that contemporary capitalist societies have transformed into true competition societies. Competition, however, disintegrates more than it unites. The formulation of a credible counter-hegemonic project can only be successful if the powerful imperative of competition can be overcome. Even though it is too early, if not wrong, to announce neoliberalism's defeat, this does not mean that a radically different type of competition regulation is inconceivable in the longer run. During the past year, hundreds of thousands of people have demonstrated on the streets against the austerity measures of European governments to overcome the sovereign debt crisis. Social unrest and protests are on the rise, which may form an important first step in a European-wide resistance against the continuation of neoliberal crisis solutions.

Conclusions: alternative forms of competition regulation

As part of the neoliberal restructuring since the 1980s, the view that market-based solutions were superior to the interventionist arm of a public authority came to prevail. More and more social and economic activities were subjugated to the anarchic pursuit of profits. Strict competition control formed the juggernaut of this process. This chapter has argued that the neoliberal market order and concomitant spatial restructuring of production to low-wage offshore places as a way to restore profitability in many ways exacerbated the problem of over-competition and thus over-accumulation in the past 30 years. The current global economic crisis is a testimony to this. At first glance, the recent crisis responses adopted in Europe seemed to contrast sharply with the orthodox neoliberal mindset that underpinned EU policy-making during the past 30 years. The neoliberal type of competition regulation is, however, still thriving and going strong. The transnational capitalist class and surely its financial fraction have endorsed the idea that more competition is an important part of the solution to the crisis.

So far the crisis has thus been a missed opportunity for countervailing social forces to break with the neoliberal type of competition regulation. What then would it take for such a break to take place? As highlighted above, competition regulation needs to be seen in the wider context of capitalist production and power relations. This means that a genuine paradigm shift in this regulatory area needs to form part of a wider transformation of the regulatory ensemble at the EU and national levels. Neoliberalism is currently, however, reworked and extended, which can be seen in the field of financial services regulation (cf. Quaglia 2011), EU trade policy (cf. De Ville and Orbie forthcoming), as well as the budget austerity programmes that are currently orchestrated by the EU-IMF tandem. Moreover, the global economic crisis has not yet seriously affected the balance of power between social forces, nor are the contours of new accumulation structures coming into view. In many ways, it seems that competition has become the central disunifying principle in the formation of political opposition. Certainly organized labour faces difficulties in articulating a political counter project, which would provide a comprehensive alternative to ongoing labour market flexibilization, the adoption of labour-saving technologies, wage stagnation and the geographical relocation of production to cheap labour areas – all offshoots of the centrifugal forces of capitalist competition.

A credible alternative to hollow mantras such as 'competition for more competitiveness' is therefore desperately needed. The search for post-neoliberal alternatives needs to take place in various social spheres and spaces simultaneously, and also encompass the field of competition regulation. A society, let alone a market, without competition is not something worth striving for, but if we want to successfully tackle problems of environmental destruction, climate change and perverse social inequalities, an overall restriction of competition forms an una-voidable part of the solution. New avenues for shrinking the econo-mies of the privileged North need to be explored, rather than finding solutions for the imperative of infinite economic growth. Downscaling may sound utopian in the current political climate, but continuing down the path hitherto followed is not an option either. Limiting com-petition to well-defined geographical boundaries could be an option. This does not imply that inter-territorial competition should be aban-doned altogether for all industrial sectors. Rather, imposing geographi-cal limits to fair competition provides, for example, an avenue for local producers of sustainable food products to evade the global war of price competition. Certainly, the restriction of competition comes at a 'cost' for those who currently benefit from it, namely competitive compa-nies. This will also affect our role as consumers and the possibility to choose from a huge assortment of products and services that may be affordable and entertaining but also environmentally and socially unsustainable.

New conceptions of what it means to be competitive are needed, namely conceptions that valorize the extra-economic dimensions and that comprehensively re-embed economic activities in a way that is more attuned to the needs of society at large. This requires a move away from microeconomic price and efficiency modelling, which assesses competition in isolation from other social spheres. The com-petitive performance of companies should instead be assessed accord-ing to various social interest criteria, such as an assessment of the social usefulness of new products, ecologically sustainable production methods, the safeguarding of employment and employee rights in the corporate governance structure, fair trade practices and investment decisions, as well as solidarity in knowledge transfer and technology sharing. Competition authorities applying social interest criteria as a judgmental basis should be democratically accountable and genuinely responsive to all inputs by different groups in society. Precisely because competition regulation is inherently political, it should also be sub-jected to political mediation.

Notes

The authors, who have contributed equally to this chapter, would like to thank the editors for their helpful comments.

1. The notion of 'over-competition' is first and foremost associated with Brenner's *The Economics of Global Turbulence* (2006), even though he does not discuss the concept in any depth in this work. In line with what we suggest here, Brenner makes the connection between competition and declining rates of profits (see 2006: 57). However, it should be noted that Brenner's general theory of competition, which is arguably problematic in a number of respects (see Duménil et al. 2001), has not informed the understanding of competition underpinning the arguments made in this chapter.

3
After Shareholder Value? Corporate Governance Regulation, the Crisis and Organized Labour at the European Level

Laura Horn

Introduction

In the context of the financial and economic crisis, corporate govern-ance has been identified as 'one of the most important failures of the present crisis' by an EU expert group (De Larosière 2009: 29). In the decade preceding the crisis, EU corporate governance regulation has increasingly become neoliberal both in content – with an exclusive focus on shareholder value – as well as form, with market-based regula-tory mechanisms such as disclosure and voluntary compliance instead of mandatory legislation. Corporate governance arrangements such as excessive performance-related remuneration have led to perverse incen-tives for risk-taking, and increasingly independent, and externalized corporate oversight bodies lacked sufficient information and willing-ness to hold managers and investors accountable. Clearly, the patholo-gies of shareholder value have become even more apparent. In a climate of widespread critique of neoliberal policies, as well as the neoclassical models on which shareholder value rests, could the crisis indeed be the catalyst through which shareholder value as prime objective for corpo-rate control can be overcome?

Many observers have looked to the 'left' for alternative strategies to deal with the fallout of the collapse of finance-dominated, market-driven policies. A common assumption holds that the current crisis not only corroborates the analyses and arguments of critics of unfettered market capitalism, but that we are indeed witnessing a conjunctural 'window of opportunity' for alternative policy proposals and political strategies to enter into the policy-making arena. Organized labour, in particular trade unions, perceived as 'regulated representative constituencies of the Real Economy' (TUAC 2008), here represents a central node of agency in emerging networks of contestation, at the national as well as the European and international level. As John Monks, then secretary general of the European Trade Union Confederation (ETUC) declared, 'the conditions are there for a trade union counter attack' (Monks 2008). At the same time, rising job losses and unemployment levels, and pressure on real wages have put organized labour (once again) in a defensive position. None of the major bailout plans have been initiated through pressure from below – that is, from trade union associations or civil society networks. Labour representation and interests are becoming more and more fragmented at the company and the national levels, while the institutional configuration of the European Union has been permeated deeply with governance structures that are conducive to market-making, neoliberal policies rather than strengthening the alleged 'European Social Model'.

The broader question is, then, what role, if any, organized labour can play in a possible movement beyond neoliberalism. In this context, this chapter seeks to engage with the agency of organized labour at the European level in the area of corporate governance regulation. Corporate governance here refers to those practices that define and reflect the power relations within the corporation and the way, and to which purpose it is run (Van Apeldoorn and Horn 2007). Questions of corporate control, as expressed in corporate governance regulation, go to the very heart of capitalism. It is in this arena that contesting ideological perspectives on ownership and socio-economic organization collide most immediately. As I have shown (Horn 2011), corporate governance regulation in the European Union has increasingly shifted towards financial market imperatives, that is towards a regulatory perspective focusing exclusively on the interests of shareholders. This marketization of corporate control constitutes a key element of the neoliberal project in Europe. Concomitantly, labour law, once an integral part of regulating the modern corporation, is more and more relegated to the area of social affairs and employment law, and provisions for workers' rights with regard to corporate control are increasingly marginalized. Labour law in the European Union has a representational rather than redistributive character, whereas collective bargaining, the right to strike and working conditions have been at the centre of trade union strategies and demands, and corporate governance and financial market regulation at the EU level has often come about out-side the focus of trade unions. It was only in recent years that corporate control and corporate governance have become more politicized and contested, often in tandem with the broader debate about corporate ownership and the debate about alternative investment structures (i.e., the so-called 'locust' debate about the role of private equity and hedge funds). This chapter hence focuses on the marketization of corporate control as an integral part of neoliberal European restructuring, and the limits and contradictions of the process, in order to examine to what extent it might be transcended in the context of the current crisis.

Following the general outlook of this edited volume, the chapter is structured as follows. The next section provides a brief discussion of the role and agency of organized labour in neoliberal European governance, as well as why corporate governance regulation as a crucial element of neoliberal restructuring at the European level is indeed a relevant field of social struggle in this context. The empirical part is structured in two parts: The first section outlines how the marketization of corpo-rate control has become the central principle in EU corporate govern-ance regulation, and how this process at the same time served to isolate labour from the regulatory process. The next section then provides an overview of regulatory reaction after the emergence of the financial and economic crisis, and the role of organized labour in this process. The chapter then concludes with some remarks on the relevance of the European level as a platform for social struggle for organized labour.

A historical materialist framework on organized labour in European integration (in a nutshell)

The emphasis in this chapter is on the social struggles underlying the political project of neoliberal European integration, and in particular the marketization of corporate control. Rejecting pluralist notions of agency at the European level, Van Apeldoorn et al. argue (2008: 13) that, in order to analyse the potential for contestation of and resist-ance to socio-economic restructuring, the position and agency of subal-tern classes in European governance have to be seen from a perspective that acknowledges the fundamental power asymmetries in the EU. At the same time as the terrain of class struggle is increasingly shifted beyond the nation state, the European state formation becomes more and more important as a locus for counter-hegemonic strategies. It is through the articulation of, and struggle between, concrete political projects that social forces shape European integration. This focus on concrete political projects is all the more important as the EU state formation stipulates a certain market-making focus in the first place. As Van Apeldoorn's analysis (2002: 78) of rival projects of European integration shows, the crucial question is *what kind* of market is being promoted. Regulation here represents a juridico-political manifestation of the struggle between particular political projects, albeit subject to political concessions and compromises. Rather than perceiving of regulation as a functional outcome or the drive to improve efficiency by correcting market failures, in the understanding of this study, regulatory developments are perceived of as part and parcel of political projects. Here, in order to discuss the transformation of a regulatory framework, it is indispensable to analyse *qualitative* changes, as well as the underlying configuration of social forces. This focus transcends a state-centric perspective, as regulatory transformation must be viewed as a transnational process in which changes take place simultaneously at different levels. Not only 'hard' regulation is taken into account, but also how political projects are being discursively formulated, as well as disseminated and contested within capitalist society.

The concept of the political project here serves as a starting point for the analysis, as its discursive and operative dimensions can be investigated empirically, while at the same time seeing it in the context of wider structural changes. As concrete and more or less coherent manifestations of social interests with regard to particular socio-economic issues, political projects are subject to internal contradictions as well as contestation by contending social forces. As such, it is through an analysis of political struggle, as well as the compromises and consensus necessary to sustain hegemonic projects, that the contours of rival political projects become most clear. Hegemony in a Gramscian sense is in fact never complete, and subordinate groups and classes may always struggle to redefine the terms of the dominant discourse and transform underlying social practices. This again points towards the open-ended nature of the process of European integration, as well as the emancipatory potential within the European arena.

Organized labour and neoliberal European restructuring

International political economy approaches have long focused on the agency of transnational capital and business actors, while a focus on labour as a political actor has been fairly marginalized (Harrod 2002: 15). A common perception is that organized labour, despite its often internationalist ideology, is still rooted at the national level and has become a conservative and inflexible force with dwindling membership, unable to adapt its strategies to the new supra- and transnational realities. And indeed, as Hyman sums up (2004: 19–20), the challenges to traditional unionism have been manifold, ranging from external factors such as the intensification of competition across countries, regions and sector, the internationalization of chains of production and the deregulation of the labour market, to internal challenges such as the erosion of the 'normal' employment relationship, extensive social and generational changes and hence the decline of trade union membership. There are different mechanisms through which organized labour can seek to advance these objectives. Traditional union strategies have been class action at the firm, sectoral or national level, as well as close political cooperation with social democratic or other (confessional) parties. Here, organized labour has long represented an interest group in national politics, manifest in, e.g., corporatist concertations. Increasingly, trade unions have also become engaged in 'partnerships' with businesses at the firm level, in firm-specific agreements (which in the case of multinational corporations can take on a transnational character). International cooperation between trade unions through international Union secretariats or the TUAC (Trade Union Advisory Committee to the OECD) has become more important for the coordination and organization of union strategies; yet the main space for action has remained at the national level. In recent years, however, unions have also increasingly established cooperation with social movements (cf. Bieler 2008). Yet as Hyman points out, engaging in 'contentious politics' potentially 'redefines unions as outsiders in a terrain where until recently the role of insiders was comforting and rewarding' (Hyman 2004: 22). As the next section shows, with regard to organized labour at the European level, the insider role seems to have been more appealing indeed, so far.

As mentioned above, in order to understand the role and counter-hegemonic potential of organized labour in the emerging state EU formation, the neoliberal restructuring of the European Union should be seen as a contested project, rather than a linear, inevitable and unchangeable trajectory. At the same time, the agency of organized labour has to be understood within the institutional and political structures of the European Union. Organized labour at the European level, in particular the ETUC, has often been perceived as, put bluntly, co-opted into the project of neoliberal restructuring (cf. Bieling and Schulten 2003). The European Trade Union Confederation and the European Industry Federations, set up as lobby organizations for worker interests at the European level, have been implicated into the emerging system of labour relations, characterized through the Social Dialogue and firm-level agreements. As Streeck and Schmitter have pointed out (1991: 147), changes in social structures, in particular a weakened social democratic movement and more flexible labour arrangements, concurred with a changing character and role of trade unions in the 1980s. In particular under the promises of Delors's vision for a *European Social Model*, trade unions entered into a tacit agreement that intensified market competition, and deregulation was unavoidable (Bieling 2001: 100). The institutionalization of the Social Dialogue in the Maastricht Social Chapter in 1991 has led to what Bieling and Schulten have called symbolic Euro-corporatism, incorporating trade union associations into the hegemonic bloc supporting neoliberal restructuring, while all the same 'keeping alive their functionalist hopes of a slow but steady expansion of European social regulation' (Bieling and Schulten 2003). The Social Dialogue channelled conflicts between capital and labour into a non-binding social partnership forum, effectively blurring the antagonistic relations resulting from the neoliberal restructuring. Concessions to labour have been mostly symbolic (cf. Tidow 2003). EU-level trade union associations have also been criticized for being integrated into the EU system of decision making also through funding and institutional networks with ambivalent consequences, while the financial and institutional support from the Commission increases the organizations' scope for action and creates political dependencies.

Trade union strategies at the European level mainly take place within the institutional framework of the European level. This, however, means that initiatives and policy objectives also remain *within* the broader political context of neoliberal restructuring, rather than pose a fundamental alternative to it. Hyman's critique is rather to the point here: 'Working for marginal adaptations to the dominant orthodoxy of actually existing Europeanisation is the line of least resistance, the new realism and practicality of a trade unionism that has lost its former utopian inspiration' (Hyman 2005: 22). This ambivalence has, for instance, been born out in the ETUC's earlier support for the Lisbon strategy as a 'balanced and integrated approach between economic, social and environmental policies' (ETUC 2005: 15). It was only when the scale of failure of the Lisbon strategy became apparent and with the austerity measures following the crisis, that the ETUC has taken a strong position against the broader EU policy programme. The question then remains in how far organized labour can indeed be seen as a potential counter-hegemonic actor, in particularly with regard to the current crisis and possible forms of post-neoliberalism, and in how far the institutional terrain of the European level would be the appropriate place for social struggles. Even though the space for agency for organized labour is limited, there remain avenues for trade unions. As Erne points out, unions are not passive victims of the EU integration process, but agents that are also capable of politicizing its contradictions (Erne 2008: 199). While labour has, in the absence of strong uniform representation at the EU level and framed in the soft model of the 'Social Dialogue', acquiesced to the previous programme under the promise of competitiveness and job growth in the context of the Lisbon agenda, there is now increasing disillusionment with the flanking measures of the European Social Model.

In the following sections, these social struggles on the terrain of the European state formation are analysed in the policy area of company law and corporate governance regulation. To clarify why corporate governance regulation constitutes a central field in the socio-economic restructuring of European integration, and is hence of immediate interest to labour as a social force in the process of European integration, a brief conceptual overview is pertinent here.

Corporate governance as social relation, and why this is important for labour

Corporate governance here refers to *those practices that define and reflect the power relations within the corporation and the way, and to which purpose, it is run* (Van Apeldoorn and Horn 2007). This understanding of corporate governance differs from a law and economics perspective through a focus on the social power relations in the corporation rather than perceiving of corporate governance mainly as technical solution for agency problems, i.e., how 'investors get the managers to give them back their money' (Shleifer and Vishny 1997: 737).

Following Berle and Means (1991), the separation between management and 'owners', and the potentially conflicting interests of these two social groups, is generally seen as constituting the core of power struggles over corporate control. Indeed, the corporate form has also fundamentally transformed the relations between capital and labour. As Marx argued, 'in joint-stock companies the function is separated from capital ownership, so labour is also *completely separated* from ownership of the means of production and of surplus labour' (Marx 1991: 568, emphasis added). Through the socialization of capital, the social relations between the actual producers of surplus value and the owners of capital became indirect and obscured, mediated by the bureaucracy of professional management. As corporate control was legally established as based on proprietary rights, that is, tied to share ownership, labour became further subordinated vis-à-vis capital. However, actual social relations between shareholders and labour are not necessarily purely antagonistic (Jackson 2001: 280; see also Gourevitch and Shinn 2005: 205–207). Just as capital is not a homogeneous social group, labour interests cannot be assumed but need to be established conceptually and empirically.

In concrete processes of class formation, these abstract categories have been manifested in the class fractions of industrial and financial capital; however, these categories must be understood in their historically specific configuration and cannot simply be assumed (Van Apeldoorn 2002: 27; cf. Van der Pijl 1998). Particularly important with regard to the rise of the shareholder value model, industrial capitalists can also take on a financial perspective, e.g., when their specific interests are tied to financial capital through for instance incentives and structural relations. Still, as Van Apeldoorn points out, there are structural limits to which extent industrial capitalists can adopt a financial capital perspective, as industrial capital ultimately remains tied to the production process. Concomitantly, in order to maintain the production process, industrial capital is more tied to social protection, that is, it is more 'embedded' than the 'autonomous' structures of the money commodity fetish that sustains financial capital (Van Apeldoorn 2002: 28–29). As power struggles and conflict between labour and capital are mainly taking place in the production, it is from an industrial capital perspective that concessions to and compromises with labour need to be negotiated to ensure production. In contrast to this, financial capital does not need to maintain an element of 'embeddedness'. In ideal-typical terms, money capital tends to have a more liberal perspective than productive capital (Van der Pijl 1998: 51; cf. Harvey's discussion of finance capitalism, 2006: 316–324). As such, a financial capital perspective is potentially at odds with an industrial capital perspective on labour relations and the 'disembedding' of production from national, more protective structures. At the same time, as financial capital has to compete to some extent, with industrial capital over the profits of the production process, it needs to ensure that its interests, in particular with regard to the distribution of surplus, are maintained.

With the marketization of corporate control the perspective of financial capital increasingly comes to reign over industrial capital (cf. Hager in this volume). At the level of the firm, this is expressed most clearly in the rise of 'shareholder value' as the new ideological paradigm for corporate governance (Lazonick and O'Sullivan 2000; Aglietta and Reberioux 2005). The marketization of corporate control puts the corporation, its management and workers more firmly under the discipline of the capital market. It implies a *deepening* of the commodification of the social relations constituting the corporation, in that they are exclusively mediated by the market. The state here has a central role in creating and maintaining the legal and regulatory underpinnings that sustain the 'legal fiction' of the corporation.

Corporate governance regulation

The organizational form of the modern corporation did not come about as the inevitable outcome of economic processes, in which it emerged as the most efficient, that is, the transaction cost-minimizing way of organizing production. Rather, the modern corporation was a creation of the state (Roy 1997). Its organizational form as well as its purpose, that is, in which interest it should be run, is continuously sustained by the legal framework provided through the state. Rather than seeing corporate governance regulation in terms of de- or re-regulation, as is often the case, it is the *qualitative change* in corporate law and other regulatory domains pertaining to the social relations of the corporation that needs to be explained. It is here that the neoliberal character of regulation becomes most apparent. The conceptualization of the corporation as a social relation, rather than a neutral 'legal fiction' or even nexus of contracts facilitates a discussion of the social purpose of the corporation which transcends efficiency and transaction costs arguments and takes into account the unequal social relations of production that sustain the corporate form. The focus here needs to be on the *political* process through which a particular regulation regime emerges, with law as a fundamental arena for political struggle.

The transformation of corporate governance regulation at the European level

In a 1975 Green Paper on Employee Participation and Company Structure, the European Commission argued that 'employees are increasingly seen to have interests in the functioning of enterprises which can be as substantial as those of shareholders, and sometimes more so' (European Commission 1975: 9). Now, just over three decades later, little is left of this strong emphasis on the role of workers in company-level decision making. Rather than *industrial democracy*, the Commission has been pushing for a *shareholder democracy* (European Commission 2005).

The focus on industrial democracy had emerged from a conjunctural shift in the power relations between (organized) labour and industrial capital in the European Union, while the demise of the corporate liberal compromise initially forced industrial capital to make concessions to labour at the national level. However, the struggle about industrial democracy abated towards the end of the 1970s (Streeck and Schmitter 1991: 139). After the Commission's failed attempt at coordinating corporate control systems in the European Community with regard to board structure and workers' participation, the diverging national systems of 'industrial citizenship' were no longer to be harmonized from the late 1980s onwards. Rather, the objective was to ensure that these different systems could be integrated in, and made to sustain, the single market, and that to this end a minimum level of workers' rights were guaranteed. Mandatory provisions were abandoned in favour of a more flexible approach providing national policy makers and companies with alternatives solutions to implement information and consultation rights. Worker rights were increasingly relegated to the area of labour law, covered by Directorate General (DG) Social Affairs (Streeck 1998). Company law and corporate governance regulation was the exclusive remit of DG Internal Market. Consequently, the focus changed towards establishing information and consultation rights, rather than participation rights with potentially redistributive consequences.

While aspects of corporate control had been present in early debates on company law, for instance with regard to worker participation or board structure, corporate governance was now increasingly perceived in a narrower sense, that is pertaining solely to the internal and external control mechanisms between shareholders and managers. Crucially, the relation between shareholders and managers came to be understood as a principal-agent one, with the share price as prime mechanism to align shareholder and manager interests; here, the market for corporate control as disciplining device plays an essential role. The objective of regulation thus turned away from protection of 'stakeholders', for instance creditors (which were increasingly to be covered by transparency provisions) or workers, towards a focus on creating a framework conducive to the 'efficient' functioning of capital markets. With worker rights consigned to social policies, this elimination of regulatory focus on any other relation than the shareholder-manager constitutes an important precondition for the establishment of the marketization project. As Zumbansen points out, 'the claim to fame of the corporate governance movement at the beginning of the twenty-first century might be the flipside of the longstanding deterioration of labor rights and an effective labor rights regime' (Zumbansen 2006: 14). To be sure, labour law as a legal field is of course far broader than questions of employee participation and works councils.[1] As such, however, the institutional and legal separation of employee rights and shareholder rights within the regulatory context of company law reflects, and at the same time perpetuates, the conceptual dichotomy between the interests of shareholders and other stakeholders of the corporation. A narrowly conceived perception of corporate governance advances an understanding of the role of regulation that precludes the inclusion of labour into the regulatory focus.

Concessions to labour at the EU level

Workers' rights were increasingly seen in the context of minimum concessions to labour to keep industrial relations stable, to facilitate smooth, nonconflictual management. The Social Dialogue, set up in 1985 between employer and employee associations at the European level (that is, BusinessEurope [previously UNICE] and ETUC, as well as the CEEP), has led to the implementation of three directives; none of them, however, related to questions of the governance of, and control over, corporations.[2] As the developments with regard to the proposals for a Fifth Directive and the Vredeling Directive have shown, employee consultation and participation rights have been highly politically contested. While company law directives had established several minimum provisions for companies, workers' rights had to be asserted and negotiated anew with every new legislative proposal of the Commission – the case of the European Works Councils and the European Company Statute illustrate this (Streeck 1998; Villiers 2006). These regulatory developments provided at best *flanking measures* which served to bind labour into the emerging project of neoliberal restructuring. Instead of the supranational harmonization envisaged, an increasingly complex level of coordination arrangements allowed firms to negotiate their own frameworks of worker rights. The increasing integration of capital markets was thus concomitant to an increasing *fragmentation* of workers' rights at the European level. With regard to labour law, corporate governance regulation is at best *defensive*, to the extent that workers are to keep acquired rights, and they are guaranteed consultation rights in a process of corporate restructuring (e.g., in the formation of an *Societas Europaea*, SE). In general, however, with the regulatory framework granting more and more scope for firm-level arrangements and self-regulatory corporate governance standards and codes, employee protection has been more and more dislodged from the regulatory focus on corporate governance. Rather, it is in the shallow waters of Corporate social responsibility (CSR) that we find employees as 'stakeholders' in a pluralist conception of the corporation, as for instance advanced in the Commission's initial Green Paper on CSR (2001).

Moreover, financial participation of workers was increasingly emphasized, for instance in Employee Stockownership Plans (ESOPs). As the High Level Group that was established to deal with 'cross-border obstacles with regard to financial participation of employees for companies having a transnational dimension' points out, the objective of financial participation with regard to corporate governance was that 'financial participation can be used to promote good corporate governance, by making it possible for the employees to participate as shareholders, ready to promote socially responsible corporate behaviour or even to become board members of enterprises' (European Commission 2003b). Employee participation, it seemed, was no longer to be established by mandatory law, but rather through turning workers into shareholders. This is indicative of the broader shift in the social purpose of company law – rather than integrating the perspectives and rights of stakeholders, and in particular workers, into the regulatory framework, the focus came to be primarily, and almost exclusively, on the rights of shareholders.

Contestation of the marketization project

As noted above, organized labour at the European level, most notably the ETUC, has been integrated in the coalition of social forces carrying the broader project of 'relaunching' the Single Market since the late 1980s. In particular through the 'symbolic Euro-corporatism' (Bieling and Schulten 2003) within the structure of the Social Dialogue, organized labour had been implicated in the restructuring of social relations according to the requirements of increasingly integrated European financial markets. The marketization project, as outlined above, has been an important part of this integration process; however, as workers' rights were relegated to social policy and employment, organized labour did not concentrate so much on the company law programme as such. The struggle over the Service Directive or the right to strike occupied labour associations at the EU level more than the Commission's initiatives with regard to corporate governance.

When the Commission presented its Company Law Action Plan in 2003, there was no mention of worker rights at all in the policy programme. This was a turning point for the ETUC's position on the Commission's project. As a senior member at the ETUC's research institute points out 'we realised that we as a trade union didn't have anything to do with this – there is this Action Plan but we're doing

Social Dialogue'.[3] The ETUC strongly opposed the underlying orientation of the Action Plan, arguing in its reaction to the consultation that 'governance is presented as a problem limited solely to the relationship between shareholders and management, as though an entreprise were a private entity that concerned the interests of shareholders alone' (ETUC 2003: 4).

In May of 2006, the ETUC Executive Committee adopted a resolution on 'Corporate Governance at the European Level', in which it was cautiously argued that the 'European corporate governance framework should lay down proper institutional conditions for companies to promote long-term profitability and employment prospects, define mechanisms that prevent mismanagement and guarantee transparency and accountability with regard to investments and their returns' (ETUC 2006).[4] The strategy through which the ETUC seeks to proceed is twofold. On the one hand, it emphasizes that Art 138 provides for the consultation of social partners on a range of issues concerning employment and social affairs. However, the structural separation of worker rights and company law/corporate governance regulation means that actual company law issues are outside the reach of social partnership now.[5] At the same time, organized labour is trying to preserve existing worker rights (for instance through the provisions in the European Works Councils and the European Company Statute), and raise people's awareness that corporate governance is more than just about shareholders. The former secretary general of the ETUC, Emilio Gabaglio, has been a member of the Corporate Governance Forum, and he has liaised frequently with the ETUC; in addition to this, the ETUC has set up its own expert groups on corporate governance (ETUI 2011). In its recent strategy and action Plan 2007–2011, the ETUC stepped up the rhetoric, demanding that

> it should not be left to managers and investors – nor the European Commission – alone to define what companies do for society. Workers participation is not a private affair in the hands of employers. It is a public matter which, if need be, must be politically imposed against the wishes of employers and investors. (ETUC 2007: 79)

However, as the structural separation between company law and labour law/employment policies has proceeded rather fast, organized labour actors are more or less consigned to writing position papers and participating in consultations in which labour is seen as but one stakeholder of the modern corporation. There is, however, an emerging cooperation between labour and the European Parliament, which could potentially be more of an actual obstacle to the marketization project.

In the context of an own-initiative report on corporate governance, the Parliament called on the Commission for 'taking the European social model into consideration when deciding on further measures for the development of company law; this also involves the participation of employees' (European Parliament 2006). In marked contrast to the Commission's programme, the Parliament stressed that

> corporate governance is not only about the relationship between shareholders and managers, but that other stakeholders within the company are also important for a balanced decision-making process and should be able to contribute to decisions on the strategy of companies; ... in particular, there should be room for the provision of information to, and consultation of, employees. (ibid.)

With regard to the regulatory developments in company law and corporate governance, organized labour is still mainly politically active in the national arena, while the control over corporations, and, crucially, the regulation thereof, is becoming increasingly transnationalized. The institutionalization of the remnants of corporatist consensus in the form of the Social Dialogue, in concert with the relegation of worker rights from the company law agenda to social policies, meant that organized labour has been implicated in the restructuring of corporate governance without much institutional power to influence or even oppose the regulatory trajectory. Also, soft law and regulatory mechanisms such as expert groups and consultations advance and encourage the participation and representation of particular interest groups, rather than a fundamentally redistributive process on the basis of mandatory regulation.

The structural selectivity of the European state formation here clearly disadvantages labour interests. What is more, the depoliticization inherent to the expert-driven process of regulatory articulation renders concrete political contestation more difficult, in particular in a discursive context in which the boundaries of corporate governance, and the regulatory debate in general, are predominantly being defined following the exigencies of capital markets. The structural position of labour actors in the framework of EU industrial relations has changed in that, as Streeck points out, 'material rewards for workers and the institutional influence for labor are more than before tied to a joint commitment with employers to success in competitive markets' (Streeck 1998: 15). Also, developments that are seen as a success for labour at the EU level can in fact weaken the position of organized labour at the national level, as in the example of the European Works Councils, where collective agreements are undermined through firm-level concessions (Bieling and Schulten 2003). Yet in the absence of a real European Social Model that could, in a Polanyian vein, mitigate the social implications of the marketization of corporate control, the limits of this political project are becoming increasingly manifest. In 2006 the ETUC agreed upon a common position on corporate governance which fundamentally conflicts with the marketization project; labour associations and representatives, mainly in concert with the socialist group Party of European Socialists (PES) of the EP, have also challenged the regulatory process as such. The market-oriented common sense articulated through expert groups and corporate governance conferences is being challenged by organized labour and members of the European Parliament. The role of expert knowledge in the regulatory process is increasingly questioned (Alter EU 2008), and 'critical expert groups' provide alternative expertise (cf. PES 2007; Euromemorandum 2007). The question then is whether this contestation has indeed gained momentum through the crisis?

After the crisis? Regulatory reactions and the resilience of shareholder value

While the crisis had, until the collapse of Lehman Brothers in September 2008, mainly been seen as confined to the housing market and specialized finance, it became painfully clear that this was indeed not just a case of tremendous market failure, but rather a manifestation of the underlying crisis tendencies inherent in financial capitalism, premised upon the continuous extension of financial markets (cf. Lewis and Perry in this volume). The expansion of financial markets is predicated on a political project establishing necessary legal and economic conditions; hence it is only through focusing on these processes, and the regulatory counter-reactions after the onset of the crisis, that we can understand in how far we are now witnessing a fundamental change in neoliberal capitalism. As Helleiner et al. (2010) have shown, responses to the financial crisis have indeed affected the public–private debate in the regulation of financial markets. New markets have been regulated (e.g., over the counter [OTC] derivatives), there is an increasing level of public monitoring of financial intermediaries, e.g., credit-rating agencies, as well as mandatory regulation instead of self-regulation, e.g., with regard to hedge funds. It became abundantly clear in the crisis that capitalism indeed needs the state to maintain itself.

While the financial crisis has been most prominently a crisis of liquidity, it has also revealed the pathologies of market-based corporate governance. The fundamental link between financialization as broader process and shareholder value as concrete manifestation has become clear even to policy makers and the public at large. Regulatory reactions, however, have without exception adopted a problem-solving approach focusing on 'fixing the flaws' in the system rather than reconsidering radically different policy choices. Given the firm entrenchment of the shareholder value paradigm within the regulatory domain, this does not really come as a surprise. Rather, it is a continuation of the corporate governance discourse that has already been articulated in response to the corporate scandals in the early 2000s. As Soederberg argues,

> the state finds fault almost exclusively with the misalignment in principal-agent relations, and therefore concentrates attention on issues of fraud, accountability of boards and CEOs and lack of transparency, as opposed to neoliberal-led forms of capitalist restructuring that have benefited a relatively small number of powerful and wealthy people. (Soederberg 2010: 55)

The question regulators are confronted with is thus not whether marketized corporate governance regulation can (or should) be maintained, but how to find best practices to make the system work better; how to fine-tune technical issues and if necessary, how to insert regulatory gussets to ensure supervision that could pre-empt market failures. This is rather well illustrated by the OECD's identification of the issues most immediately linked to financial crisis: the governance of remuneration process; effective implementation of risk management; board practices and the exercise of shareholder rights (OECD 2009: 2). In particular this last aspect is instructive for an analysis of whether we are indeed witnessing a shift away from neoliberal corporate governance regulation; at the same time the re-emergence of the debate on corporate ownership and governance shows the possibilities and limits of the role and agency of organized labour in this process, as argued below.

Failure of external control: how to turn shareholders into good corporate citizens?

The marketization of corporate control has been a fairly successful political project to subject the control over listed companies more and more to 'the market', aimed almost exclusively at generating shareholder value. However, as has become abundantly clear even before the crisis, 'the market' does not appear to be so keen on making necessary investments in time and information to exercise these control rights in voting and monitoring companies. As the OECD points out, 'shareholders have contributed importantly to failures of boards and companies by being too impassive and reactive' (ibid.: 53). Investors are often highly concentrated or have holdings across the market so that it cannot be assumed that they have a strong interest in a particular company. It also requires expertise and comprehensive information for shareholders to take a position on strategic issues. There have, of course, been prominent cases of shareholder activism in recent years, but it is very much the question whether activist shareholders indeed represent the interests of (minority) shareholders in general. It is quite instructive in this context that shareholder activism is often portrayed as an act of emancipation, echoing the parallel to voting rights in a liberal democracy. Indeed, *The Economist* already detected 'a glimmer of hope for corporate democracy' (*The Economist* 2009a). That one of the core constituencies of the company, that is the workers, is indeed excluded from the corporate democratic utopia seems to be irrelevant.

So what can be done to encourage shareholders to take a long-term perspective and exercise their control rights? A range of regulatory proposals have been suggested to get shareholders, in particular the rather unwilling institutional investors, to become 'good corporate citizens' (ibid. 2009b).[6] In most countries, concrete regulatory measures still have to be introduced. Most problematic, as *The Economist* points out, is that these initiatives would run counter to the '*moral* argument against depriving property-owners of their rights' (ibid. 2010a, emphasis added). The limits of the marketization of corporate control clearly demonstrates the contradictory nature of regulatory projects geared at safeguarding the rights of owners of capital; having pushed an extensive political project to hand the control of companies to the shareholders, the state is now at a loss as it simply cannot force them to then exercise prudential ownership. This is a development we see in most capitalist market economies in which the shareholder-value paradigm has become dominant.

Crisis management and regulatory developments at the EU level

Initial reactions to the financial crisis came from the Member States, in the form of bank bailouts and rescue programmes, rather than as a concerted European action. Following the report by the *De Larosière* group, a reconstruction of financial market supervision at the European level has been initiated.[7] The Commission has also drawn up regulatory initiatives as the direct response to the failure of several external corporate governance mechanisms that have become central in corporate governance practices in the European Union. However, the crisis prompted the OECD to announce that it would also re-examine its general corporate governance principles, arguing that 'ineffective board oversight, significant failures in risk management in major financial institutions, incentive systems that encouraged and rewarded high levels of risk taking... are also relevant for non-financial systems' (OECD 2009: 3). In this context, the *De Larosière* group also noted that corporate governance failures in the unfolding of the credit crunch and the subsequent crisis have to be seen against the background of the broader financial and macroeconomic system.

> It is clear that the financial system at large did not carry out its tasks with enough consideration for the long-term interest of its stakeholders. Most of the incentives – many of them being the result of official action – encouraged financial institutions to act in a short-term perspective and to make as much profit as possible to the detriment of credit quality and prudence. (De Larosière 2009: 9)

While the actual impact of the Recommendation on Executive Remuneration of 2004 has been minimal (European Commission 2007), the EU has launched several initiatives in this field in the wake of the crisis.[8] The *Recommendation on Remuneration in the Financial Services Sector* advises Member States to improve risk management in financial firms by aligning pay and bonus incentives with sustainable and effective risk management.[9] Another recommendation complements the 2004 and 2005 Recommendations, with the objective to further align remuneration with a long-term/sustainable company perspective.[10] The Commission has announced that it will pursue further legislative proposals, in particular with regard to the revision of the Capital Requirements Directive. Most provisions for more disclosure and control mechanisms over executive remuneration, however, pertain to shareholders and the board only, rather than granting other stakeholders voice, or at least a consultation status (outside boards in which employee representatives are present) on these important issues. It is clear that the kind of regulatory response we have witnessed so far does not correspond to the far-reaching changes that organized labour has been advocating. It is notable that the bulk of regulatory initiatives in response to the crisis have been regulation of policy areas pertaining to market mechanisms (e.g., with regard to Accounting Standards or Rating Agencies), which had previously been questioned by trade unions and the European Parliament, but were only taken up by the Commission in reaction to the crisis. At the same time, though, the *De Larosière* group made it very clear that the failures and excesses in risk management and executive remuneration were also closely related to the failure of a corporate governance system that increasingly relied on independent directors. In particular in financial services, boards did not grasp the complex structure of financial instruments and exposure of banks and companies to financial markets. As the Commissioner for the Internal Market, Michel Barnier, argued, 'we need stronger corporate governance' and to consider 'targeted measures' to strengthen the independence of boards and look at the role played by shareholders and external auditors' (Barnier 2010).

And yet the European Commission seems to have developed doubts about its own policies, as a recent Green Paper by the Commission confirms:

> The financial crisis has shown that confidence in the model of the shareholder-owner who contributes to the company's long-term viability has been severely shaken, to say the least...The Commission is aware that this problem does not affect only financial institutions. More generally, it raises questions about the effectiveness of corporate governance rules based on the presumption of effective control by shareholders. (European Commission 2010d)

This is quite remarkable, given that just a couple of years ago the Commissioner at the time, McCreevy was still keen on declaring shareholders 'king or queen' of the corporation. However, this tentative expression of a potential change in regulatory orientation raises several important questions. At this stage, it remains to be seen whether the by now firmly embedded marketization of corporate control will prove resilient to these regulatory changes spurred on by the immediate and mid-term regulatory responses to the crisis. It is important to not here that while the Commission's statement is very interesting indeed, as argued above, the 'common sense' of corporate governance had not changed in its core.[11] Despite the public discreditation of underlying dogmas such as the Efficient Market Hypothesis, corporate control is still perceived as bifurcated – control for shareholders within the corporate governance and company law domain, while all issues pertaining to 'stakeholders' are situated within Social Affairs and Employment. Corporate social responsibility, environmental reporting and socially responsible investing might all be significant avenues to explore within the regulatory terrain of the European Union, but as long as control remains firmly isolated and exclusively allocated to owners of capital, the core of the marketization project remains intact – and with that the core of neoliberalism as a capitalist class project (see the introduction to this volume).

What role for contestation and organized labour?

And yet the discussion about corporate governance has become increasingly politicized, with the European Parliament taking an ever more critical position on the Commission's policy initiatives. The case of the Commission's decision to drop the Fourteenth Company Law Directive for the cross-border transfer of the registered office of a company, which resulted in an EP resolution, or the debates over the Alternative Investment Fund Manager Directive, demonstrate that in contrast to just a decade ago, corporate governance has indeed become a contested concept also at the EU level.

As the financial crisis and its consequences have exacerbated the growing asymmetries in the European Union, class inequalities have become more and more apparent. Initially through the socialization of banks' losses, incurred through excessive risk-taking, served as short-term crisis management. But as a monetary response was impossible for the members of the Eurozone (and other Member States, in particular in the Baltic and CEE region, suffered severe currency depreciation), fiscal reactions have now initiated welfare cuts and higher taxation. In the context of the sustained legitimacy crisis of the European Union (Van Apeldoorn et al. 2008), these initiatives also provide more opportunities for political contestation. Several ideas and demands that have been put forward by organized labour, the European Parliament and NGOs prior to the crisis are now being openly discussed – for instance, who would have ever expected to see governments and the European Commission embracing the idea of a financial transactions tax (even though the debate on the FTT was eventually dropped at the G20 level). Other demands that have been taken up by the Commission, if only partially, include regulation of credit-rating agencies and alternative investors. There has also been a notable increase in the *epistemic* contestation of regulatory principles, with trade unions, civil society organizations and academics producing alternative frameworks for corporate governance regulation and broader financial market frameworks (see e.g., Vitols and Kluge 2011).

However, with the 'obvious' culprits, that is, in the case of this financial crisis, investment bankers and credit-rating agencies dealt with the scope for further regulatory action increasingly limited by the established market-making regulation and the legal basis of European integration. What is more, the assumption that the crisis would be a turning point for neoliberal market integration is premature as long as the structural dominance of financial capitalism is still prevalent in the European Union. More concretely in the context of corporate governance, strategic selectivities are still at play when it comes to the politics of resistance. As Soederberg argues, 'resistance of corporate power...framed by, and limited to, a structured and sanitized exchange between those who own and those who control' (Soederberg 2010: 4). By flanking issues of corporate control with CSR, consultations and stakeholder dialogues, class struggle is obscured from the political process.

Concluding remarks

Whether the current financial and economic crisis represents indeed a conjunctural terrain upon which opposition to neoliberal European governance can be formed remains to be seen in the coming years. As the previous discussion has shown, it is very much the question whether organized labour at the European level can indeed (and aims to) assume a stronger role in a counter-hegemonic struggle. With regard to corporate governance and company law at least, organized labour has been mainly struggling to maintain and defend the concessions made by capital at the European level, rather than establishing an alternative to neoliberal restructuring. As I have argued, here we also need to look at the institutional and structural forms of state power, which renders it even more questionable whether the European level can indeed be turned into a space for Social Europe. As recent rulings by the European Court of Justice have indicated, the tension within the politico-legal framework of the European Union between the 'capitalist' freedoms of movement and establishment and the fundamental lawfulness of industrial actions that could potentially limit those freedoms is increasingly decided towards the benefit of economic liberalization.[12] However, this does not necessarily mean that trade unions have no option but to revert to mainly national strategies, as Scharpf implied by stating that 'hoping for a Social Europe actually prevents politicians from taking the action that is still possible at the national level' (Scharpf 2008: 16). Trade unions are increasingly using the European level as an alternative space for mobilization, and are also increasingly voicing criticism about European governance. At the same time, the European Parliament is becoming an important ally for trade union organizations (e.g., the call for a Social Progress Clause in the Lisbon Treaty). However, in order to overcome the neoliberal bias of the European state formation, trade unions would indeed have to participate, or even initiate, in the articulation of a counter-hegemonic project that would transcend their respective particularistic interests. While there have been successful instances of cooperation with social movements (e.g., against the Services Directive), there are also wide-ranging internal discussions and tensions within the labour movement. The debt crisis in Greece, Ireland and several Mediterranean countries has called into question the underlying idea of European solidarity, with mass protests in those countries failing to encourage broader expressions of support among citizens in other Member States. With the prospect of strengthened macroeconomic coordination in the Eurozone in a climate of severe debt problems, labour interests are unlikely to be at the heart of the negotiations. Without a concertation of social forces rallying around a coherent alternative socio-economic programme for European integration, it seems that despite the crisis of neoliberalism, shareholder value will remain at the core of European corporate governance.

Notes

1. See Zumbansen 2006 for an overview of the 'parallel worlds' of labour law and company law. As he points out, this separation is also prevalent in most textbooks and law courses (Zumbansen 2006: 16–17).
2. On parental leave in 1995, on part-time work in 1997 and on fixed-term contracts in 1999. The Social Dialogue has been criticized as 'symbolic Euro-corporatism' (Bieling and Schulten 2003; cf. Streeck 1998)
3. Interview with senior researcher at the ETUI-REHS, 22 November 2006.
4. Available at http://www.etuc.org/a/2250 (last accessed 10 January 2011).
5. As a member of the ETUI puts it, 'we complain that they should have consulted the Social Partners under Art 138, but they tell us that employee participation wasn't concerned, and we should go and talk to DG V (Employment) about consultation information' (Interview with a senior researcher at the ETUI-REHS, 22 November 2006.
6. It has been suggested to give shareholders of longer tenure extra voting rights (as is the case in several French corporations), or to bar new shareholders from voting until they have held the stock for a certain amount of time. In the US, the Employee Retirement Income Security Act (ERISA) legislation obliges investors to use their voting rights and publicly disclose. A new rule at the New York Exchange ends discretionary voting by brokers who hold shares on behalf of their clients.
7. For detailed analyses of the regulatory reactions in financial market integration, see the special issue 'European Perspectives on the Global Financial Crisis', *Journal of Common Market Studies* 47(5), edited by Dermot Hodson and Lucia Quaglia.

8. For an explanatory statement, see European Commission, Communication accompanying Commission Recommendation complementing Recommendations 2004/913/EC and 2005/162/EC as regards the regime for the remuneration of directors of listed companies and Commission Recommendation on remuneration policies in the financial services sector, COM (2009) 211 final, Brussels, 30 April 2009.
9. European Commission, Recommendation on remuneration policies in the financial services sector, C(2009) 3159, Brussels, 30 April 2009.
10. European Commission, Recommendation complementing Recommendations 2004/913/EC and 2005/162/EC as regards the regime for the remuneration of directors of listed companies, C(2009) 3177, Brussels, 30 April 2009.
11. And, it should be noted, expert groups are still very much at the centre of policy formulation. The European Corporate Governance Forum has issued several statements on executive remuneration and voting, and the De Larosière group is a case in point within the financial markets domain.
12. For more information on these ECJ cases, see the extensive collection of documents and analysis on the ETUC website, available at http://www.etui.org/en/Headline-issues/Viking-Laval-Rueffert-Luxembourg (last accessed 13 May 2011).

4
Investment Bank Power and Neoliberal Regulation: From the Volcker Shock to the Volcker Rule

Sandy Brian Hager

'The bank is something else than men. It happens that every man in a bank hates what the bank does and yet the bank does it. The bank is something more than men, I tell you. It's the monster. Men made it, but they can't control it.'
–John Steinbeck, *The Grapes of Wrath*

'I'm doing God's work.'
–Lloyd Blankfein, CEO of Goldman Sachs

Introduction[1]

In 1941, Paul Sweezy (1910–2004), a founding member of the 'monopoly capital' school of Marxism, published an article on the power of US investment banks in light of the 1929 stock market crash and ensuing depression. His assessment of their relative position and future prospects within the corporate hierarchy was bleak. Although the major investment banks had survived the turbulent 1930s, Sweezy argued that they failed to reassert the dominance they secured during the initial transition from competitive to monopoly capitalism around the turn of the twentieth century (see Veblen 1923). Firms that once embraced the guidance of investment bankers had matured into giants capable of expanding their operations through internal financing. As a result, most of the securities market activity that took place involved routine refunding operations that required little investment bank expertise, while those few securities that were newly issued were privately placed with increasingly powerful institutional investors.

Taken together, Sweezy (1941: 66, 1942: 265–269) suggested that these changes signified a 'simple atrophy of functions' for investment banks, whose remaining business was 'being carried on to an increasing extent by new methods and by new agencies better suited to the task'. Investment banks played a crucial role in the consolidation of monopoly capitalism. Yet once this process was completed, Sweezy (1941: 67–68; emphasis in original) argued that they ceased to 'play a *special* role in the economic life of the country'. The power vacuum left in the wake of their decline was likely to be filled by the state and family-controlled industrial empires.

Forty years later, Sweezy followed up the themes of this original article by reassessing the power of investment banks during the heyday of monopoly capitalism, the postwar 'Golden Age'. Investment banking had proven to be highly profitable in this period, but the community of large investment banks, Sweezy (1981: 249) claimed, had still not 'regained any of its old aura as the aristocracy of the business world'. Competition for underwriting and merger services had become increasingly fierce, and the diffusion of power created by competition was further aided by the growing tendency towards conglomeration. Much like corporate legal or auditing services, Sweezy (ibid.: 250) suggested that investment banks played an essential role in the 'smooth functioning of the corporate system'. But this did not provide them with a position of power relative to their corporate clients, nor did it stem their relative long-term decline within the financial sector. In short, Sweezy reaffirmed his earlier claim that investment bank power was a transitory phenomenon strictly confined to an earlier phase of capitalist development. Upon reaching this unambiguous conclusion, Sweezy never again revisited the issue of investment bank power and its implications for US capitalism.

What is most remarkable about this final assessment is that it came on the cusp of what Sweezy and other members of the monopoly capital school would later identify as a new phase of capitalist development in the US. This phase, which emerged in the early 1980s and which now appears to be drawing to a close with the global financial crisis, has recently been referred to as 'the age of monopoly-finance capital' (Bellamy Foster 2010). According to monopoly capital theorists, the main feature of the monopoly-finance phase is the 'financialization' of capital accumulation, a process that involves the stagnation of investment in the 'real' productive economy and the explosion of 'fictitious' claims to wealth. While Keynesianism was the 'ideological counterpart' of monopoly capitalism, neoliberalism, with its free market mantra of 'sound money', liberalization and deregulation, has emerged as 'the economic policy most conducive to today's monopoly-finance capital' (Bellamy Foster and McChesney 2010: 52).

The monopoly capital school argues that this shift to financialization and neoliberalism has led to the resurgence of 'financial capital'.[2] Power, according to this argument, is increasingly wielded by large finance, insurance and real estate sector (FIRE) corporations at the expense of the industrial giants that dominated the postwar period (Sweezy 1994; Bellamy Foster and Holleman 2010). This argument seems to conflict with Sweezy's earlier claims about investment bank decline. Investment banks are, after all, a part of FIRE, so doesn't the apparent resurgence of that sector suggest that investment bank power is not in fact a 'transitory' phenomenon confined to an earlier phase of capitalism, but a very real part of the contemporary period? Sweezy provides us with little insight into this question because, as was noted above, the issue of investment bank power was completely neglected in his work after 1981. Unfortunately, the works of other monopoly capital theorists are also of little help. The few brief references that are made to the power of investment banks merely reassert Sweezy's original arguments (Bellamy Foster and Magdoff 2009: 149).

How do we explain this indifference, especially given the monopoly capital school's recent emphasis on financial power? The answer may lie in the enduring influence of Sweezy's conclusions. With this justifiably influential figure reaching such unambiguous conclusions about the transitory nature of investment bank power, it is little wonder that others working within the monopoly capital school since then have never seriously re-examined the issue. Another reason may have to do with the growing trend towards conglomeration, which Sweezy (1981) not only regarded as a further sign of investment bank decline, but which he also saw as eliminating any meaningful distinctions between financial firms. If investment banks are indeed indistinguishable from other financial services conglomerates then there is little need to re-examine the power of investment banks as a separate category of firms.

My purpose in this chapter is to challenge this indifference and re-examine Sweezy's arguments about the transitory nature of investment bank power. Through extensive qualitative–quantitative analysis, I argue that there has in fact been a rapid increase in the power of large investment banks from the early 1980s up until the current financial crisis. This power is wielded in almost every facet of financial market activity and therefore extends far beyond their traditional power in underwriting and merger advisory services. But this diversification of power, I suggest, does not render the distinctions between investment banks and other financial services conglomerates meaningless. The trend towards conglomeration is undoubtedly significant, and now, with the disappearance of independent investment banks in the wake of the current crisis, the distinctions between FIRE firms may have been irreversibly erased. I argue that the rapid rise of investment bank power over the past three decades, as well as its apparent decline with the crisis, cannot be adequately explained if investment banks are lumped together with the FIRE sector as a whole. Though functional boundaries between firms may have faded, the course of investment bank power over the past three decades has been bound up with the unique ways in which they have manoeuvred within US financial regulation.

This alternative empirical account does not arise within a theoretical vacuum. The arguments here have developed out of an engagement with the theory of monopoly capital, and particularly with its conceptualization of the relationship between power and the central process of capitalist societies, capital accumulation. Specifically, the theory of monopoly capital relies on a bifurcated view of accumulation, one that separates capital into 'real' and 'financial' spheres. The interaction between these spheres is supposed to explain the power of investment banks, but as will be discussed in detail below, this bifurcated view is logically circular and empirically inoperable. Because of this, the monopoly capital approach is unable to explain or measure the oscillations in investment bank power over time.

My own approach, anchored within the capital *as* power framework pioneered by Jonathan Nitzan and Shimshon Bichler (2009), takes its point of departure in explicitly rejecting the real/nominal duality underlying monopoly capital's theory of accumulation. Instead, it argues that the central logic governing accumulation is capitalization: the discounting of risk-adjusted future earnings into present value. As a symbolic quantification of capitalist power to restructure society, capitalization provides an alternative starting point for investigating investment bank power. I argue that linking the quantitative architecture of capitalization to the qualitative manifestations of power provides a more compelling account of the changing power of investment banks since the 1980s.

Finally, this alternative theory of accumulation also leads to a rather different assessment of neoliberalism's role within contemporary capitalism. For the monopoly capital school, neoliberalism is said to serve the interests of 'financial capital'. Yet my empirical study suggests that this assertion is far too general (see also Kotz 2010: 6). Even if financial capital is narrowly equated with so-called financial intermediaries, the claim that neoliberalism has served their collective interests glosses over the ways in which neoliberal policies and regulations have at certain points served to enhance the competitive struggles *within* the FIRE sector (compare the chapter by Paul Lewis and James Perry in this volume).

The rest of the chapter is roughly organized into two halves. The first half offers a systematic critique of the monopoly capital school's approach to capital accumulation, and outlines an alternative approach based on the notion of capital *as* power. The second half then offers an empirical analysis of investment bank power since the 1980s, with particular emphasis on the linkages between investment bank power and the rise of neoliberal regulation. It then offers some tentative thoughts about US financial sector power and the limits and possibilities of new regulatory initiatives in light of the current crisis.

Finance, Power and Monopoly Capital

The monopoly capital (hereafter MC) school's explanation for the power of financial intermediaries is anchored within a theory of capital. Most of the time, this theory is not explicit in Sweezy's writings on investment banks, but it is still possible to retrace how this theory informs Sweezy's arguments about the changing role of investment banks.

Before the rise of giant corporations in the early twentieth century, Sweezy argued that accumulation in the US was governed by Marx's competitive laws of motion, including the tendency for the profit rate to fall (Baran and Sweezy 1966: 72). It was in the nineteenth century within an environment of fierce competition that the investment banker, enriched by the financing of the Civil War and the construction of the railroads, began to exert incredible influence over the nascent US industrial apparatus. Desperate to stem the tide of excess output, deflation and falling profits, the industrial firms of this period welcomed the oversight that investment banks, led by J. P. Morgan, provided by sitting on corporate advisory boards, facilitating the combination of firms into holding companies, and underwriting new securities.

In orchestrating the combination of small firms into a tightly knit network of colluding giants, the investment banks helped to restore these sectors to profitability; but Sweezy argued that in doing so the investment banks also planted the seeds for their own demise. As mentioned in the introduction, the once-feeble industrial corporations had become powerful by the early twentieth century, capable of self-financing their operations. Growing profits meant that the industrial corporations were gradually able to shed their reliance on investment banks.

According to Sweezy, these developments had deeper implications for the US because they annulled the competitive tendencies that Marx predicted would bring about a collapse of the capitalist system. While the competitive phase was dominated by the tendency of the profit rate to fall, the monopoly phase was governed by a new tendency for the surplus to rise. Within this phase, the investment banker's position as the most powerful figure in the US was usurped by the large industrial corporation.

Space constraints prevent a thorough discussion of the tendency of the surplus to rise[3], but the basic dilemma of that tendency is that collusive, 'price-making' industrial corporations no longer face a problem of falling profits, but instead a shortage of profitable, productive outlets for their surplus. In order to counteract the tendency towards stagnation that this causes, capitalists come to rely on wasteful expenditures to absorb the economic surplus. The sales effort, government (especially military) spending and the 'financial superstructure' are all singled out as primary 'outlets' for surplus-absorption.

The growth of the 'financial superstructure' can be seen with the explosion of private and public debt, consumer finance, financial instruments and the ballooning of the financial sector that intermediates the proliferating relations of credit and debt. As such, 'finance' still plays a role within advanced monopoly capitalist societies, but under monopoly capitalism, financial power becomes a dependent force since, as an outlet for surplus, the precise oscillations of the financial superstructure ultimately depend on, and can only be explained with reference to, the underlying oscillations in the industrial 'base'.

In MC's analysis of the postwar golden age, finance took a back seat to military spending and advertising as the predominant wasteful outlets for excess surplus. But from 1980s, the MC school turned its attention to the re-emergence of finance as the 'largest countervailing force' to stagnation (Bellamy Foster and Magdoff 2009). Since the early 1980s, MC has argued that stagnation, coupled with financial explosion, has caused the financial superstructure to de-couple significantly from the underlying 'real' economic base. As a consequence, financial intermediaries have moved beyond their supporting-role as 'facilitator[s] of the production and distribution of goods and services' (Magdoff and Sweezy 1987: 20), to become the primary drivers of accumulation.

The MC school offers plenty of data to demonstrate the connection between industrial stagnation and financial explosion over the past three decades, but it is unclear to what extent this data actually supports MC's theoretical claims. One of the less serious problems has to do with diversification, which according to Magdoff and Sweezy (ibid.: 97), made it impossible '...to define or delineate the financial sector with any accuracy'. Since corporations classified as 'industrial' and 'financial' are both increasingly engaged in intermediation, it becomes difficult to separate their financial and industrial activities, and impossible to pin down the financial and industrial components of profitability.[4]

This ambiguity has its origins in a more pressing problem: MC's bifurcation of capital into 'real' and 'financial' spheres. This duality can be tied back to Marx's labour theory of value (LTV), which is supposed to explain the interactions between the two spheres. For Marx, the 'real' sphere of industrial capital is denominated in the universal unit of 'abstract labour' and the 'fictitious' sphere of money capital in prices. Because the LTV assumes that productive labour expended within the 'real' sphere is the source of surplus value, what happens within this sphere is meant to explain the epiphenomenal world of prices.

However, there is one crucial difference between Marx and the monopoly capital school: the latter completely abandoned the LTV as a guide to quantitative empirical research (Sweezy 1942). Given that no one has been able to identify or measure abstract labour, it could be argued that the MC school, which has been careful not only to theorize, but also to explore accumulation empirically, made this move out of necessity. But the abandonment of the LTV came at a hefty price. Recall that in the MC framework, what happens in the 'financial' sphere ultimately hinges on what happens in the 'real' economy. But without a 'real' unit of its own to replace abstract labour, all of MC's empirical measures rely on national accounting data denominated in 'fictitious' prices. To make matters worse, 'real' measurements created by statisticians involve a series of circular assumptions about equilibrium and utility – liberal concepts that are antithetical to Marxism (Nitzan and Bichler 2009). Magdoff and Sweezy (1987: 94) recognized the impossibility of separating the 'real' from the nominal, but never considered the logical circularity of relying on nominal data to explain so-called 'real' phenomena.

Yet even if we take a pragmatic approach and assume that price measurements offer a meaningful proxy for 'real' capital, the explanation still runs into trouble. According to the theory, although the financial superstructure can de-couple from its 'real' base 'to a considerable degree' this cannot happen indefinitely (Bellamy Foster and Magdoff 2009: 72–82). And so the argument follows that periods of speculative excesses eventually unravel, and 'fictitious' capital comes crashing back to 'real' capital. In order to know whether this actually is the case, we need to measure real and fictitious capital to determine if: (1) there was a coupling between them at some point; (2) periods of de-coupling are eventually followed by re-coupling through financial crisis. To address these issues we first need reasonable and comparable proxies for 'real' and 'fictitious' capital. The MC have offered plenty of data on stagnation and financialization, but they have thus far neglected to bring measures for these types of capital together in order to analyse their long-term historical relationship.

By MC's own definitions, 'real' capital is represented by 'the stock of plant, equipment and goods generated in production', while 'fictitious' capital is represented by 'the structure of financial claims produced by the paper titles to this real capital' (Bellamy Foster 2010: 6). Employing these definitions, we would have to compare some measure of the capital stock alongside the market value of debt and equity that has capitalized this 'real' wealth. In research that explores the thesis of a 'mismatch' between 'real' and 'fictitious' capital, Nitzan and Bichler (2009) provide such measures. Figure 4.1 reproduces and updates their data, which analyses the relationship between the rate of change in the current cost of corporate fixed assets ('real' capital) and rate of change in the market value of corporate equities and bonds ('fictitious' capital).

According to the MC approach, in 'normal' times (i.e., prior to the 1980s), 'fictitious' capital is coupled with 'real' capital. Finance may become de-coupled from its real base for a while (i.e., from the 1980s), but this deviation from the rule is short lived and eventually, through the onset of crisis, fictitious capital must come crashing down to its underlying base in the real economy.

The contemporary situation seems to support this account. From the early 1980s to around 2001 'fictitious' capital accelerates while 'real' capital declines, and then stagnates. Throughout the 2000s, a series of crises have seen 'fictitious' capital come crashing down, while 'real' capital has continued to move sideways. Since we are dealing here with long-term trends that unravel over decades, it is too early to say with any certainty that the current crisis has led to a re-coupling of 'fictitious' and 'real' capital. Thus far, however, the results seem to fit with the theory.

How do we know, though, that the situation since the 1980s has been a deviation from normality? And since it is too early to draw definitive conclusions about the current crisis, how do we know that past periods of financial deceleration actually resulted in a re-coupling of 'fictitious'

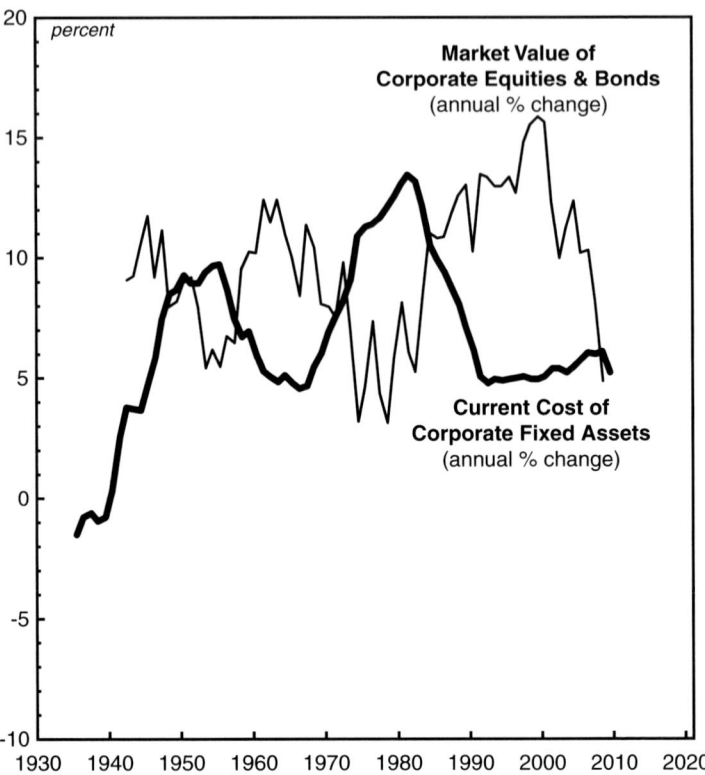

Figure 4.1   'Real base' and 'financial superstructure'

Note: Series smoothed as ten year moving averages.

Source: Nitzan and Bichler (2009); Global Insight (series code: FAPNREZ for current cost of corporate fixed assets).

and 'real' capital? To address these questions, we have to go back further. It is within the broader historical picture that the MC explanation starts to break down. Notice that the alleged coupling of finance with the 'real' before the 1980s never actually happened: finance has *never* been coupled with 'real' capital. So what is explained as a 'deviation' from the norm since the 1980s is in fact the theoretical rule. Since the two are never coupled in the first place, there is no sense in talking about a period of de-coupling since the 1980s. Furthermore, this inverse relation between the two means that periods of financial decline have not resulted in its re-convergence with 'real' capital, but in upswings in 'real' accumulation!

The complications created by diversification, the logical circularity of using prices to measure 'real' phenomena, and above all, the absence of a meaningful relationship between proxy measurements for 'fictitious' and 'real' capital, should be enough to raise serious doubts about monopoly capital's bifurcated theory of accumulation. Without a meaningful way of distinguishing between the 'real' and financial spheres, MC's explanation of the precise movements of finance and the historical changes in the power of financial intermediaries breaks down. Sweezy's research provides useful insights into the changing role and power of investment banks from the turn of the twentieth century through the postwar period, but these insights are inevitably limited by the theoretical assumptions that underpin his account. Though the MC school draws linkages between power and capital accumulation, their explanation of these linkages lacks theoretical coherence and empirical grounding. Consequently, it is not sufficient to uncritically adopt the tools of MC in order to update Sweezy's analysis of investment banks. Instead, we need to first rethink the linkage between power and accumulation.

Capital *as* power

In this section, I outline some features of a capital *as* power (CasP) alternative. Like the MC school, CasP explicitly rejects the quantitative dimensions of Marx's LTV, precisely because of the logical and empirical impossibility of the theory's underlying unit of abstract labour. However, it goes further in also abandoning the circular assumption that the quantities of price are somehow representative of unmeasurable 'real' quanta that are supposed to explain them. The problem with the real/nominal duality is that it assumes an impossible *dual quantity* relationship between values and prices.

Instead, CasP argues that there is only one universal quantitative reality for capitalists, and that is the market value of their assets.[5] As a system of commodification based on private ownership, capitalism is particularly amenable to numerical ordering: anything that can be privately owned can be priced, and that is why the history of capitalism has witnessed an exponential expansion of the price system.

While prices are the fundamental unit of the capitalist order, the central logic governing this order is capitalization: the discounting of risk-adjusted future earnings into present value. Of course, earnings have a lot to do with production, but they extend far beyond the factory floor; anything that is expected to impact the course of future earnings can be capitalized. Since the fundamental unit and pattern of the capitalist order are financial, capital accumulation itself is to be understood with reference to a single rather than a dual entity: capital is finance and only finance.

But why capital *as* power? The answer can be traced back to the institution of private property. As was mentioned above, anything that can be privately owned can be priced, and the price of that asset is determined by discounting its risk-adjusted expected future earnings. To understand the nature of private ownership, Nitzan and Bichler (2009: 228) argue, we need to look no further than the root of the word 'private', whose etymology can be traced back to the Latin 'privatus', meaning 'restricted'. It follows that since private ownership is organized around the principle of *exclusion*, the ability to exclude others from using that property is itself a matter of organized power. Since accumulation is impossible without this institutionalized exclusion, power needs to be integrated into our definition of capital from the very start.

Though capitalization is usually treated as a benign technical exercise in mainstream theories of finance, it is recast within the CasP approach as a symbolic quantification of capitalist power to restructure and reshape society. Whether capitalists own claims on the earnings of governments, consumers, industrial or financial corporations, their goal is always to accumulate by having the capitalized value of their assets grow over time. This dynamic process is inherently relative: capitalists seek to increase the value of their assets relative to some average benchmark. As capitalists boost their capitalization relative to other capitalists, they accumulate *differentially*, and as a result, augment their power.

The universalizing struggle to achieve differential accumulation provides the point of departure for CasP. Though this process is mapped quantitatively, its effects are always manifested qualitatively. Thus in place of Marx's *quantitative* (labour) theory of value, CasP offers a *qualitative* (power) theory of value that analytically links together the quantitative architecture of capitalization with an account of the broader societal manifestations of power. The link is always speculative, but its advantage is that, unlike Marx's LTV, it provides both a theoretical explanation *and* empirical tools for exploring the nature of contemporary capitalist power.

Investment banks: differential accumulation

So how does this framework help us to explore investment bank power since the early 1980s? Figure 4.2 provides the starting point for such an investigation by plotting the differential capitalization and profits of the top five US investment banks relative to a proxy for what Nitzan and Bichler refer to as 'dominant capital': the top 100 US corporations (ranked by market capitalization).[6] Both series indicate rapid growth in favour of the large investment banks.[7] In 1973, the relative capitalization and net profit of a large investment bank were a paltry 0.08 and 0.1 times the dominant capital average. In 1981, when Sweezy was sounding the final death knell of investment banks, they were still insignificant. However, since then, both measures have increased rapidly and steadily, so that by 2006, the differential net profit of the top five was slightly *larger* than the dominant capital average. From this high point in 2006, we see the impact of the crisis on the differential profits of the investment bank, which fell back down 0.8 times the average in 2008.

The differential capitalization of the large investment banks mirrors the pattern of differential profits, but its overall magnitude is lower. This suggests that, due to the perceived differential riskiness of investment bank earnings, investors have been reluctant to translate the increases in profits into equal increases in capitalization. Still, at 59 per cent of the dominant capital average in 2007, and even taking into account the crisis-era decline to 54 per cent in 2008, the differential capitalization of the large investment banks has seen a marked upsurge over the past three to four decades.

As a first step, the data in Figure 4.2 bring into serious doubt Sweezy's 'transitory power' thesis. Investment bank power appears instead to be a rapidly growing feature of contemporary capitalism. From their subordinate position in the 1970s and early 1980s, the large investment banks have achieved rapid differential accumulation, the levels of which are now comparable with the uppermost echelon of dominant capital.

The task that remains is to offer some explanation for this remarkable transformation. We can start by exploring how the power of contemporary investment banks differs from their predecessors. At the turn of the twentieth century, investment banks wielded their power over corporations who sought financing in securities markets. In this 'traditional' role as agents, the earnings of investment banks are dependent on the fees and commissions they charge for bringing together the two sides of securities market transactions. If we look at the pricing power over these activities, there is evidence to suggest that investment banks no longer dominate them. For example, average brokerage commissions on the New York Stock Exchange have fallen 60 per cent to 80 per cent since fixed commissions were abandoned in 1975 (Hoover 2005). During the

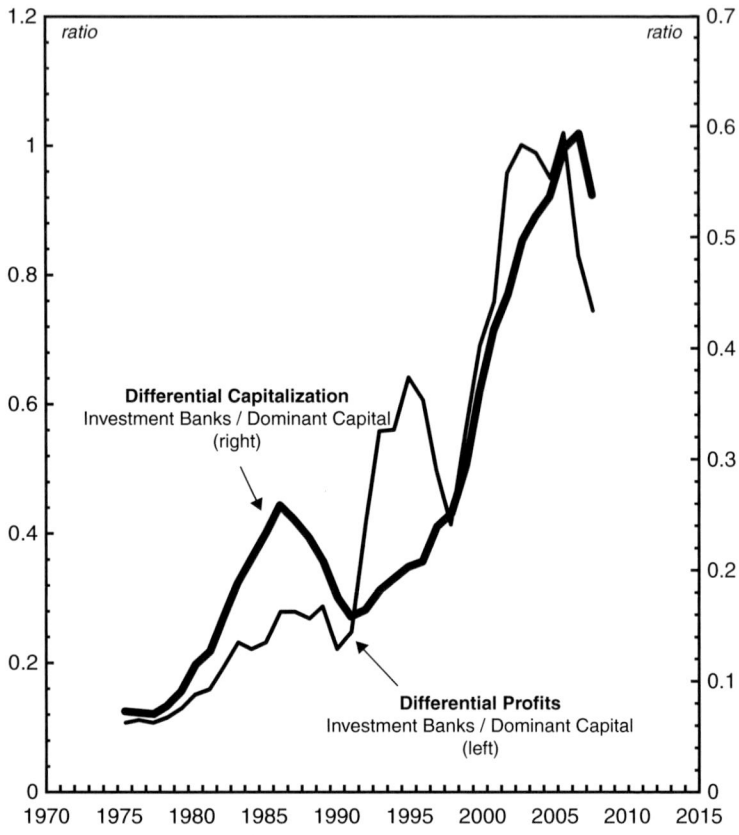

Figure 4.2   Investment bank differential accumulation

Note: Series smoothed as five year moving averages.

Source: Compustat through WRDS (series codes: CSHO for common shares outstanding; NI for net income; PRCC_F for price close fiscal).

heyday of investment banking in the early 1900s, common stock under-writing spreads were as high as 20 per cent to 25 per cent, and for bonds they ranged from 5 per cent to 10 per cent (Calomiris 2000: 280).[8] The spreads on underwritten common stock declined around 11 per cent for the years 1945 to 1949, and 7.5 per cent in 1963 (Mendelson 1967: 408–409). Recent data published in Morrison and Wilhelm Jr. (2007: 25) show that in 2000 bond underwriting spreads fell to 0.5 per cent. Data from Thomson SDC indicate average common equity spreads in the US of just 4.5 per cent in 2008.

The decline in pricing power has gone hand in hand with the movement of foreign banks and domestic commercial banks into investment banks' traditional territory. In 1990, all of the top ten underwriters of common stock in the US were stand alone investment banks, and by 2003 this was reduced to five (Merrill Lynch, Goldman Sachs, Morgan Stanley, CS FirstBoston and AG Edwards), as three US commercial banks and two foreign banks entered the league table rankings (Morrison and Wilhelm Jr. 2007: 17).

In response to the decline in their traditional power, large investment banks have moved far beyond their role as securities market agents, to become significant principal actors, lending and committing their own capital in transactions. The extent of this shift away from this traditional agent role is shown in Table 4.1.

Large investment banks' investment banking and commissions business has been halved from 1982–1986 to 2004–2008, while their income from interest and principal trading (from their own inventory of securities) has jumped from 60 per cent to 76 per cent over the same period. These trading operations now take place on a global scale, and include everything from asset-backed securities, currencies and derivatives to commodities, insurance and real estate (*The Economist* 2007).

In the past, investment banks relied primarily on the obedience of corporations to seek out their services, which allowed them to exact a substantial mark-up for these services. Yet the long-term reduction in spreads and fees for investment banking services indicates that this pricing power has declined significantly, while the decreased reliance of investment bank revenues on traditional investment banking suggests that their power is now wielded in other areas. Investment bank

Table 4.1 Large investment bank revenues (% of total revenues)

Period	Commissions and fees	Investment banking income	Interest and related income	Principal transactions
1982–1986	17.7	13.2	46.8	13.6
1993–1997	13.8	9.7	50.5	16
2004–2008	6.4	8.8	59.7	16.3

Notes: The cut off point for large investment banks in Table 4.1 is determined by annual revenues. From 1982 to 1990 the cut off point is revenues of $1 billion or higher. From 1990 to 1999 it is $1.5 billion or higher. For 2000 to 2008 it is $3 billion or higher.

Source: Compustat though WRDS (series codes: CFBD for commissions and fees; IBKI for investment banking income; IDIT for interest and related income; PTRAN for principal transactions; REVT for total revenue).

power has become diversified into many other facets of global securities markets and the growing complexity of these markets means growing complexity for investment bank power relations.

Consider, for example, the investment banks' recent role in global commodities markets. Since the early 1990s, Goldman Sachs in particular has been buying heavily into 'long' positions in commodities futures, leading some to suggest that it played a key role in orchestrating the dramatic spikes in oil and wheat prices in 2008 (Taibbi 2009; Kaufman 2010). Regardless of whether Goldman Sachs single-handedly orchestrated these price spikes or not, it is clear that their power now extends far beyond corporate finance into areas that impact the very survival of humanity: food and energy.

It could be suggested that this diversified power is now qualitatively indistinguishable from the power of other financial conglomerates. This may be the case as far as functions are concerned, especially with the disappearance of independent investment banks in 2008. But if we want to explain why investment banks rose from insignificant players in the early 1980s to diversified giants in the 2000s, then I argue that it still makes sense to analyse them separately. This is not because of any distinctiveness in their functions, but due to the rather unique ways they have manoeuvred within, and also shaped, the global shift towards neoliberal regulation from the 1980s to the current crisis.

Diversified power and neoliberal regulation

The 'Volcker Shock' (1979–1982) is often considered to be a 'founding moment' in the history of neoliberalism (Panitch and Gindin 2009: 23). Little consensus exists as to the exact causes of the 1970s inflation, nor as to what allowed the Federal Reserve under Paul Volcker to raise interest rates in order to combat it, but one important consequence of the Volcker Shock seems clear-cut. The Federal Reserve's 'sound money' crusade, which saw prime lending rates increase from 7 per cent in 1976 to 19 per cent in 1981,[9] irreversibly disrupted the 'live-and-let-live compact' that had up till then existed between investment and commercial banks on opposites of the Glass-Steagall Act of 1933 (Hayes and Hubbard 1990: 110).[10]

Volcker's interest rate hikes had a negative impact on the commercial banking side of the Glass-Steagall wall. Interest rate ceilings on bank deposits imposed as part of Glass-Steagall's Regulation Q served as a particular disadvantage to commercial banks, whose deposit base was being stripped away by the investment banks' money market mutual funds. These investment vehicles proved popular in the context of high interest rates, offering market rates of return and all the basic features of a bank account. On the assets side, rising interest rates made bank loans more costly relative to securities markets, and the issuance of commercial paper became a favoured option in corporate financing. This directly benefitted the investment banks that underwrote these and other debt issues.

The commercial banks started to voice complaints that Glass-Steagall was being applied unevenly to the benefit of investment banks, but they did not respond by advocating the re-establishment of Glass-Steagall barriers. While they may have been negatively impacted by the onset of neoliberalism, the commercial banks felt that neoliberal financial deregulation would help restore their once-dominant position. As Thomas G. Labrecque, former president of Chase Manhattan, put it, '[t]he solution is not to rid ourselves of the invaders on our turf...Rather we've got to be allowed to compete more fully in the marketplace' (cited in Bennett 1982: 12). In other words, commercial banks wanted access to securities market business that the neoliberal monetary policy had made so appealing.

Some commercial banks tried to invade investment banking turf by exploiting loopholes within the legislation (Bleakley 1984). However, this was staunchly resisted by the investment bankers' main professional association, the Securities Industry Association (SIA), and led to protracted legal battles (Hall 1986). During this time, the weight of the government was firmly tilted in favour of the investment banks. Federal Reserve chairman Paul Volcker (1979–1987) and Treasury Secretary Donald Regan (1981–1985), a former Merrill Lynch CEO, were lukewarm towards dismantling Glass-Steagall barriers (Schlesinger 2002). In 1981, the government did, however, agree to phase out Regulation Q, but this was done only gradually over a five-year period, and by the time the final ceilings were abandoned in 1986, the damage to commercial banks' deposit base had already been done. Even though inflation was 'tamed' and interest rates declined through the early to mid-1980s, there was little sign of commercial banks recapturing their traditional business from securities markets (Hager 2010).

Government reticence towards dismantling Glass-Steagall underpinned the investment banks' power to exclude commercial banks from their business, but to what extent did this actually impact accumulation? The accumulation trajectories of investment and commercial banks during the early phase of neoliberalism were impacted by a myriad of factors. As a result, any attempt to empirically assess the impact of the Volcker Shock on their accumulation is necessarily speculative. Issues concerning regulation were, however, constantly debated in the financial press during this period, and for some, the regulatory barriers of Glass-Steagall were regarded as the 'most urgent issue for the US financial community' (*The Economist* 1987: 5).

With this in mind, there is evidence to suggest that the ushering in of the neoliberal era, specifically the switch to monetarism and deregulation, led to the dramatic restructuring of power from commercial banks to investment banks. Figure 4.3 plots the differential capitalization and profits of the top five investment banks relative to the top five commercial banks (again ranked by market capitalization).

Here we see that from 1975 to 1985 the differential profits of the investment banks doubled from 0.17 to 0.34 times commercial banks, before doubling again to 0.68 in 1987. Meanwhile, their differential capitalization rose from 0.1 in 1975 to a high of 0.67 in 1985.

In the early stages of the 1980s 'bank wars' (Prins 2004), investment banks were the clear victors. Yet as Figure 4.3 also shows, by the mid-1980s the course of accumulation would turn against them. Reeling from the 1987 stock market crash and insider-trading scandals, the differential capitalization and profits of large investment banks started to plummet. The onset of this fallout was doubly fortuitous for the commercial banks as it coincided with the 1987 appointment of Alan Greenspan, the high priest of neoliberal deregulation, to replace Volcker as Federal Reserve chairman. Greenspan, who previously held posts on the board of directors for commercial banks J.P. Morgan and Morgan Guaranty Trust, immediately set his sights on dismantling Glass-Steagall. The Fed never made reference to the disadvantaged position of commercial banks in trying to justify deregulation. Instead, it argued that Glass-Steagall stood as an unnecessary barrier to the more efficient forces of free market competition (Greenspan 2007). Given deregulation in other parts of the world, the Fed feared that Glass-Steagall was hampering the global competitiveness of the US financial system (Rosenstein 1989). Soon new provisions were passed allowing commercial bank subsidiaries to underwrite some securities. From a position of weakness, the investment banks, led by the SIA, finally dropped their opposition to Glass-Steagall reform in 1989 (Bush 1989).

With dominant financial intermediaries now united in pushing for neoliberal deregulation, the Glass-Steagall Act was gradually chipped away throughout the 1990s and was officially repealed in 1999. The deregulation wave of the 1990s was accompanied by a wave of mergers/conglomerations which effectively removed most of the remaining

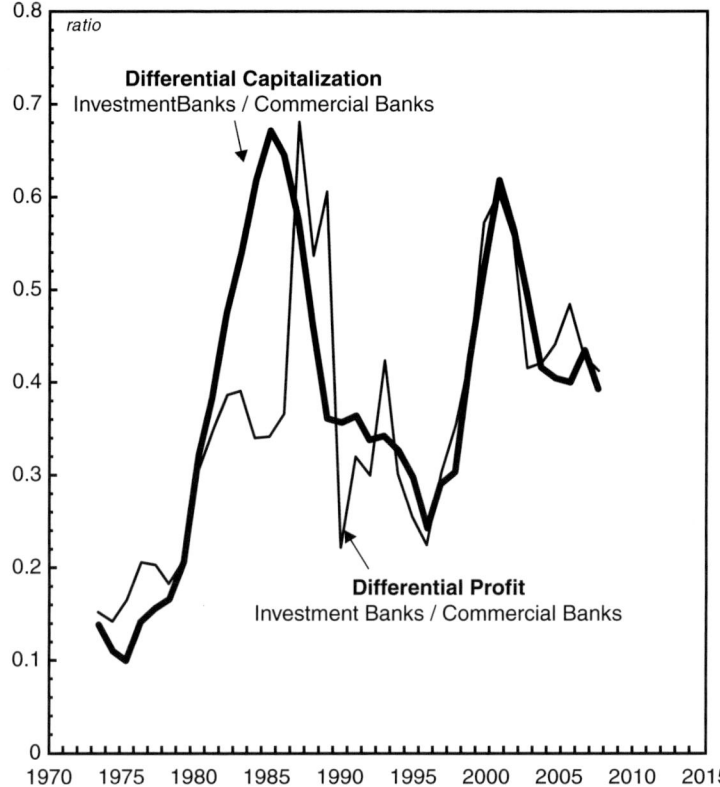

Figure 4.3 Differential accumulation: investment banks v. commercial banks
Note: Series smoothed as three year moving averages.
Source: Compustat through WRDS (series codes: see Figure 2).

functional and regulatory distinctions between commercial and investment banks. The 'main divide' was no longer between commercial
and investment banks, but between giant financial conglomerates and
their smaller, less diversified banking counterparts (Johnson and Kwak:
2010: 86).

The data suggest that the repeal of Glass-Steagall did not have a negative impact on investment bank accumulation. Relative to dominant
capital as a whole (see Figure 4.2), the differential capitalization of the
investment banks grew rapidly in the 2000s. Relative to dominant commercial banks (see Figure 4.3), the investment banks were able to 'tread
water' from 2003–2007 after a decline which likely had more to do with

the dot com crisis than with the repeal of Glass-Steagall. However, as the current crisis has now made plain, the ability of investment banks to keep up in the post-Glass-Steagall world was built upon an edifice of (leveraged) sand. Like the initial rise of investment bank power, the collapse of the independent investment bank model can only be explained with reference to the unique ways in which investment banks experienced neoliberal deregulation. In other words, the analysis here suggests that the generally accepted explanation of neoliberalism as a class project of 'finance' in general, or of 'big finance' in particular, is misleading insofar as it neglects the inter-sectoral power struggles between financial firms over the course of regulation.

After the demise of Glass-Steagall commercial banks remained subject to the regulations of the Federal Reserve, the Federal Deposit Insurance Corporation and the Comptroller of the Currency, whereas investment banks continued to be supervised by the Securities and Exchange Commission (SEC). It was during this time that the large investment banks wanted to expand further into booming businesses such as asset-backed securities and derivatives (Labaton 2008). The only thing that stopped them from doing so was the SEC's 'net capital rule', which required investment banks to limit debt to twelve times their equity. This rule made it difficult for the investment banks to compete with commercial banks in the increasingly complex world of finance. Despite the long-term decline of their deposit base, the balance sheets of commercial banks were still significantly larger than the investment banks, and this allowed them to take significant investment positions without resorting to excessive leveraging (Prins 2009). Led by Goldman CEO Henry Paulson, the investment banks began in 2000 to lobby for changes to the net capital rule.[11] In a now-infamous decision in 2004, the SEC gave into pleas by the 'big five' investment banks to self-monitor their investment positions through their own risk models (Ritholz 2009).

Investment bank leverage increased 42 per cent from 2002–2007, and by 2007, assets were 31 times equity (Roxburgh et al. 2010). This explosion was funded primarily through short-term instruments (70 per cent of total assets in 2006) such as repurchase agreements (repos). Under stricter regulations and with bigger balance sheets, commercial bank gross leverage actually decreased three per cent from 2002–2007, and at the height of the 2007 boom the ratio of commercial bank assets to equity was 12 to 1, and only 11 per cent of their funding in 2006 was short term.

The precariousness of this situation became painfully obvious with the onset of crisis in 2007–2008. As doubts about the quality of the mortgage-backed securities held by investment banks grew, repo market creditors began to demand more collateral in exchange for financing (Gorton and Metrick 2010). Faced with difficulties in rolling over their debt, the investment banks were pushed towards insolvency in 2008. The smallest of the big five, Bear Stearns, was taken over by J.P. Morgan in March. Unable to orchestrate a similar commercial bank takeover, Lehman Brothers collapsed in September. Merrill Lynch then agreed to be taken over by Bank of America. Meanwhile the two survivors, Goldman Sachs and Morgan Stanley, voluntarily converted into bank holding companies in order to gain access to the Fed's emergency lending facilities.

In the course of several months in 2008, any of the remaining vestiges of the 75-year-old regulatory separation of commercial and investment banks vanished. One of the most notable outcomes of the crisis has been the sudden disappearance of independent investment banks from the US corporate landscape. This collapse, as well as the dramatic rise in investment bank power that preceded it, are intimately bound up with the neoliberal project's own rise and descent with the current crisis. Faith in neoliberal deregulation has been shaken, and as a result, calls for reform of the US financial system have been growing. Some of the more far-reaching proposals have even called for a reinstatement of the Glass-Steagall Act. But how serious are these proposals? Is financial regulation entering a new phase 'after neoliberalism'? My task now will be to outline some of the possibilities and limitations of this regulation drive.

From the Volcker shock to the Volcker rule

If the collapse of independent investment banks was one of the most notable outcomes in the early stages of the crisis, one of the more notable outcomes since then has been the rapid recovery of the FIRE sector more broadly. The extent of this recovery can be seen in Figure 4.4. After seeing their share of total US market capitalization fall from 23 per cent in January of 2007 to 13 per cent in March of 2009, the US FIRE sector had by the summer of 2010 recovered nearly half of its market share. This would come as little surprise to some analysts. With the disappearance of their main competitors, and with the support of government bailouts, there is a widespread belief that survivors have become *more powerful* as a result of the crisis (Stephens 2010). Simon Johnson (2009: 49), former chief economist at the IMF, argues that the crisis has laid bare the existence of a 'financial oligarchy' in the U.S., one that possesses political weight 'not seen in the US since the era of J.P. Morgan (the man)'.

Even before this recent FIRE recovery, calls for regulation were gaining support, but persistently high unemployment, coupled with the record breaking profits and massive executive bonus announcements by firms such as Goldman Sachs, have served as the real catalyst rallying public support for regulation. In the financial press, the merits of reinstituting the Glass-Steagall Act are constantly debated, but even most progressives claim that Glass-Steagall is ill-equipped for the complexities of modern finance (Kregel 2010). There are, however, some other proposals that aim to combat the power of financial conglomerates by erecting regulatory barriers between various financial activities. One such proposal has been spearheaded by none other than former Federal Reserve Chairman and now presidential advisor, Paul Volcker. In its original formulation, the 'Volcker Rule' would ban deposit-taking banks from owning or investing in hedge funds and private equity firms, as well as prevent them from short-term trading with their own capital ('proprietary trading'). This provides a somewhat ironic twist to the history of neoliberal deregulation. It was, after all, Volcker's shock that is thought to have provided the initial stimulus for the emergence of the neoliberal project. However, he was reticent on the issue of deregulation in the 1980s, and now in the current environment of scepticism towards unfettered markets, Volcker's ideas on regulation have again gained political currency.

The Volcker Rule was passed into law as part of the *Dodd-Frank Wall Street Reform and Consumer Protection Act* in the summer of 2010. Yet through months of intense political wrangling, the version of the rule included in the act was significantly watered down, and critics doubt whether the act will have any meaningful impact (Taibbi 2010). While most of the main tenets of neoliberalism were already being challenged well before the current crisis, the central pillar of neoliberal ideology, financial deregulation, has proven far more difficult to reverse. With FIRE now rebounding from a position of weakness, the opportunity for meaningful reform may have already passed.

Any assessment of the limits and possibilities for US financial reform must also take into account the wider global context. When anchored in the global political economy as a whole, a paradox surfaces: while FIRE's domestic *resurgence* appears to have limited the prospects for reform, the persistent *weakening* of US FIRE globally may serve to reinforce these limits. As Figure 4.4 illustrates, US FIRE's share of total world FIRE capitalization and its share of total US capitalization have both

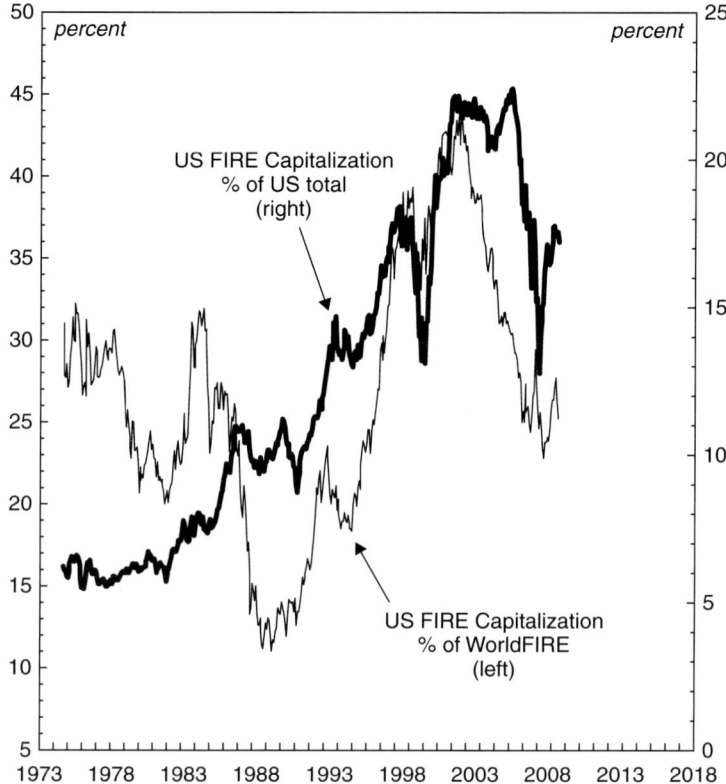

Figure 4.4   US FIRE's share of market capitalization

Note: The final data point is for September 2010.

Source: Thomson Datastream (series codes: TOTMKUS(MV) for total US capitalization; FINANUS(MV) for US FIRE capitalization; FINANWD(MV) for World FIRE capitalization).

rebounded – the former by 12 per cent and the latter by 38 per cent. What matters here is not only that US FIRE's domestic rebound has been much larger, but also the longer-term historical pattern in which it has taken place. The decline in US FIRE's share of US capitalization is recent, cyclical and tied to crisis, whereas the decline in its share of world FIRE capitalization is long-term, secular and already evident in 2003.

As was mentioned above, Greenspan's initial calls for neoliberal deregulation in the 1980s were motivated by concerns about the global competitiveness of US FIRE. Deregulation did have the intended effect: after losing its global market share in the 1980s, US FIRE recovered through the wave of consolidations and conglomerations in the 1990s. How then can we expect re-regulation in a context similar to that in the 1980s and without a concerted effort towards global regulatory cooperation? Fears about US global competitiveness, whether justified or not, stand as a formidable obstacle to efforts aimed at reversing neoliberal deregulation.[12] The recent backlash towards the 'financial oligarchy' may point to a widening chasm between dominant FIRE and the wider population, but the widespread belief in the sanctity of global competitiveness helps to defray these domestic cleavages. When this global context is taken into account, Lloyd Blankfein's assertion that 'what's good for Goldman Sachs is good for America' finds few serious challengers (Brenner 2009).

Conclusion

The analysis here has been framed primarily as an engagement with Sweezy's 'transitory power' thesis. Rather than merely updating Sweezy's analysis, it has developed new empirical tools for analysing investment bank power based on a capital *as* power approach. The research results are unambiguous. They show with various differential measures that the power of investment banks grew rapidly alongside the rise and consolidation of neoliberalism through to the onset of the current crisis. What this analysis suggests is that investment bank power is not transitory, but transforming. The resilience of investment bank power is bound up with their abilities to constantly transform their accumulation strategies. Investment banks have diversified their activities far beyond their 'traditional' role as securities market agents, but the distinctive experiences of investment banks in manoeuvring to secure advantages within neoliberal regulation highlights the dangers of dwelling on the functional similarities they share with other diversified financial services conglomerates.

Whether or not the surviving investment banks will continue to transform and augment their power is an open question. The current crisis has brought the most serious challenges to the investment banks since the 1929 crash. The collapse of three of the big five is evidence that the so-called 'Masters of the Universe' (Wolfe 1987) are by no means omnipotent. At the same time, the ability of surviving investment banks to not only weather, but in some cases also to profit from, the recent turbulence points to the resilience and flexibility of their power.

In the end, one of the main questions dividing those on the 'critical' side of political economy is strategic: should the goal be to harness power through regulation or eliminate power altogether? The alternative focus on differential capitalization suggests that regulation has a significant impact on power. At various points in the history of neoliberalism, the struggle over regulation has been at the heart of accumulation. It has not merely 'affected' accumulation from the outside. To the extent that regulation is perceived to impact the course of future earnings, it becomes a key facet of accumulation. At the same time, the analysis also highlights how dominant capital groups are able to effectively limit the imposition of meaningful regulatory change even through periods of crisis. Here too, a focus on differential capitalization provides tools to analyse the ways that capitalist power shapes and limits regulation. Whatever the precise answer to the strategic question, the analysis here argues that in order to confront power we must first radically rethink our categories and concepts, and that involves rethinking capital accumulation, the process through which dominant capitalists actively reshape and restructure society.

Notes

1. Earlier versions of this chapter were presented at the 2009 Rethinking Marxism conference at UMASS Amherst, the 2010 International Studies Association conference in New Orleans and the 2010 Eastern Economic Association conference in Philadelphia. The chapter has benefitted from the insightful comments and criticisms of many people, especially Bastiaan van Apeldoorn, Joseph Baines, Joe Francis, Elif Genc, Jeremy Green, Brenda McComb, Jonathan Nitzan and Henk Overbeek. The usual disclaimers apply.

2. Of course, the monopoly capital school is not the only school of Marxism to analyse the dynamics of financialization and the rise of finance capital over the past three decades. An exhaustive review of this literature is outside the scope of this chapter, but many of the critiques that I make here, especially concerning the problematic bifurcation between the 'real' and 'nominal' spheres, could apply equally to these other accounts.

3. For more detailed explications of this tendency and its relation to the laws of motion of orthodox Marxism, see Baran and Sweezy (1966); Howard and King (1992).

4. On the problem diversification poses for profit accounting, see Nitzan and Bichler (2009).

5. My overview of CasP in the next five paragraphs draws on Nitzan and Bichler (2009, 2010).

6. Differential measures are calculated as a ratio of the average market capitalization (or net profit) of a top five investment bank relative to the average market capitalization (or net profit) of a top 100 corporation.

7. Whether we focus on the top five investment banks or all investment banks in the Compustat database makes little difference because the top five are clearly dominant. For example, in 1971–1975 they held 85 per cent of the net profits of the sector and 93 per cent in 2004–2008.

8. The underwriting spread is the difference between the price paid by the investment bank to the issuing corporation for its securities, and the price the issue is then sold for in securities markets.
9. Data is from the IMF through Global Insight (series code: A111L60P.A).
10. The most important feature of the Glass-Steagall Act was that it barred deposit-taking commercial banks from engaging in the securities underwriting and trading undertaken by their investment bank counterparts.
11. Paulson would later go on to serve as Treasury Secretary from 2006–2009. For an eye-opening account of the revolving door between Goldman Sachs and the US federal government, see Johnson and Kwak (2010: 92–94).
12. These are certainly the fears that are driving the Republican Party's resistance to the Volcker Rule. In the words of Republican Congressman Spencer Bachus, '...the Volcker rule may spark a mass exodus of clients from US banks to banks based abroad' (cited in Braithwaite 2010: 15).

5
Price Wars: The Crisis and the Future of Financialized Capitalism

Paul Lewis and James Perry

Introduction

Popular theoretical explanations of the recent financial crisis suggest that finance, due to a combination of cheap credit, speculative invest-ment and 'irrational exuberance', created a bubble in particular asset prices that proved impossible for underlying cash flows to justify. In this case, the inability of subprime borrowers to keep paying their debts undermined confidence in the value of financial assets constructed upon those cash flows. The central claim in such explanations is that finance periodically 'overreaches' the 'fundamental' capacity of some part of the 'real' or 'productive' economy to support it.

While this theory appears consistent with events, in the sense that the recent crisis and many others before it were preceded by a finance-led boom in particular assets, it leads to a partial and oversimplified account of the crisis. As we argue in this chapter, the chief shortcom-ing of the finance-overreaches-production type of explanation is that it analyses finance and production as discrete and independent sectors of the economy. This overlooks the ways in which finance has increased its power over all other economic activities during the last 30 years.

In the next section, we explain how mainstream neoclassical eco-nomics-inspired accounts of the financial crisis rely on two discrete the-ories of finance and production: First, there is a theory explaining how financial asset prices periodically rise above the level justified by the legal claims on production which they represent, fuelled by an expan-sion of credit. Second, there is a theory for the generation and distribu-tion of economic products in the 'productive' economy, which limits the capacity of the financial sector to act as a *rentier* upon it. Regulatory responses to the crisis have relied on the possibility of achieving a stable equilibrium between these two economic spheres and distinct bodies of theory. This is largely to be achieved through limiting the amount of credit in the economy. However, as we emphasize, there is in fact no theoretical basis for why this equilibrium should occur.

Following this, we present an alternative account of finance and production, with finance as both an active manager and demanding claimant of the economic product generated in the nonfinancial sector. Using this framework, we trace the historical emergence of the crisis in terms of finance's intensifying search for yield. Focusing particularly on the period since the 1980s, we review how finance, through the corporate governance framework of shareholder value, was able to temporarily boost its return by forcing industrial capital to downsize capital assets, increase debt, reduce retained earnings, increase the capital share at the expense of the majority of workers and return a greater proportion of profits to shareholders. As we explain, this strategy ultimately exhausted the ability of companies to absorb any more debt.

Given the subsequent wave of cheap credit in the 2000s, this led financial services, with government consent, to look to the household as the next absorber of debt and provider of cash flows. Taken together, the strategies of shareholder value and expanded household debt meant that, by the late 2000s, the nonfinancial sector was unable to take on and service sufficient new debt burdens to maintain the supernormal profits to which finance was now accustomed.

As we conclude, none of the regulatory responses to the crisis now on the table deals with this central aspect of the crisis – namely, the paradox that finance has reconfigured the 'real' economy in such a way as to reduce its long-term ability to service finance. Instead of addressing the level and mode of profit accumulation in the financial sector, and the consequence of this for distribution more generally, governments' focus in this policy area has been almost entirely concerned with regulating the amount of credit. This is highly unlikely to succeed on its own terms for both theoretical *and* political reasons; the political will for reducing *leverage* through regulation is extremely limited. It also does nothing to resolve the tensions of the distribution of economic products that are becoming increasingly apparent across developed economies.

A neoclassical explanation of the current crisis – the financial instability hypothesis

The theory that has attracted most adherents in explaining the current crisis is one that suggests financial crises are an inherent feature of capitalism, they are recurrent and they may be explained using a general framework known as the 'financial instability hypothesis' (FIH). Elements of this theory have a long history that may be traced back to the classical political economists, but it is the work of Hyman Minsky (1982) and elaborated by Charles Kindleberger (2000) that has attracted recent attention (Barrell and Davies 2008; Authers 2009).

FIH starts with an initial 'displacement' in the economy, an exogenous shock to the macroeconomic system which creates new profit opportunities in at least one important sector of the economy. This leads to investment opportunities for companies and individuals with either savings or access to credit. If the new opportunities are large enough to dwarf the redirection of investment out of other sectors that have a comparatively negative outlook, then a boom gets underway. The boom is fed by an expansion of bank credit, which feeds the money supply. Credit can be expanded through banks increasing their own leverage, through the development of new funding or credit instruments – for example, derivatives and securitized debt. It may also be expanded through the creation of credit by nonbank institutions, for example via hedge funds, off-balance sheet vehicles, private equity companies, etc. 'Crucial questions of policy turn on how to control all of these avenues of monetary expansion' (Kindleberger 2000: 15).

A positive feedback loop may develop, whereby increasing demand for certain assets drives price increases, creating further speculative opportunities and increasing use of credit, further investment and income increases. Minsky referred to this as 'euphoria', Adam Smith and contemporaries as 'overtrading'. The result is a 'bubble' or 'mania' in one or more asset classes. At some point, the bubble reaches its plateau as some speculators begin to liquidate their positions but for a while these are balanced by new entrants. Finally, a signal occurs, which changes market sentiment triggering a rush for the exits and a vicious circle of sales reinforcing price declines. At this point, the vast majority of investors have a preference for liquid and low-risk assets (e.g., hard currency or precious metals), rather than less liquid and riskier financial assets.

The downward spiral is halted by one or more of three possible events: (1) Prices may fall so low that people are again tempted to move back into less liquid assets. (2) Trading is artificially limited – for example by setting limits on price falls or closing exchanges. (3) A lender of last resort emerges providing confidence among market participants that sufficient cash is available to meet demands for liquidity (ibid.: 13–18 outlines the model).

FIH is distinct from orthodox economic theory in the view of agents that it takes. Rather than being rational optimizers who create efficient markets whereby all available information is incorporated in equilibrium prices, the agents of the FIH are prone to the 'animal spirits' of Keynes.

However, despite this departure in terms of how it understands economic actors, FIH is still based on neoclassical foundations. The value of capital is still the sum of future expected cash flows, discounted with an interest rate. Crisis occurs when it becomes clear that the expectations of future cash flows, as anticipated by financial investors, ultimately exceed the ability of the nonfinancial sector(s) of the economy to produce them. Asset values are then said to have departed from any 'fundamental' value as suggested by discounted future cash flows. Most importantly for our analysis, FIH thus implies that the system would be stable so long as the expectation of those providing money capital remains in equilibrium with those generating returns in the productive economy.

The financial instability hypothesis and the regulatory response to the financial crisis

The extent to which FIH, as outlined above, drives today's regulatory reforms becomes clear when one considers that achieving a stable equilibrium between financial asset values and productive-sector profitability remains the fundamental aim of regulating credit creation. Indeed, it has been precisely this outcome on which most attention has been focused since the 2008–2009 financial crisis.

One of the most frequently cited factors in the official (even critical) discourses of the 2008–2009 financial crisis has been that banks were over-leveraged in the long boom of the past decade (BIS 2009; FSA 2009; IMF 2011). The banks essentially created too much money, which pushed up the price of financial assets beyond a level that could be sustainably serviced by the nonfinancial sector. The overriding imperative of the new banking framework that emerged following the crisis (so-called 'Basel 3') was to reduce the leverage of the banking system (BIS 2009: paragraph 60).

A bank's leverage is the ratio of its assets (e.g. loans) to its core capital:

Leverage Ratio = Total Assets (e.g. loans) / Core Capital

A higher leverage ratio means a higher volume of bank lending. The reason for limiting leverage, from a regulatory perspective, is that banks are thus better capitalized and so can absorb losses without defaulting on their liabilities (deposits). To achieve this, core capital is (supposed to be) the most subordinated claim on a bank. This means that the providers of core capital cannot demand its repayment, and – in the case of bank failure – providers are only entitled to whatever is left over when everyone else has been paid. In short, the more core capital banks have relative to their assets, the safer the financial system. However, this also makes the banks less profitable because core capital is expensive; it pays no return or very little return *to* the bank, yet the bank must still pay a market-based return to those who provide it, usually shareholders.

There are thus three aspects to the regulatory equation, each of which can be tinkered with: First is the actual numerical value of the leverage ratio (how many 'assets' compared with how much 'capital'); second is the definition of 'assets'; third is the definition of 'capital'.

Obviously, banks want a high numerical leverage ratio, a narrow definition of assets (meaning one that is favourably risk-weighted so that the 'low-risk' loans count significantly less), and a broad definition of capital (meaning one that is cheap to maintain). In September of 2009, Bank for International Settlements (the Basel-based international banking regulator) issued a proposal for a comprehensive set of measures to cut back on excessive leverage (BIS 2009):

- Broadening the definition of assets
- Narrowing the definition of what constitutes a bank's core capital
- Introducing a simple (and suitably low) leverage ratio, under which assets are *not risk weighted at all*
- Stipulating a longer-term 'net stable funding ratio' that aligns the maturity of bank assets and liabilities

Taken together, these four measures aimed at moving the credit system towards an equilibrium between financial asset values and productive-sector profitability, exactly as the FIH implies would be necessary for long-term stability.

The interesting question that is rarely asked is *on what basis would such equilibrium exist*? As we explain in the remainder of this section, it is difficult to find an answer: We compare the different approaches used to justify the return to capital viewed (1) as a financial claim on future output, and (2) as a 'factor of production'. It turns out that these approaches not only offer no inherent reason for equating quantitatively, but also disagree fundamentally about what 'capital' actually is, and employ different justifications for the income that it generates.

Furthermore, both approaches are also hampered by their own internal logical and empirical inconsistencies that render them highly questionable even when they are considered separately from one another and only within their respective spheres of finance and production.

A finance theory of capital – CAPM

As mentioned above, the financial approach to valuing 'capital assets' is based on discounting the stream of expected future cash flows they generate back to a net present value. The rationale for these cash flows has been developed from the work of Böhm Bawerk (1890) and Irving Fisher (1930).

'We may think of the rate of return of any asset as separated into two parts: the pure rate of interest representing the "price for waiting", and a remainder, a risk margin, representing the "price of risk" (Mossin 1966: 774, cited in O'Sullivan 2000: 45)'.

The 'price for waiting' is known as the 'risk-free rate of return', which in practice is taken as the historical average return on short-term low-risk assets, such as US Treasury bills. The additional risk element for riskier assets is derived from the covariance between the asset returns and the return on 'an efficient market portfolio'. For example, the expected/target return of a company share may be derived from the historical volatility of that asset relative to a benchmark, i.e., the stock market. This creates a risk-reward correlation in valuation models, the majority of which are extensions of the seminal capital asset pricing model (CAPM) (e.g., Markowitz 1952; Sharpe 1964).

The favoured finance metric is 'return on capital employed' (ROCE), which is a return on the combination of the two basic components of corporate finance: equity (shares) and debt (bonds). The equity component is calculated using a volatility premium to the average risk-free return, using a historic company/sector measure of volatility and an average market premium over a given period.[1] Similarly, the target return on the debt component adds a risk of default premium to the return on a standard nondefaulting bond of the same duration; usually government-issued treasury bonds or gilts. Ratings agencies are central in calculating the risk premia for debt and equity attached to each firm and sector. A weighted average return on equity and debt, which is the target ROCE, is calculated for each firm based upon a standard split of equity and debt financing in order to make the metric comparable. Rappaport (1998) calculated the target ROCE to be 10 per cent to 12 per cent across sectors.[2]

The approach just outlined, which is meant to justify the return to capital in terms of waiting and risk, contains a number of theoretical problems. Most fundamentally, 'the explanation of distribution is completely divorced from the explanation of production, as though incomes "just growed"' (Seager 1912, cited in O'Sullivan 2000). To say that risk justifies a return does not identify any process by which risk is inherently productive. Second, and related, the return to waiting and the risk margin are based on the idea that finance has been invested in productive processes that take time and are inherently risky. However, secondary trading on the stock market is completely divorced from providing finance to nonfinancial companies. Companies generally only come to the stock market once they are generating steady cash flows and the stock market provides a means for the owners to 'cash out'. Hence, there is no notion of investing in production and waiting for it to pay off because that has already occurred. The financing of subsequent investment comes largely from retained earnings, not shareholder equity. Similarly, due to limited liability and incomplete contracts for suppliers of inputs, it is not clear that all of the risk of companies is borne by shareholders. O'Sullivan suggests that the true purpose of today's stock markets, which are dominated by secondary trading, is in fact to *separate* saving preferences from the productive process (O'Sullivan 2000: 49).

Empirically, there is evidence that the CAPM target is unachievable for many industries (Froud et al. 2006). Studies by Fama and French (1997) and Gregory and Michou (2007) of the US and UK respectively, find that the CAPM model (and various more sophisticated adaptations of it) fail to 'estimate the cost of capital of any firm or industry with any degree of accuracy' (Gregory and Michou 2007: 3, 16). Furthermore, comparing the volatility of classes of assets, such as equities with 'treasury bills', makes it difficult to justify the equity premium on 'risk-reward' grounds. Over some time periods the standard deviation of annual rates of return on treasury bills, a measure of risk, is greater than on equities, yet there remains a consistently large 'equity premium' (O'Sullivan 2000: 50).

However, the fact that real performance does not appear to follow theory does not mean that the strategies followed by corporate managers are not influenced by theory, or their interpretation of it, at any point in time. It is the intention, and the consequences from having that intention, that matter, not necessarily the ultimate result. If company managers believe that the only way to increase their share price is to focus upon an exogenously set and extremely high return on capital, then this influences the strategies available to them in order to generate such returns. It is certainly consistent with events that stock market analysts and the senior management of companies were aware of the target rate of return for their companies. However, rather than treating this as a discount rate on realistic earnings projected into the future, it seems that simpler, more short-term measures have been used as a proxy to drive the share price. The logic seems to be inductive; an organization needs to demonstrate that it is at least moving towards its risk-related rate of return in order to provide confidence in its future performance. Indeed, Rappaport suggests that it takes more than 10 years of expected cash flows to justify the stock price of most companies (2006: 68).

A productive theory of capital – marginal productivity theory

The neoclassical theory of production is marginal productivity theory. Formalized in the work of John Bates Clark at the end of the nineteenth century (Clark 1965 [1899]), marginal productivity theory explains how market mechanisms allocate society's productive resources (labour and capital) to their most efficient uses, and simultaneously ensure that the owners of these resources are paid (wages and profits) in direct proportion to what they contribute.

Although Clark did not invent marginalist economics, he was the first to use its toolkit of ideas to demonstrate why, in a properly functioning market society, there would be no exploitation and hence no economic grounds for conflict. As he put it:

> It is the purpose of this work to show that the distribution of the income of society is controlled by a natural law, and that this law, if it worked without friction, would give to every agent of production the amount of wealth which that agent creates. (Clark 1965 [1899]: 1)

In short, Clark argued that the level of wages and profits (return on capital, ROCE) are derived from the respective marginal productivities of labour and capital. Among mainstream economists, the 'results' of Clark's theory are now beyond doubt, presented as truths in intermediate macroeconomics textbooks before advanced students move on to learn derived models applying higher mathematics (see for example Mankiw 2007). Marginal productivity theory today forms the kernel of neoclassical economic thought and it is widely invoked to lend scientific authority to policies encouraging the growth and openness of capital and trade flows, and the ensuing deregulation of financial markets and labour markets (see, for example, EC 2005: 21–22; OECD 2008a: 1–4; WTO 2007: 5–9).

Although it is perhaps the most ideologically influential theory within neoclassical economics, the marginal productivity theory of income distribution is in fact a tautology. For it not to be would require the existence of homogeneous factor inputs that are divisible and substitutable for one another, having a measure of input quantity that is independent of their price. However, there are no such substances. Particular capital equipment and particular workers are not examples of homogeneous capital and labour.

This has created a situation wherein the price of capital has to be taken as the *measure* of its quantity and hence its productive contribution. However, the price of capital, being future cash flows discounted at the ROCE, is supposed to be a consequence of its quantity in the marginal productivity model. The same problem occurs for labour. This precise problem came to a head in the so-called 'Cambridge Capital Controversies' of the 1950s and 1960s (Robinson 1953; Sraffa 1960; see Hodgson 1997; Mongiovi 2002; and Cohen and Harcourt 2003 for overviews). Despite considerable theoretical and empirical victories against the neoclassical conception of capital as a homogeneous substance, mainstream economics has largely ignored the conclusions from this episode or regrouped around disaggregated economic models that treat each piece of capital equipment separately, with the latter offering no attempt to rationalize the 'equilibrium' posited by financial instability hypothesis.[3]

The incommensurability of CAPM and MPT

On one hand, the target 'normal' rate of return, which the financial sector expects the productive-sector to achieve, derives from the historic and sectoral volatility of the firm considered in terms of the payments it generates to investors. On the other hand, the rate of return generated by marginal productivity theory derives from marginal productive contributions. The latter unrealistically treats capital as a homogeneous productive factor and does not distinguish between the source of finance (equity or debt) and the idea of risk to the investor. A further distinction is that the finance theory of the firm includes the notion of surplus, residual earnings, paid to equity capital investors. In Marginal Productivity Theory (MPT), there is no surplus. All factors including capital are paid their marginal products, which exhausts all revenues. In short, the finance theory of capital is simply irreconcilable with the economic theory of production; there is no clear theoretical rationale for why the returns predicted by these two approaches should be in equilibrium. Moreover, given that both approaches also appear to be theoretically and empirically wanting in their own spheres, the likelihood of stability between finance and production in the real world seems even more remote.

The current crisis as a reflection of the power of finance

The mainstream understanding of this crisis, and the regulatory responses which it has prompted, are based on the idea that so long as the quantity of credit in the system does not expand beyond the 'fundamental value' of the nonfinancial sectors to which it is linked, then the economy can remain healthy and stable. As discussed, this theoretical view is of two distinct spheres, production and finance, brought into equilibrium when the latter invests in the former based on realistic and shared expectations of future cash flows.

This is a benign, and in our opinion, unrealistic view of how capitalism functions, and an oversimplification of this financial crisis. Through its separation of capital into discrete productive and financial spheres, it misses the key story of how this crisis occurred, namely the rising power of finance *over* all other sectors of the economy, productive and household (cf. Sandy Hager's contribution to this volume). It is this story which we outline in the current section.

Rather than viewing economic output as generated by abstract homogeneous, productive inputs, as in neoclassical economic theory, we consider it best viewed as created by the central economic units of capitalism: firms. A firm's ability to generate economic product, measured in economic statistics as '*value added*', depends upon a number of external and internal factors, but it can rarely be attributed to individual inputs. A firm's – or one level higher – an industry's ability to generate economic product per input depends upon its ability to generate margin and volume of sales.

Raphael Kaplinsky (1998, 2001), writing in the global value chain literature (see Gibbon et al. 2008), has begun to explain this by reference to a variety of rents.[4] Kaplinsky suggests that anything which allows a firm to construct barriers to entry and limit competition will allow it to generate rent. In his taxonomy, some rents are due to access to scarce inputs – resource rents; some rents arise from the historical strategies and actions of firms – organizational, human resource, technology, product and marketing rents; others are due to the legal, institutional and infrastructural environment in which firms operate – policy, infrastructural and finance rents. Lastly, there are rents arising from specific relationships with other firms, relational rents. Clearly individual rents may fit into more than one category and constellations of rents will be key to the generation of high levels of economic product per input.

As well as being quite different from the neoclassical approach, this kind of framework is also distinct from Marx's labour theory of value, which views value as created from the uniform exploitation of living labour. It is logically possible to view all economic output as the product of labour and nature, where capital goods are reducible to dated labour, without assuming the uniform class exploitation of Marx's labour theory of value. If we are to view at least some workers as autonomous agents, capable of innovation and making good or bad judgements, then it follows that contributions to production cannot be reduced to the input of abstract labour power. Rather than attempting an objective theory of value, the more pertinent question, in our view, is how economic output is valued and appropriated by economic agents. This is best understood through the ability of firms to generate rents, which is a measure of their relative power over each other, and over their suppliers and customers.

The economic product of firms is distributed among a range of stakeholders or claimants. There are three main groups: *government* in the form of corporate taxes, *capital* conceived as the financing of firms, and *labour* as the multiple types of workers that are employed by firms. Traditionally in accountancy and finance theory, shareholder finance (equity) is understood as receiving the residual product once all other claimants have been paid. However, as we argued in the previous section, finance has become increasingly powerful in determining target performance metrics for companies, such as ROE and ROCE, and continually scrutinizing performance in the competitive market for corporate governance.

This increasing centrality and power of finance in developed economies has been referred to by some academics as a period of 'financialization', the most recent phase of neoliberal capitalism (Crotty 2002; Duménil and Lévy 2001; Epstein and Power 2002; Krippner 2005; Froud et al. 2006). This understanding of finance suggests an increasingly obtrusive and demanding rentier upon all other activities in society. Financial instruments in and of themselves cannot generate a yield as though isolated and disconnected from all economic activities. As mentioned in the previous section, the rationale of risk is insufficient to *explain* where reward comes from. Rather, finance is dependent upon the nonfinancial activities that it historically invested in, or more recently speculated upon,[5] for its returns. As increasing areas of life are opened for private finance, the opportunities to generate a return are increased.

As we will see in the subsequent historical tracing of the crisis, the power of finance is exercised at a number of levels. It enables the direct squeezing of the distribution of economic product to other stakeholders, labour and governments. It influences nonfinancial capital, on which it is dependent, to reorganize its activities, its structure, costs, level of retained profits and its level of investment and debt. Furthermore, once new high-yielding investments are no longer available from productive capital, the financial sector turns its attention to other sectors of the economy, such as real estate and household consumption, in an attempt to generate its target yield. However, as this crisis demonstrates, such opportunities have a clear limit. This is because in demanding a higher return, finance is doing nothing directly to bring about the creation of a sustainably higher level of economic product. Instead, the financial sector is promoting short-term corporate strategies that undermine the incomes of workers upon which it increasingly depends.

To elaborate on this argument, we next briefly examine the perform-ance of the nonfinancial and financial sectors of the economy in the postwar period.

The rate of profit in the nonfinancial sector

The period during the 1950s and 1960s has been described as a 'golden age' of industrialization – a virtuous circle whereby productivity increases in manufacturing resulting in lower relative prices, *increased* demand, *rising* real wages and high and stable profits[6] (Appelbaum and Schettkat 1995; Glyn 2006: 6–7; Brenner 2009: 10). During the 1970s, profits began to be squeezed by a combination of international compe-tition, which served to restrain pricing power in manufacturing, and by powerful organized labour, which pushed up earnings. This was combined with a weakening of productivity growth and an increase in the cost of imported goods, particularly oil. As a consequence, the gross profit share of manufacturing fell dramatically in the 1970s (Glyn, 2006: 7), accompanied by a large rise in inflation that proved difficult to control through collaborative incomes policy.

From 1980 onwards we witness the politically supported backlash by capital (Overbeek 2005), led in the US and UK. Contractionary monetary policy is used to curb inflation, leading to recession and a large growth in unemployment. This weakens the bargaining power of labour in the Anglo-Saxon countries, which is further diminished by policies explicitly aimed at reducing union power and ultimately creating 'flexible' labour markets. The falling share of labour in value-added and the increasing inequality of wage distribution, greatest in the Anglophone countries, has been well documented (Duménil and Lévy 2004; Glyn 2006: 6, 52; Millberg 2008: 443). So too has been the inability of wages to keep pace with productivity increases in the US and the stagnation of real wages for the bottom 90 per cent of US families since 1973 (Mishel and Bernstein 2007; Luce 2010). Governments' capacity to tax corporations has also been reduced through the threat of relocation to more favourable tax regimes (Cerny 1997). Nevertheless, despite the squeeze on distribution to other stakeholders, the profit rate has failed to return to its pre-1969 levels (Brenner 2009: 10).

In the 1990s, further performance strategies, linked to the demands of finance, included (i) distributing a greater proportion of profits to shareholders, and (ii) managing the assets and financial structure of companies to boost short-term performance metrics. Earnings per share (EPS) could be boosted through the company repurchasing its own stock and/or through raising the proportion of dividends to profits. The latter was raised to the historically high level of 55 per cent during the 1990s, reducing the capacity of firms to retain earnings for investment purposes (O'Sullivan 2000: 192–193, table 6.4; Crotty 2002a). Return on capital employed (ROCE) could be raised by downsizing existing capital stock and outsourcing production, while return on equity (ROE) could be boosted by taking on increasing quantities of debt (see Brenner 2002 on the US case). The role of debt was particularly important. The net effect was an ongoing transfer from the nonfinancial to the financial sector, much of it through interest payments (as Duménil and Lévy (2001) demonstrate was the case in France and the US).

The rate of profit in the financial sector

At the same time that nonfinancial capital was struggling to raise its profit levels, financial capital was achieving a position of heightened strength in Anglo-Saxon economies. In many regards, this rise can be ascribed to the increasingly dominant 'shareholder value' approach to corporate governance. Shareholder value started as a range of performance metrics[7] invented in the 1980s by management consultants, and employed as a means of selling consulting products to their clients (Williams 2000), but subsequently became the central pillar of an economic ideology which placed the interests of investors above all others, particularly workers. As Aglietta and Reberioux (2005) explain, by the mid-1990s, delivering maximum financial returns to shareholders became the unquestioned and, for the most part, socially acceptable objective of corporate governance. OECD-brokered intergovernmental agreements on corporate governance principles are highly prescriptive on shareholder rights, but significantly less so on worker rights (OECD 2004: part 2, section IV).

The process of 'financialization' was escalated by the increasing concentration of investment wealth under professional management, and an increasing trend to invest in the stock market. Accounting techniques and information technologies made it considerably easier to compile and analyse the necessary financial data. Investment fund managers, and a range of specialized analysts, intensified their comparisons of the value created by each firm against benchmarks set by the best performers across all industrial sectors (Harmes 2001). Against an increasingly active market for corporate control (Aglietta and Breton 2001), firms and their management were now actively competing not only in product markets but also in the financial markets (Froud et al. 2000). This often resulted in over-ambitious rate-of-return targets and unsustainable corporate strategies to meet them (Williams 2000; Froud et al. 2006; Gregory and Michou 2007). By the end of the 1990s, the wage-labour nexus of the Fordist era was subordinated to a financial regime with shareholder value as both the new form of competition and the new mode of governance (Boyer 2000b).

The result of this form of corporate governance was a further rise in the proportion of corporate profits made from financial activities relative to that made directly from production. A study by Epstein and Power (2002) calculated the 'rentier' share of income[8] as a time series for 17 countries and found strong evidence of this shift in composition of profits across a wide range of OECD economies. Rentier income as a share of private-sector GDP grew dramatically between the 1960s and 1990s; its share doubled in Denmark, France, the UK and US, and increased by over 50 per cent in Austria, Belgium, Germany and Norway.

Behind this lay two connected dynamics: the growth in profitability of the financial sector relative to the nonfinancial sector of the economy, and the financialization of the remaining profits in the nonfinancial sector itself. Regarding the latter, data on the earnings composition of nonfinancial corporations shows that by the mid-2000s they were making as much as 40 per cent of their profits from financial investments compared to just 10 per cent in the 1950s and 1960s (Krippner 2005, Duménil and Lévy 2001, Crotty 2002). As for the first dynamic, Krippner (2005) shows that the relative positions of manufacturing and finance were reversed during the last half-century. The US financial sector's share of profits quadrupled between the start of the 1950s and

2000, growing from 10 per cent of all corporate profits in the early 1980s to 40 per cent by 2006 (Crotty 2009: 576). During the same period, the manufacturing sector's share fell sharply to end at only a fifth of what it had been. Duménil and Lévy (2001) show France following the same pattern from the mid-1980s. By the end of the 1990s, the profit rate in the French financial sector was four times higher than in the nonfinancial sector.

This rise in profitability of financial services was mirrored by an increase in its indebtedness. US financial services share of total debt grew from 10 per cent to almost 30 per cent between 1975 and 2005, at the expense of the share of nonfinancial business and local, state and federal government (Bellamy Foster and Magdoff 2009: 48). Essentially financial services in the US were borrowing short to invest long in assets whose prices were rising in a boom. This had the effect of multiplying profits and generating fantastic shareholder returns and bonuses for bankers.

Taken as a whole, this debt-driven financialization of profit was unsustainable. With increasing leverage,[9] financial investors require assets to invest in. These take the form of debts and other financial instruments connected to the nonfinancial economy. However, nonfinancial companies can only service a certain quantity of financial obligations, restricted by their net earnings and other claimant obligations. While some companies and even industries may temporarily be in unique competitive positions, and hence able to generate supernormal profits, most sectors of the economy are not able to achieve this (Froud et al. 2006; Gregory and Michou 2007). There is a sense in which nonfinancial companies became saturated with debt in order to meet performance targets. This is a major reason why finance turned to the household, and those previously considered less creditworthy, as the new frontier for debt.

Policy, easy credit and the transition from corporate to household lending

The trends of financialization that began in the 1980s resulted in two distinct booms or bubbles, from 1995 to 2000 and from 2003 to 2008 (Brenner 2000, 2004, 2009; Perez 2009). The most important distinction between these booms, for our analysis, is that the recipients of credit were very different in each.

In the first boom, although richer households consumed more, reducing their saving rate as asset appreciation provided paper wealth, the major borrowers were nonfinancial corporations. Firms connected to technology found it particularly easy to tap equity and debt markets, producing an annual growth in investment of around 10 per cent between 1995 and 2000. Whether it was innovation-led capital or capital more generally that was looking for an outlet, there was a stock market and venture capital boom centred on new technology companies and supporting infrastructure (Morgan 2009: 56–61). When the bubble burst due to the inability of corporate profits to meet expectations,[10] this debt overhang had to be managed by the borrowing companies and the pension and other funds which had provided capital (Gjerstad and Smith 2009: 284). Repairing balance sheets overloaded with debt and excess productive capacity became the focus of corporate America post-2000 (Brenner 2004). This meant that any future surge in liquidity could not be absorbed by nonfinancial corporate borrowing.

As such, the second boom was characterized by the steadily increased indebtedness of households, especially in advanced OECD economies. This was possible for two reasons. First, the tremendous boost in liquidity that resulted both from OECD central bank actions post-9/11, and the recycling of current account surpluses via the US bond market, particularly by Germany, Japan and China. The macroeconomic environment facilitated by global imbalances created an excess of capital looking for a home within the international financial system. This surge in liquidity lowered the real world interest rate and thus, in combination with loose monetary policy, increased asset values.

Secondly, and of at least equal importance, the financial sector escaped from the bust of 2000–2002 with a relatively permissive regulatory environment still intact. As Perez (2009) points out this was in stark contrast to the crackdown on finance witnessed after similar historic crashes, and it was probably in large part due to the fact that the headline-grabbing frauds of the 1995–2000 boom were predominantly in the *non*financial sector (e.g., Worldcom, Enron and Parmalat).

Taken together, the growth in liquidity and permissive regulation created the incentive structure and available funding for banks to expand their balance sheets using short-term debt. At the same time, there was a growing demand for yield from investors faced with relatively low returns from low-risk government bonds. As the ensuing boom gathered pace, with rising house prices, the volume of mortgage lending and housing equity withdrawal increased in tandem (see IMF 2008a: 9; see Reinhart and Rogoff 2008: figure 3). The resultant consumption stimulus was harnessed by Anglo-American politicians and regulators, and their emulators elsewhere during the post dot com boom, and presented as a social good (Crouch 2008: 481). Lending criteria were loosened, allowing a greater volume of borrowers to become homeowners with smaller deposits and on greater multiples of income. This allowed potentially higher interest rates and charges to be made that, down the line and combined in innovative ways through several different financial products, could support higher risk-return yields to investors. The term 'subprime' originally referred to loans that did not conform to the standards that Fannie Mae and Freddie Mac[11] in the US demanded in order to purchase loans for securitization. One of the conditions, for example, was that deposits be a minimum of 20 per cent of purchase value. However, between 2000 and 2005, nonconforming loans grew 10-fold to $800 billion, representing almost half of all mortgage-linked bonds in the US (Tett 2009: 111–112). From 2005, Fannie Mae and Freddie Mac themselves loosened their conditions to a 3 per cent deposit which could be paid up front by the lender, effectively re-categorizing many subprime borrowers as prime (Mendales 2009: 1393). A further example of relaxing lending conditions, which has led to accusations of deliberate misselling, was the introduction of 'teaser rates' at 2.5 per cent for the first two years of a loan, rapidly increasing after that, often to well over 10 per cent. Many borrowers could only just afford their teaser rate. However, it was widely assumed that low rate refinancing would be available due to the huge surplus of capital available in the market and competition between lenders (Tett 2009: 145).

Clearly, the quantity of lending to households in certain economies had grown massively. Looking at the G7 countries, only Germany and Japan remained relatively stable in their level of household indebtedness as a proportion of gross disposable income. Between 1995/6 and 2007/8, Canada, France, Italy, the UK and US recorded increases of between 35 per cent and 86 per cent (OECD 2010). However, even with the increasing leverage available to banks that was being recycled from global imbalances, regulatory capital reserves should have acted as a buffer to control expansion. Here, financial innovation and a permissive regulatory environment were again crucial, initially in reducing the capital reserves required, and latterly in enabling 'synthetic' products to be created that did not even require ownership of the underlying loans and that could be used as 'arbitrage' opportunities by investors. That is to say, they enabled a greater return to be achieved for the apparent level of risk than the 'referenced' loans would provide if owned directly (Partnoy and Skeel 2007: 1028–1029). With corporate America unable to fulfil the role of chief borrower as it had during the dot com boom, households became the main absorbers of capital and temporary providers of investment return, facilitated by a housing bubble.

Marxist theory and the financial crisis

It is in foreseeing the growth of interconnected and tiered financial products, that we consider Marxian approaches most useful in helping to understand the present financial crisis. Marx understood that the credit system is necessary to facilitate and smooth the circulation of capital, temporarily overcoming a lack of effective demand and serving several other purposes. Credit allows the mobilisation, concentration and allocation of slack resources to be invested as capital, facilitating an increasing scale of fixed capital. It reduces the turnover time for commodities through the option of paying by instalments and allows uninterrupted circulation to occur for production processes of radically different periods. However, he was also aware these benefits entailed the creation of instruments such as shares that he labelled 'fictitious capital'.

Credit in its simplest form is money that is lent for conversion into capital and demands an interest rate payment from the surplus value/economic output created by the subsequent circulation of that capital.[12] This is 'money capital'. However, because this conversion from money into capital is irreversible for the duration of production, such money capital loses some of the co-ordinating power associated with the mobility of money. The creation of fictitious capital solves this problem. It is 'fictitious' because it is a paper claim to income that is not tied into real capital or even backed by existing collateral. Its value depends on the future circulation of real commodities that have not yet been produced or realised as money through exchange. Therefore, the value of the claim may turn out to be less than its face value, less than the money capital advanced, because of all the possibilities for the circuit of capital to be interrupted and surplus value not to be extracted as anticipated (Harvey 2006: 266–268).

There is also a second way in which paper claims to future income may be considered fictitious capital. This is if they are not actually investments related to capital at all and therefore are not a claim to future surplus value generated from production. Lending to households for mortgages, government bonds, lending against land on the basis of rents or other assets on the expectation of price rises are all examples of investment in appropriation rather than investment in production (ibid.: 268–269).

Such paper claims to future income, whether surplus value or other forms of revenue, may obviously multiply and be traded as forms of money themselves so long as those holding them have confidence in their value. There is nothing stopping layers of ever more sophisticated financial instruments as claims to future surplus value or the future income streams of labour, government or landlords, being constructed one upon another and this is essentially one way to understand derivatives and their use in the creation of mortgage-related securities. The cost of having a credit system, and creating the fictitious capital that is necessary for the functioning of capitalism, is the tendency for the creation of claims that far outrun the capacity of real production to service them. This is the nature of a financial crisis.

Conclusion

This chapter has argued that mainstream theory that depicts finance as a disconnected rentier upon production, resulting in crises when the implied size of the rent becomes unjustifiable, fails to recognize the increasingly active dominance of finance over all other activities performed within developed economies. Central to this power is neo-classical finance theory that justifies reward in terms of risk but that is disconnected from those processes that generate reward.

Rather than conceiving finance as a detached *rentier* periodically over-reaching production, we suggest that the financial sector is better understood as an increasingly powerful manager of the business structure in which the nonfinancial sector must operate. If share capital demands a particular rate of return, but the degree of intra-industry competition means this rate cannot be achieved from normal operations, then we have seen how industrial capital is pushed towards a range of short-term strategies in an attempt to satisfy finance. These include increasing debt, reducing retained earnings, downsizing capital assets and distributing greater proportions of profit. They also include altering the framework for the division of surplus between labour, capital and government (and between different types of labour).

Any credible account of this crisis accepts that finance 'over-reached' the ability of its borrowers to pay. Just as the dot com crash resulted when confidence in the future cash flows necessary to justify hugely inflated asset prices evaporated, the 2008–2009 crash occurred when repayment confidence in the US real estate market was undermined. Because the financial system was so highly leveraged, interconnected and complex, the mountain of structured finance constructed would have destroyed the international financial system if it had not been for unprecedented public sector intervention. However, what the mainstream account does not tell us is the way in which the relentless demand for financial return first reshaped the strategies of companies in the real economy, and second, and related to the first, exhausted the ability of labour to take on any more debt.

The story of the financial crisis that began in 2008 should better be understood in terms of an increasingly powerful financial sector that, in its pursuit for yield, first restructured industrial capital, and upon exhausting that potential, turned to the consumption of households. The irony is that in reshaping production, the consequent squeeze on average household income ultimately reduced the capacity of this potential absorber of debt and source of yield. None of the regulatory responses to the crisis now on the table deal with this aspect of the crisis. Instead of addressing the level and mode of profit accumulation in the financial sector, the cost of the crisis has so far been almost entirely paid for through taxes and wage restraint. Moreover, via the direct and indirect bailout of banks, plus the countervailing fiscal stimuli that governments implemented, private debt has been transformed into public with minimal political appetite to allow private bondholders to realize losses on either banking or sovereign debt. This has been justified in terms of fears about contagion and renewed crisis. For those countries in greatest financial difficulty, bailouts, austerity measures and the retrenchment of the state have been the 'necessary' political responses.

Aside from bailouts and fiscal stimuli, the main policy response has been almost entirely concerned with regulating the amount of credit in the financial system, and even in this regard the results are rather limited. Early in the aftermath of the crisis there was much tough talk from politicians and regulators, with especially strong pledges emanating from the Pittsburgh G20 summit in September of 2009. However, although the Bank for International Settlements initially translated this into quite harsh regulatory proposals that would have seen financial sector leverage cut dramatically (pp. 96–7), successful lobbying by the banks since then has led to a significant watering down of the proposals, both conceptually and numerically. Indeed, in early 2011, even the chairman of the UK's national financial regulator stated that leverage should ideally be *two to three times lower* than the new rules will require (Turner 2011).

As such, despite the rhetoric, there appears to be little *real* political willingness, even in those countries with (relatively) smaller dependence on their financial sectors, to enact substantive reform. Partly this is a function of the embeddedness of the ideational mindset that has accompanied neoliberalism; in essence, while there may be much criticism of 'free' markets, there is no developed alternative presently on the table. Furthermore, there is also a degree of 'lock-in' which may in fact, at least in the near term, be still more significant in preventing change. In short, if the financial system were to be de-leveraged too quickly, that would amount to a monetary contraction (the money-multiplier would be reduced) with the concomitant threat of deflation. This would be the exact opposite of the textbook policy response to a debt overhang, namely *inflation* to erode debt. In other words, even if the political will was organized and mobilized, today were are at possibly the worst point in the macroeconomic business cycle to attempt a rebalancing of economies via credit curtailment.

In some ways, this may be viewed as an unlikely victory of neoliberalism, a crisis caused by free market ideology in finance resulting in a strengthening of the role of private enterprise in societies and a further undermining of the postwar social compromise. However, the crisis has also opened up new cleavages of political awareness, protest and resistance. Resentment of the banking class and mistrust of the role of finance in society has not diminished, even in those economies with a significant structural dependence upon the sector, such as the UK. The potential for social discord increases as the cumulative impact of cuts and neoliberal 'solutions' to the fiscal problems facing national governments feeds into public consciousness. However, at present, the Left has failed to articulate a popular alternative political project.

It is also far from clear that this crisis has run its course. Global imbalances remain, with signs of new asset bubbles in food and basic commodities, overheating in developing economies, and muted consumer and small business lending in developed economies. The overhang of bad debts on the books of private and central banks continue to exert a significant drag on economic growth, which remains fragile and sensitive to shocks from any of the major areas of the world economy. It is too soon, and conditions are too uncertain, to suggest that we are truly 'beyond neoliberalism'. The political elite appear to be seeking a return to pre-crisis 'normality'. However, what *is* certain is that such normality is wishful thinking. It is not plausible to expect a benign return to the conditions of the financialized boom period. Just what sort of social compromise the new normal brings remains to be seen.

Notes

1. There is an internal contradiction in using the CAPM model to provide an ROE target. ROE is calculated using yearly income data, whereas CAPM is traditionally used to give a total shareholder return (TSR), which includes dividends *and* capital appreciation in the stock price. Capital appreciation may be affected by exogenous events such as the proportion of wealth invested in the stock market.
2. It is noteworthy that the ROE component is much higher than the return on debt for most companies. Indeed this difference provides the opportunity for 'financial engineering' on which most private equity purchases of companies are structured (Froud et al. 2006: 122).
3. To be consistent, each worker or bearer of human capital would also have to be treated separately.

4. This understanding of rents draws upon Ricardo, Marshall and Schumpeter, and it is distinct from neoclassical understandings of the term, which remain factor-centric (see Alchian 1987: 142).
5. Even synthetic instruments, constructed using derivatives, reference instruments or measures relating to the nonfinancial economy. This explains the demand for high-yielding subprime mortgages at the base of the inverted financial pyramid.
6. Defined as net profit/net capital stock.
7. Froud et al. provide a summary of the major consultancies' different methodologies and metrics for measuring shareholder value (Froud et al. 2000: 83).
8. Rentier income is calculated as financial sector profits, plus interest and capital gains by nonfinancial, non-government institutions.
9. The ratio of borrowed financing with a fixed-term repayment obligation to non-repayable financing in the form of retained earnings and shareholder equity.
10. Brenner attributes this to global overcapacity, specifically in manufacturing, and insufficient demand from consumers. US consumers had experienced real wage squeezes, despite rising productivity, in an attempt to improve profitability and other economies were too export oriented, relying on US demand (Brenner 2004).
11. These organizations, originating from the Great Depression, are referred to as government-sponsored enterprises. Although private corporations with shareholders, they are tasked with achieving social objectives with regard to private home ownership. Their debt, asset-backed securities sold into private credit markets, is backed by an implicit government guarantee.
12. Clearly, if we do not accept the labour theory of value, our view of the generation of economic output is different from Marx's view of the creation of surplus value. However, this does not alter Marx's insight into fictitious capital.

Part II
Beyond Neoliberal World Order?

6
The Rise of the 'B(R)IC Variety of Capitalism' – Towards a New Phase of Organized Capitalism?

Andreas Nölke

Introduction

It is somewhat ironic that scholars of international political economy take inspiration from a 10-year old study by Goldman Sachs. Still, it has become more than obvious that the future face of capitalism will be influenced in fundamental ways by countries such as Brazil, Russia, India or China (BRIC). In order to understand the development of capitalism after neoliberalism/financialization,[1] we need to link the study of global regulation – the focus of the previous section of this book – with an investigation into the capitalist developments within these countries. In order to do so, this chapter combines approaches from international political economy with concepts derived from comparative political economy, thereby complementing a historical diachronic perspective on capitalism with a spatial synchronic one. In doing so, it shares the concerns of the notion of 'variegated capitalism' (Peck and Theodore 2007; Dixon 2010; Jessop 2011) that is highlighting the commonalities of capitalism besides the specifics of national models. Still, for the purpose of complexity reduction, this analysis is based on rather precise and operational models that have been developed for the analysis of national and inter-temporal variation of capitalism, instead of the rather broad notion of 'capitalism in the singular, but more importantly as a dynamic polymorphic process whose development is uneven and "variegated"' (Dixon 2010: 5).

The basic question of this chapter is what a post-liberal phase of capitalism might look like if the BRIC economies become decisive in the global order. In order to answer this question, we will first look at theoretical concepts for highlighting the specifics of different phases of capitalism. The focus is on the juxtaposition of more liberal and more organized phases of capitalism, with neoliberalism/financialization being the most recent liberal one, following upon the more organized phase of Fordism. The basic argument here is that we might be witnessing the end of a rather liberal phase of capitalism, to be followed by a more organized one. This phase will arguably be influenced by the type of capitalism that has emerged within the BRIC. In order to get a better grip on this type of capitalism, the focus of the chapter will be on applying a Comparative Capitalism heuristic to the economies of Brazil and India, with some brief illustrations on China.[2] It highlights the various ways in which the state permeates the capitalist institutions within these organized economies. The conclusion focuses on the question of whether a coming organized phase of capitalism will be more desirable than the current one.

Financialization as current phase of capitalism: spatial and inter-temporal perspectives[3]

Over the last decade, more and more scholars have conceptualized the current phase of capitalism as 'financialization', broadly conceived as the growing dominance of finance in economy and society (Boyer 2000; Froud et al. 2000; Epstein 2005; Krippner 2005; Windolf 2005; Engelen 2008; Stockhammer 2008). While there is fairly broad agreement on the importance of financialization for any understanding of contemporary capitalism, there is much less attention for the degree of financialization of individual economies (Nölke 2009). We argue that the degree of financialization in individual political economies depends in particular on their historical context and on the timing of their integration of into the global economy. Thus, a more comprehensive perspective on capitalism does not only have to account for different phases of capitalism (of which Fordism and Financialization are but two), but also for different spatial configurations of capitalism. For this purpose, we do not propose a new, elegant and parsimonious theory, but rather an eclectic combination of existing approaches. In order to conceptualize the changing logics of capitalism in its different historical phases and in countries, we seek inspiration by some classics of political economy, such as Polanyi, Sombart and Hilferding, but also by more recent authors such as Höpner, Overbeek and van der Pijl.

Our point of departure is the backward-looking observation that capitalism develops in phases. These phases have recently each lasted – very roughly – some two to four decades:[4]

2000s, 1990s, 1980s, 1970s:	Financialization/Neoliberalism
1960s, 1950s, 1940s, 1930s:	Fordism
1920s, 1910s, 1900s:	Progressive Era (Antitrust)
1890s, 1880s, 1870s:	Monopoly/Financial Capitalism/New Mercantilism/Protectionism[5]
1860s, 1850s, 1840s:	Laissez-Faire/Free-Trade Capitalism

To be sure, we do not assume a continuous historical evolution of capitalism through pre-defined stages (typical for some materialist approaches, Jackson and Deeg 2006: 8), but rather observe a typical Polanyian pendulum between theses phases, with phases of embedding and disembedding of capitalism within society.[6] The core question is whether capitalist actors (owners and managers) are allowed to pursue a pure individualist capitalist rationality (such as maximizing shareholder value) or whether they are forced to negotiate with other economic, political and societal actors. The first is typical for various forms of liberal capitalism, the latter for different emanations of negotiated or organized capitalism.

Liberal capitalism carries an inherent instability and regularly leads to major economic crises, usually induced by gross speculation on the financial markets. These crises regularly lead to the mobilization of opposition against liberal capitalism, within society, governments, but also among capitalist actors themselves. Thus, the first era of Laissez-Faire Capitalism ended with the 1873 economic crisis ('Gründerkrach' in Germany, Long Depression in the US), the Progressive Era with the Great Depression of 1929 and the era of Financialization (possibly) with the Subprime crisis of 2007. While Laissez-Faire/Free Trade Capitalism was followed by a period of increased state intervention (protectionism, imperialism) and societal mobilization (formation of cartels, unions, employer association), the Progressive era was followed by the New Deal and Fordism. However, both of these negotiated settlements slowly but steadily were eroded by mobile capitalist forces, leading to periods of greater liberalization. Correspondingly, we see an alteration of more liberal and more negotiated (or 'organized', Höpner 2003) orders:

liberal	Laissez-Faire Capitalism, ended by 'Gründerkrach'/ Long Depression

> organized   Monopoly Capitalism
> liberal   Progressive Era[7] ended by the Great Depression
> organized   Fordism
> liberal   Neoliberalismended by the Subprime/Fiscal Crisis?

Following Höpner (2003) and his re-reading of theorists of organized capitalism such as Hilferding (1910), Naphtali (1928) and Sombart (1932), the distinction between liberal and negotiated (or organized) capitalism is crucial to our model, although it runs contrary to some popular assumptions about the nature of certain capitalist formations. From our perspective, Monopoly Capitalism has a lot in common with Fordism, given that both share a rather high degree of organization of economic activity (on the national level), and both oppose highly competitive liberal capitalism. Both models (cartels, trusts and monopolies on the one side, and corporate interlocks and corporatism on the other side) share a high degree of organization. In both cases, the leadership of a private company has ceased to be the private owner (Höpner 2003: 302–303) and has to give way for considerations of the entire cartel or the entire national economy or one of its sectors. Moreover, due to this high degree of organization, this type of capitalism becomes more amenable to purpose-driven societal influence than competitive capitalism (Hilferding 1910). Thus the General Commission of the German Federation of Trade Unions led by Naphtali (1928) saw the development towards organized capitalism as a major step towards economic democracy, whereas the (Progressive) demand for a return to more competitive capitalism has been rejected as reactionary by observers such as Sombart (1932). Fascism, however, destroyed the positive connotation of organized (Monopoly) capitalism, at least in Germany.

Of course, those liberal and negotiated phases of capitalism do not come about automatically or functionally. They rather are the product of specific social struggles, prominently studied by Neo-Gramscian researchers. These struggles are not only fought out between capital and labour, but also between different fractions of capital with different paradigmatic scales of operation (e.g., productive versus money capital, national versus cosmopolitan outlook, Overbeek 2005). Thus, the liberal phases of capitalism are not alike, in particular since they tend to be dominated by different fractions of capital. Whereas early struggles mainly took a local or national character, they increasingly have been fought out on the transnational plane (van der Pijl 1984, Overbeek 2005). The focus of these struggles is intellectual hegemony for a specific form of capitalism, but also the establishment of international institutions (organizations, regimes) that support these forms. International institutions have become increasingly important for the stabilization of certain phases of capitalism (Murphy 1994). Thus, the system of Bretton Woods was essential for the 'embedded liberalism' (Ruggie 1982) of Fordism, whereas the IMF, the Basel Accord and the IASB are important pillars of the 'neoliberal constitutionalism' (Gill) that is supporting Financialization. In this perspective, we need to combine studies of the historical evolution of capitalism with concepts and findings within international political economy.

However, not all socioeconomic systems are simultaneously formed by these phases of capitalism. This is where the spatial dimension of capitalism comes into play. Some systems are more advanced in their exposure to these developments of global capitalism. In particular, the US and the UK have had a vanguard role in the recent past. In contrast, successful latecomers (such as Germany, France, Italy, Japan or South Korea) enter these phases much later, or in the case of late-latecomers (such as China and India), possibly not (yet) at all, if they are not yet fully integrated into the capitalist world system. Moreover, this observation should not be understood in the perspective of a simple modernization theory. Depending on the timing of their integration into the global economic system, national socioeconomic systems may never completely converge on the 'advanced' liberal model. Most importantly, we can observe a striking distinction between the economies of the liberal 'Lockean Heartland' comprising the white-majority, English-speaking countries and the 'contender states', latecomers of the industrialization process (van der Pijl 1998). The latter tend towards a far more organized and coordinated version of capitalism (typically steered by banks, families or the state), given the need to catch up with the advanced liberal economies (but to avoid colonization), as argued by observers such as List (1841).[8] This finding is even more valid for the last round of successful latecomers; a striking aspect of the capitalist model developing in countries like Brazil, China or India is a strong role for the state and/or for families, as will be demonstrated below.

Even if these (late-) latecomer economies will also be thoroughly affected by the liberalizing phases of global capitalism, they will always remain more organized (or coordinated) than the US. Sometimes the coordinated versions of capitalism hardly become affected at all, thus the emphasis on trust busting that was an important element of the Progressive era in the US, but which never became a major issue in early twentieth-century Germany (although it was articulated there as well (Sombart 1932)). At the same time, the crises that regularly end periods of liberal capitalism do not affect all socioeconomic systems equally and at the same time. The original damage caused by the final crisis of a liberal phase of capitalism is most extensive in the liberal heartland. Still, second round effects may bring about at least as devastating crises within the economies of latecomers and late-latecomers, in particular by decreasing their exports.

What might a next phase of organized capitalism look like? a comparative capitalism perspective on the B(R)IC

During the last decade, studies of Comparative Capitalism have mainly been preoccupied with countries of the triad (i.e., Japan, Western Europe and the US). In particular, the 'Varieties of Capitalism' approach as developed by Hall and Soskice (2001a) was strongly focused on the US and Germany. Only very recently the approach has been utilized in order to analyse economies outside of the triad, as demonstrated by the modelling of dependent market economies in East Central Europe (Nölke and Vliegenthart 2009) and of hierarchical market economies in Spanish-speaking Latin America (Schneider 2009). This chapter extends the Comparative Capitalism (CC) perspective to Brazil, India and China. On the one side, the focus is on the classical questions of CC, i.e., the determinants of economic development; on the other side, the focus is on the differences to alternative types of capitalism.

Over the last years, the Comparative Capitalism perspective has become somewhat canonical in the study of the political economy of Northern industrialized countries (Blyth 2003: 215). The research programme that has been founded by authors such as Shonfield (1965) and popularized by Michel Albert (1993) has led to numerous typologies of national models of capitalism, with theoretical roots in the regulation school (Amable 2003; Hollingsworth and Boyer 1997), Neo-Marxism (Coates 2000) and New Institutionalism (Hall and Soskice 2001a). In particular, the last version has led to many empirical studies, based on its juxtaposition of liberal market economies (LME), illustrated with the case of the US, and of coordinated market economies (CME), illustrated with the case of Germany. The basic assumption of this theoretical programme is that specific institutional complementarities inherent to each variety are able to explain the divergent patterns of innovation of the leading sectors within liberal and coordinated market economies. Hall and Soskice (2001b: 17–33) distinguish – similar to other approaches within Comparative Capitalism (Jackson and Deeg 2006: 11–20) – five interdependent institutions: (1) corporate finance, (2) corporate governance, (3) industrial relations, (4) education/training and (5) the transfer of innovation within the economy. Based on this distinction, the Comparative Capitalism research programme was able to deliver a parsimonious, but still fairly sophisticated analysis of Northern capitalisms.[9]

Still, over the last years, more and more limitations of this research tradition have become apparent (Hancké et al. 2007: 4–9; Jackson and Deeg 2006: 37–39, Jessop 2011: 5–6). These limitations include the narrow focus on the countries of the triad, the overly strong dualism between LME and CME within the dominant Varieties of Capitalism approach, the omission of transnational influences and the neglect of the role of the state. A second generation of Comparative Capitalism studies tries to overcome these limitations. In line with Drahokoupil (2009), Nölke and Vliegenthart (2009), Schneider (2009), ten Brink (2010) and Taylor and Nölke (2010), this contribution will enlarge the spatial confines of Comparative Capitalism; ask for the existence of additional basic types beyond LME and CME; analyse the role of transnational influences (in particular of multinational enterprises) and highlight the role of the state for the establishment of particular types of capitalism outside of the triad.

The focus of this contribution is on the mode of capitalism within the industrialized sectors of 'emerging markets', in particular the Brazilian and Indian cases.[10] Particularly in the context of the rise of the BRIC (Brazil, Russia, India and China) this question has gained considerable importance, and it has also gained importance for the development of the world economy as a whole. The core question is whether these economies develop into a similar direction as those of the triad, or diverge in more or less permanent ways. In the following, we will try to give a preliminary answer to this question, by developing a rough sketch of a 'B(R)IC' model of capitalism and illustrating this model with the case of Brazil and India.[11] The focus is – similar to Schneider and Soskice (2009) – on an outline of the current status of these economies, while the historical evolution within colonialism, class conflicts and neo-liberal reforms will be neglected (Schrank 2009). Although it is yet too early to judge the long-term stability of this model, we can identify some highly specific elements, in spite of some parallels to institutions in liberal and coordinated economies.

State-permeated market economies as a B(R)IC-variety of capitalism

The LME/CME juxtaposition as developed by Hall and Soskice (2001b) allows for a rough typology of most Northern industrialized economies, although with some limitations in case of the Mediterranean countries, where the state plays a more important role than allowed for by Hall and Soskice (Schmidt 2003). New basic varieties should not be introduced without necessity, given that the parsimony of the Hall and Soskice model was a crucial factor for its success (Hancké et al. 2007: 16; Jackson and Deeg 2006: 31–32). Still, there are limitations to this dualism, at least with regard to the economies at the periphery of Western Europe and the US, with their strong dependencies on multinationals based in their neighbouring centres. For these economies, we have coined the model of 'dependent market economies/DME'(Nölke and Vliegenthart 2009), given their dependence on decisions taken within the hierarchies of western multinational enterprises (see Table 6.1).

Foreign direct investments are also important for 'emerging economies', such as Brazil, Russia, India and China, but they are much less dependent on these investments, if compared with countries such as Hungary or the Czech Republic. The B(R)IC variety of capitalism is rather dominated by dense relationships between public authorities and major domestic enterprises as a central coordination mechanism. In marked contrast to DMEs, these political economies are rather dominated by national capitalists, not those of the centre. The focus is on the role of the state, as already described by Peter Evans (1979) – a state that is cooperating closely with national elites and does not have to give in to the demands of multinational enterprises, but that is able to impose certain conditions onto the latter. In a more abstract way, we are witnessing a fourth mode of social coordination, besides markets (LME), networks (CME), hierarchies (DME) and now clans, as developed by Ouchi (1980) based on transaction cost economics. These clans are central within the B(R)IC-model of 'state-permeated market economies (SME)'. Clans are, similar to markets, hierarchies and network a basic mode of social coordination, with a particular focus on a background of common values (Ouchi 1980: 130f.). SMEs are dominated by a particularly close cooperation between public and business actors that is at least indirectly based on informal personal relations – partially even family ties – supported by common values and a shared social background. The importance of the latter also distinguishes clans from networks (in the context of Comparative Capitalism), given that the latter are not based on common values and social backgrounds, but rather an exchange based upon rational gains, also involving cooperation between very different social classes (e.g., between employer associations and labour unions). A close cooperation between public authorities and companies can also be found within other modes of capitalism, but in no case

Table 6.1   Three basic varieties of capitalism

Variety Institution	Liberal market economies/LME	Coordinated market economies/ CME	Dependent market economies/DME
Distinctive coordination mechanism	Competitive *markets* and formal contracts	Inter-firm *networks* and associations	Dependence on MNC intra-firm *hierarchies*
Financial system	Domestic and international capital markets	Domestic bank lending and internally generated funds	Foreign direct investments and foreign-owned banks
Corporate governance	Outsider control: dispersed shareholders	Insider control: concentrated shareholders	Control by headquarters of multinational enterprises
Industrial relations	Pluralist, market-based, hardly any collective agreements	Corporatist, rather consensual, sector-wide or even national agreements	Appeasement of skilled labour, company level collective agreements
Skill formation	General skills, high research and development expenditures	Company- or industry-specific skills, vocational training	Limited expenditures for further qualification
Transfer of innovations	Based on markets and formal contracts	Important role of joint ventures and business associations	Intra-firm transfer within transnational enterprise
Comparative advantages	Radical innovation in technology and service sectors	Incremental innovation of capital goods	Assembly platforms for semi-standardized industrial goods

Source: Nölke and Vliegenthart 2009.

is this equally predominant, and strongly based on personal relations and common values (but rather on formal contracts or laws). State permeation does not necessarily entail the existence of a 'strong', centralized state, a dominance of public enterprises and centralized economic planning, but rather an omnipresence of public authorities that may also follow their particular concerns as fragmented parts of a state class (Elsenhans 1996). At the same time, these authorities and their cooperating companies that are tempted to pursue rent-seeking activities are largely kept in balance by a relatively autonomous role of private capital, thereby preventing the comprehensive capture of public policies by private interests as witnessed in patrimonial regimes (although this capture clearly is not completely absent in SMEs).[12]

Foreign direct investments (and selective acts of privatization) are welcome as modernizing factors within this neo-mercantilist model, as long as they do not undermine the general preponderance of national capital. Moreover, it is not coincidental that the SME model emerged within the big economies outside of the triad, and that this model differs somewhat from the strongly export-oriented model of the East Asian tiger states. The rise of the SME model was based on several interrelated developments. On one side, it coincided with the reorientation of (North-South) foreign investments during the 1980s and early 1990s that shifted from a focus on access to raw materials and cheap labour towards access to the internal markets of the (semi-) periphery. This re-orientation requires a fairly close cooperation with national capital and contributes to the modernization of the latter (Abu-El-Haj 2007: 96). On the other side, national capital depends on foreign direct investments for its expansion – even entailing wholesale privatization – for the modernization of those economic sectors that are providing basic economic services (e.g., telecommunication and other public utilities).

The notion of 'clans' as mechanism for social coordination, the symbiosis of national capital and public authorities and the selective modernization via foreign direct investments enable us to describe the central elements of the SME variety, addressing the five typical elements of Comparative Capitalism. The focus is on the interrelationships between corporate governance and the other four institutional domains, in line with the usual approach towards western capitalism (e.g., Hall and Gingerich 2004; Höpner 2005): (1) In contrast to minority shareholders (LMF), institutional block-holders (CME) or control by multinational corporations (DME), major SME companies usually are either dominated by families or by the state, in any case by organized national capital. These ownership structures lead to obvious complementarities with corporate finance (2), as far as they make SME companies fairly independent from short-term fluctuations on global capital markets as well as from profit expectations of international investors. Moreover, control by national capital or even public ownership frequently allows SME companies to tap into public support (e.g., subsidized credit by state banks). A close cooperation between major companies and public authorities is also helpful with regard to industrial relations (3), given that public regulations (and their selective implementation) may serve as a key contribution to keeping labour costs low, an important ingredient to the competition strategy of companies from these countries.

The same is true for education and training (4) that are geared towards those sectors in which national companies are most active. In addition, the class background is an important factor for the transformation of educational capital into labour market success, thereby contributing to the reproduction of class structures. Finally, public interventions also assist with the transfer of innovations and competition policy (5). Soft protection of intellectual property rights allow for reverse engineering that is an important ingredient for technological catch up. At the same time, competition policies are geared towards the temporary protection of individual companies, e.g., to enable expansion into other markets based on monopoly profits. All in all, these complementarities enable companies from emerging markets to be competitive in particular on a medium level of technology and in the procession of raw goods, based on rather low costs.

It is impossible to test this model empirically within the limited space of this chapter, but we can hint at some broad commonalities between individual aspects within the modern economic sectors of Brazil and India. Departing from the model of state-permeated capitalism as described above, the following section will provide a very rough and simplified sketch of the Brazilian and Indian political economy.[13] The focus is on the modern sectors of the economy, in particular on multi-national enterprises expanding from these economies. To be sure, there is not one Indian variety of capitalism or one Brazilian one, but many, given the strong fragmentation between, e.g., urban and rural areas. Moreover, the historical evolution of capitalism in these economies was very different. Still, we can highlight some obvious parallels by illustrating the model developed above. The focus of the next section clearly is on depicting commonalities between the economies in question, not on their differences, in order to gauge what a new phase or organized capitalism might look like. Since not all economies can be presented in great detail, the focus is on the less well-known Brazilian economy, complemented by observations on the Indian case.

Comparative advantages

Both countries share broadly similar comparative advantages, typical for the semi-periphery: they operate on a labour-intensive medium level of technology, based on cheap labour. Within this context, specializations differ between the procession of raw materials (mainly Brazil) or labour-intensive services (mainly India). This observation points towards a general difference between the 'SMEs' and other less successful (smaller) countries of the semi-periphery: Brazil and India are not limited to the export of raw materials, but show fairly successful attempts to move up on the value chain in certain sectors, combined with fairly large internal markets serviced by domestic companies.[14]

Corporate governance

National capital plays the dominant role within the Brazilian economy. Most major Brazilian companies are exchange-listed, but they usually are dominated by family shareholdings or other block holders. In addition, the Brazilian state keeps substantial shareholdings, particularly in case of former public enterprises that have been privatized (e.g., Embraer). Direct state intervention, however, is rather rare. More important are indirect channels, in particular via institutions such as the national development bank BNDES (Banco Nacional de Desenvolvimento Econômico e Social). In nearly all cases, major Brazilian companies are fairly independent from short-term fluctuations on the financial markets. There is no open market for the control of companies – as characteristic for LMEs – but rather an 'insider'-dominated mode of corporate control, more in line with traditional CME-structures. Completely dispersed shareholding is very rare, and minority shareholders tend to be disadvantaged by dominating shareholders. Correspondingly, the recent 'Corporate Governance' movement met considerable resistance in Brazil (Grün 2010), even if the dominant role of family capitalism has been modernized: 'Family-controlled companies, the typical business arrangement of the Brazilian bourgeoisie, fell from 23 to 17 units of the 100 largest between 1990 and 1997. Meanwhile, a new mode of local bourgeoisie organization, dominant minority property (companies whose controllers hold between 20 and 50 per cent of the voting shares, with the remainder being offered to the public) increased from 5 to 23 of the largest 100 companies. This shift reflected the legal changes made to attract international investors' (Abu-El-Haj 2007: 106).

Similarly, major Indian companies typically are not dominated by dispersed shareholders or the organized forces of global capital markets (mutual funds, pension funds, investment banks, hedge funds, etc.), but often are rather family-owned/kin-based or state-controlled. In the majority of listed firms today, the largest blocks of equity typically remain in the hands of the founding family or controlling shareholder (Allen et al. 2006: 21). Family ownership might even be counted among the 'distinguishing features' of Indian MNCs (ibid.: 31).

Corporate finance

During the last decade, capital markets have gained increasing relevance for the financing of Brazilian companies. However, the latter still are protected by families and other stockholders, thereby moderating the pressure and turbulence emanating from internationalized finance. Typical, though less dominant as in other economies of Latin America, are also large conglomerates that have drawn on their diversification in order to survive the massive crises and adjustment programs of the 1990s. The focus is on internally generated funds as well as bank loans, in part subsidized by institutions such as BNDES. Direct and indirect state support can take many forms, including tax rebates, state guarantees and subsidized credit provided by state banks, all contributing to financing conditions that are more favourable than usual. Besides BNDES, semi-public pension funds and straight state subsidies have to be mentioned. Global capital markets are tapped selectively in order to modernize the domestic economy. In contrast to dependent market economies, however, we do not witness a 'sell-out' of domestic banks: 'In 2000, domestic banks combining public and private institutions, still controlled 72, 6% of the total financial endowment' (Abu-El-Haj 2007: 104). This distribution of ownership was very advantageous during the most recent financial crisis; the retreat of international banks (and the more careful operations by national private banks) was compensated by a massive expansion of public banking (Grün 2010: 14).

Similar features can be observed for major Indian companies. Despite the fact that India currently harbours the highest number of listed firms in the world (10,000), trading on its exchanges has remained extremely concentrated, which has meant that the bulk of shares in the most significant markets are rarely actively traded (Allen et al. 2006: 12–14). Means of corporate financing tends to be significantly correlated to the stage of development a firm is at, combined with the size of the firm and its ability to make use of informal business and kin networks. A common tendency among Indian firms during the start-up phase has been primarily to generate funds through family, friends and business connections. Later, many have turned to special financial institutions such as the Small Industry Development Bank (a wholly owned subsidiary of the state-owned Reserve Bank of India) or to a state financial institution. (ibid.: 19-20). Past the initial start-up phase, internal financing in the form of retained earnings remains the most significant source of long-term financing, whereas with short-term financing, most typical Indian firms have preferred to utilize trade credits and current liabilities, something which has been supported by the significance of informal business networks at work within the economy. Furthermore, we note that many Indian companies, similar to Chinese ones, can make use of some kind of direct or indirect state financing, including fiscal incentives, financial guarantees and credits from state-owned banks, while the allocation of these support measures frequently is decided in informal networks between business and public officials.

Industrial relations

The importance of cost advantages is very important with regard to Brazilian industrial relations. Although there are fairly sophisticated labour laws, this only pertains to a relatively small (but important) share of the Brazilian workforce – not an unusual situation in the Latin American context. Generally, labour markets are fragmented between a small, well paid, organized and protected segment of core workers in the public sector as well as in major companies on the one side, and the semi-informal economy on the other side, without any substantial union protection. Again, state permeation is important, as far as the 'labour aristocracy' is being protected by law and – in spite of the neoliberal tendencies of the last decades – well integrated into the collusion between national capital and the state (Phillips 2004: 161–164). Small and medium scale enterprises that operate in fairly close relationship to the informal sector, however, are much more critical towards stringent labour protection. Still, major companies also would be hardly keen to introduce powerful unions and better working conditions on a comprehensive basis, since affordable services by the informal sector contribute considerably to the cost advantages of the Brazilian economy. And even in those parts of the economy where labour unions are important, they operate less based on collective action and negotiations with employer associations, but rather by direct political ties with the state – a highly significant contrast to the role of unions in coordinated market economies.

The largest share of employment in India is found in the informal and unorganized sectors. Official regulation of the labour market is very complex and stringent, but there are significant deviations between what has been written on paper versus what is actually enforced, particularly in the services sector (Sharma 2006). Given that the services sectors are the primary drivers of growth in the Indian economy, a blind eye has been turned on these regulations in order to foster and ensure growth of firms. At the same time, the large informal sector helps to keep wages in the formal sector very low, due to its abundant provision of cheap services and products for daily use (Mayer-Ahuja 2006).

Education and training

Traditionally, Brazilian companies did not invest much into education and training of their workforce, but rather relied on activities of their own government (Arbix 2010: 19; Dahlmann and Frischtak 1993: 415). Thus, they did not only follow the priorities of the given government, but also suffered quite considerably during the heavy macroeconomic crises of the 1990s. Moreover, public investments in these activities generally are low, if compared to those of Northern countries. Public support, in particular for science and technology, has existed since the 1970s, but rather in basic instead of applied sciences. Cooperation between universities and companies was limited, but it has intensified more recently (Arbix 2010: 18–20; Dahlmann and Frischtak 1993: 415). Most employees have very few incentives for investments into their own education, due to their short-term and insecure employment relations (World Bank 2006a). Similar to the field of industrial relations, we find a fragmentation between small groups of highly qualified labour (education from private secondary schools and/or foreign universities) and a much larger group of hardly qualified labour with a focus on general skills, a much larger and less qualified group than in CME, LME and DMEs. Only very slowly we are witnessing a process of increased secondary education, but again this is dominated by students stemming from middle and upper classes with higher social capital, supported by a system of private schools and spatial segregation.

In contrast to Brazil, the Indian government has contributed substantial funds to the promotion of skilled workforce for the industries deemed as the backbone of Indian economic development. In the direct post-independence period, it was typical for India to prioritize tertiary education over primary education. This has fueled an ever-increasing gap between middle and lower-income classes. While the Indian higher education system is constantly pumping out thousands of new graduates per year, these graduates do not quite have all the necessary and up-to-date skills needed to match the advances in Indian industry. Correspondingly, many Indian firms have begun their own in-house training programs, such as Saytam, which has set up a campus adjacent to its headquarters in Hyderabad, thereby further intensifying the segregation of the education system.

Transfer of innovations

Due to the traditionally very limited role of internal research and development in Brazil, innovations are usually imported from abroad, usually via Northern multinational enterprises. Even a leading high tech company such as Embraer has to get along without comprehensive internal research and development. Instead, it has to mobilize innovations via its network of international partners (Goldstein 2002;

Salles-Filho, Marcio da Silveira and Bonacelli 2009). Public institutions are involved in the transfer of innovations to a limited degree. More obvious is the close collaboration between public authorities and major public enterprises in case of competition policy. However, competition policy in the strict American/European sense hardly exists at all (if so, only on paper). Over many years, a number of sectors were protected from international competition, thereby leading to the developments of monopolies or oligopolies. This is to the short-term disadvantage of consumers, but to the advantage of a few major Brazilian companies that were enabled to mobilize the resources needed for successful cross-border expansion. Competition policy, however, lately was also targeted in order to create competitive domestic companies. This can entail the selective attribution of market access to foreign companies, in order to give domestic companies strong incentives to get rid of the dangerous rent-seeking perspective that goes hand-in-hand with import substitution and the corresponding focus on state protection (Abu-El-Haj 2007: 97). At the same time, competition policy is used in order to give way to the efficient provision of those services that are necessary for the expansion of domestic capital, e.g., in telecommunications, power supply and, more lately, in certain sectors of banking (Dowbor 2009: 125). Generally, this has given rise to the consolidation of two patterns: sectors with oligopolies dominated by national capital on the one hand; and rather fragmented, competitive sectors with strong international participation on the other (Abu-El-Haj 2007: 100).

Competition policy has also been used to selectively protect and (re-) open economic sectors in India, in order to allow domestic firms to grow and later team up with foreign partners (Taylor and Nölke 2010). More specifically, something that has significantly helped the transfer of innovation has been the networks of CEOs and upper management in which many Indian firms are involved. These networks include various government officials and former state enterprise employees who have created their own spin-off firms. These ties have been extremely useful in terms of providing firms with additional financial leverage and the ability to steer domestic public policies in a manner conducive to the needs of each respective firm as well as industry as a whole. This also pertains to the (somewhat limited) protection of intellectual property rights. For instance, in India the development of the pharmaceutical industry is directly correlated to establishment of a 'soft patent system to legalize reverse engineering' post-1970 (Goldstein 2007: 95).

Central coordination mechanism

To conclude, it becomes obvious how strongly Brazilian companies are profiting from their close collaboration with the state, to a much higher extent than most triad companies are. Particularly in the field of natural resources, close cooperation with public authorities is essential for company success. At the same time, Brazil has witnessed a policy of purposeful diversification of economic structures on the basis of state-led import substitution and targeted protection of individual economic sectors. More recently, economic elites have pleaded more fervently for liberalization that is more comprehensive. Although the old protection is inefficient and may lead to wasteful rent seeking, a literal implementation of the Washington consensus, however, is perceived to be an unacceptable sell-out and subordination to (Anglo-American) capital markets (Abu-El-Haj 2007). Compared to the US or Western Europe, the internationalization of Brazilian capital is relatively limited (Phillips 2004: 194), although it is partially integrated into global capitalist networks (Flynn 2007). The typical 'thick ties between the traditional oligarchy and the state' (Phillips 2004: 55) in Brazil are not only a recipe for success, but also a liability for economic development, as indicated by many episodes of corruption. Still, we may distinguish Brazil from many much more problematic regimes in other countries of Latin America: 'The government adopted relatively autonomous policies that advanced the interests of the entire bourgeoisie without degenerating into clientelistic support for particular firms' (Abu-el-Haq 2007: 110). Correspondingly, the model of a 'clan' appears to be the best approximation of the central mode of social coordination in Brazil: Based on a rather similar (class) background, the political economy is dominated by informal, personalized relations, thereby easing the creation of trust and social coordination. In contrast to coordinated market economies, nonmarket coordination is not provided by formal institutions; business associations, for example, are rather weak, a marked contrast to the powerful role of Brazilian capital (Phillips 2004: 195). At the same time, we do not find a powerful, centralized state as in East Asia. In contrast, the state is strongly fragmented internally (ibid.: 237-239). Still, we witness a high degree of social coordination, supported by the social capital that is accumulated in clan-like relations between private and public elites.

Similarly, support by the state and its public policies have been a crucial factor contributing to the rise of Indian MNCs, as already witnessed with financial support schemes or innovation and competition policies.

These policies have been complemented by a number of other public policies, such as inward and outward investment regulation. Thus, the Indian state has been the major player in creating, shaping and fostering the growth of today's Indian MNCs. (Gupta and Dutta 2005; Gupta 2006), based on close collaboration with major capitalists. Given these strong interconnections between Indian MNCs and the state, it is more and more difficult to clearly demarcate the dividing role between the state and the private sector, thus leading to the emergence of public private 'hybrids' which have become the driving force behind the Indian national innovation production system (Clifton 2007: 7; Gupta and Dutta 2006).

Conclusion

The purpose of the chapter was to develop a theoretically informed speculation about the outline of a post-neoliberal phase of capitalism. It was based by two general assumptions. First, the next phase of capitalism will not be a liberal, but an organized one. Second, it will be dominated by the variety of capitalism evolving in the B(R)IC. In order to describe this variety, we have coined the notion of 'State-permeated Market Economies' as a fourth basic type of capitalism. In contrast to markets, networks and hierarchies, the central coordination mechanisms of the other three types, this variety is based on the 'clan' mode of social coordination, linking state authorities with domestic capitalists.

The empirical illustrations within this chapter were based on Brazil and India. Still, one could argue that we are witnessing the emergence of a more general model that also encompasses the case of China, given the high degree of coincidence with recent accounts of 'Sino-Capitalism' (Chu 2010; ten Brink 2010; McNally 2008). The industrial sector of the Chinese economy is focused on a labour-intensive medium level of technology, based on cheap labour. Chinese companies also show fairly successful attempts to move up on the value chain in certain sectors, combined with fairly large internal markets serviced by domestic companies. Obviously, state ownership and state-controlled companies are still a very prominent feature in mainland China. Furthermore, we note that many Chinese companies can make use of some kind of direct or indirect state financing, including fiscal incentives, financial guarantees and credits from state-owned banks, while the allocation of these support measures frequently is decided in informal networks between business and public officials. A low-cost workforce obviously assists Chinese companies in basing their business model on price competition in mature industries, a feature that is similar to the use that Korean and Taiwanese have made of low labour costs in some of their neighbour countries (Goldstein 2007: 76–78). Moreover, China is notorious for its weak implementation of intellectual property rights regulation. In a more general perspective on the type of economic coordination, not only the obviously crucial role of informal relationships between major companies and the state has to be highlighted, but – in particular for the expansion into the 'Greater China' region – also the support by interpersonal networks particularly based on ethnic ties (ibid.: 117–122). These networks reduce information costs by the provision of trust and other forms of social capital. Here, we also find interesting parallels to the networks supporting the Chaebol in South Korea and the Guanxi Chixe in Taiwan (Feenstra and Hamilton 2006).

Our brief analysis of the modern sectors of the Brazilian and Indian economy, with some afterthoughts on the case of China, has demonstrated that this 'B(R)IC Variety of Capitalism' is based on specific economic institutions that are quite different from the neoliberal Anglo-Saxon type of capitalism that is currently dominating on the global level. Correspondingly, we might expect increasing conflicts over global economic regulation in the near future (Nölke and Taylor 2010). Moreover, if (one of) the 'BIC' countries becomes hegemonic and would be willing as well as able to put its imprint on global economic institutions to a similar degree as the US, we might be witnessing considerable changes in the general mode of capitalism towards a much stronger role of the state within economic activities. In this context, one should also notice that the role of the state has increased quite considerably within the capitalist heartland, as indicated by the fiscal guarantees of private bank lending to the semi-periphery of the Eurozone, as well as by major public stakes in financial institutions, not only in Continental Europe, but also in the US/UK.

Although many observers might cherish a decline of neoliberalism/ financialization, a post-neoliberal phase of capitalism might be less pleasant than hoped for if this phase is dominated by the state-permeated market economies that have developed in countries such as Brazil, Russia, India or China. These economies are shaped by the strong role of public authorities and very rich families, with a very limited role for organized labour and huge parts of the population living under highly problematic conditions. These countries are hardly democratic (even in Brazil and India) and highly unequal, although the SME variety of capitalism has also proven to be able to lift hundreds of millions of people out of absolute poverty. While not all of these observations are equally valid for the economies of the triad, the growing role of the state, increasing levels of inequality and decreasing levels of democratic participation can also be noted for the US or Europe. At least the capitalists dominating in SMEs usually are not allowed to pursue a pure individualist capitalist rationality (such as maximizing shareholder value), but are forced to negotiate with political actors, thereby pointing towards (very faint) options for social reform.

Notes

1. In the following, we will use the term 'financialization' instead of 'neoliberalism', since the focus is more on the mode of capitalism (financialization) than on the political project behind it (neoliberalism).
2. Russia will be excluded from the analysis, due to its somewhat less dynamic economy.
3. This section of the chapter is based on a joint conference paper written with Marcel Heires.
4. For reasons outlined below, (national) socioeconomic systems enter these phases at different points of time. This periodization focuses on the US; in particular, the Progressive Era was not a global one.
5. From this perspective, the notion of financialization is somewhat unwelcome, since it depicts a very different capitalist system than the earlier Monopoly/Financial Capitalism (Höpner 2003). To avoid confusion, we will use Monopoly Capitalism for the latter.
6. Polanyi (1944/1997: 40) based his studies on the end of the free trade/laissez-faire era in the 1870s and, more importantly, on the breakdown of the late 1920s/early 1930s (ibid.: 41–54).
7. The characterization of the Progressive Era as liberal is certainly not self-evident, given that it not only disorganized the US economy by trust busting, but it also introduced some regulatory policies for the first time, such as the US Food and Drug Administration. Still, the progressive movement was clearly a liberal pro-free enterprise and pro-competition movement of the middle class, mobilizing against the 'Robber Barons' on the one side and radical political movements of farmers and workers on the other. Correspondingly, Polanyi (1944/1997: 196) observes that the 1920s was the period when economic liberalism was most popular.
8. One could even argue that the latecomers will in part be formed by the characteristics of the phase of capitalism that was predominant during their first-time integration into the global economy. Thus, the German and Japanese coordinated economies were organized in the protectionist late nineteenth century and South Korea was influenced by Fordism. In contrast, China and some of the transformation economies in Eastern Europe carry some more liberal traits, given their global integration under financialization.
9. Following Jackson and Deeg, I prefer to use the more general notion of Comparative Capitalism in order to highlight the plurality of approaches developed in this research programme, over the narrow notion of Varieties of Capitalism that gives too much credence to the somewhat functionalist approach developed by Hall and Soskice.

10. Given the heterogeneity of the countries involved, it does not make sense to develop a model of the full economies. Thus, the focus is on the most dynamic sector. Interrelationships with other sectors, e.g., the informal sector or agriculture/mining will be taken into account when relevant.
11. Given the space constraints of this chapter, involving the rather complex Chinese case would lead to a much too superficial analysis. I will briefly return to the Chinese case in the Conclusion, in order to strengthen my argument that we are dealing with an emerging additional (and potentially dominating) variety of capitalism.
12. Arguably, less successful checks on rent seeking are responsible for the less dynamic economic development of the Russian economy.
13. The representation of the Brazilian case is based on Nölke 2011, the Indian case on Taylor and Nölke 2010. Please refer to these studies for more detailed country case studies.
14. Based on this observation, countries such as Mexico, Turkey or Indonesia can be expected to take a similarly dynamic development.

7
Sovereign Wealth Funds in the Global Political Economy: The Case of China

Henk Overbeek

Introduction[1]

This book deals with the crisis of neoliberalism and the forces determining its future trajectory. One of those forces seen in the early days of the crisis, or so it seemed, was the rise of government-owned investment funds or 'sovereign wealth funds' (SWFs) from China, Singapore and the Arab Gulf countries. These countries invested billions of dollars in failing Western financial institutions such as Citicorp, UBS, Merrill Lynch and Barclays Bank (Farrell, Lund and Sadan 2008: 10). Ironically, the billions of Communist China were called in to save some of the most prominent icons of Western financial capitalism. Headlines in the international press increasingly referred to 'the return of the state' and the rise of 'state capitalism' (e.g., Bremmer 2008, Lyons 2007). Where these SWFs originate in what Van der Pijl has called Hobbesian contender states (see Van der Pijl 1998, 2006) such as China, their increasing prominence has gone hand-in-hand with an emerging geopolitical and geoeconomic rivalry. In this chapter, we will analyse the role of the China Investment Corporation (CIC), the Chinese SWF established in 2007, from a comparative perspective.

The chapter is organized as follows. First, a brief factual summary is given of the establishment and structure of CIC.

Then, the chapter presents a general discussion of the rise of SWFs. The aim of this part is to develop a rudimentary framework with which to analyse the SWF phenomenon more generally, and especially to make some sense of some of the observed contradictions and paradoxes surrounding their appearance on the stage of the global economy. It will be argued that SWFs in general need to be analysed against the background of the specific nature of the political economy of the country in question, specifically looking at the ways in which domestic economic and political characteristics and dynamics are articulated with the ways in which the national political economy is inserted in the structures and dynamics of the global political economy. Here we will present, as a heuristic device, two ideal-typical models: the *rentier model* and the *mercantilist-developmentalist model*.

The fourth part of the chapter will turn specifically to the Chinese case: to which extent we can speak of a coherent Chinese 'sovereign wealth strategy'; how big exactly are the Chinese currency reserves which were used to create the China Investment Corporation, where do they originate and what form do they take? How can we characterize the Chinese management of these financial reserves?

In the fifth part, attention will be turned to the theoretical interpretations of the politics of China's sovereign wealth policy. What forces are involved, how are discussions over the strategy of CIC related to broader cleavages in China's political elite? In what way does this affect the global financial and economic order? What impact does China's sovereign wealth strategy have on global power relations?

In conclusion, the findings of the preceding analysis will be contextualized: how do these inform our understanding of the political economy of China, and what research agenda does this suggest?

The *China Investment Corporation*: a brief portrait

On 29 September 2007, the Chinese government established the China Investment Corporation (CIC) as a ministry-level state-owned enterprise, directly under the management of the State Council.[2] Its ministerial status puts CIC on the same level as the Ministry of Finance (MoF) and China's central bank, the People's Bank of China (PBoC) (Zhang and He 2009: 103–104; see also Cognato 2008: 12–15; Li Hong 2011: 410).

Mission

The Chinese government took the Singaporean SWFs, and especially Temasek, as its model when contemplating the creation of a sovereign wealth fund (Zhang and He 2009: 103; Shih 2009: 333–334). The main objective was to create a vehicle for more active management of part of the foreign exchange reserves held by the PBoC, which until the establishment of CIC were managed for the PBoC by its subsidiary, the

State Administration of Foreign Exchange (SAFE) (Zhang and He 2009: 102–103).

Governance

Deputy Minister of Finance Lou Jiwei was appointed as deputy secretary general of the State Council to prepare the creation of CIC, and subsequently appointed chairman of CIC. Lou Jiwei, a computer scientist and economist, had enjoyed a successful career as a technocrat, and he is considered (like current Prime Minister Wen Jiabao) to be a protégé of former Prime Minister Zhu Rongji (Shih 2009: 336; Cognato 2008: 16).

CIC is governed by a board of directors, appointed by and directly answering to the only shareholder of CIC, the State Council. The board of directors in turn appoints a management committee responsible for the daily operational activities. Next to the board of directors, there are also a supervisory board and a CPC (Communist Party of China) committee (Zhang and He 2009: 104; the authors add that the lack of clarity about the roles of these two bodies 'makes the corporate governance of CIC more sophisticated'). Victor Shih provides more information on the role of the CPC committee, or what he calls the CIC party group: 'Like most government agencies and state companies, the party group, rather than the board, makes most of the important decisions' (Shih 2009: 337). Overall, following Shih, the management of CIC consists of 14 individuals. Seven hold executive positions, and only Vice Manager Wang Jianxi (also known as Jesse Wang) is not also a member of the party group. Four of these have a history of close association with former Prime Minister Zhu Rongji: Chairman Lou Jiwei, CEO and Vice Chairman Gao Xiping (who was persuaded by Zhu to return to China after a career on Wall Street), Zhang Hongli (vice manager and executive director, from the MoF), and Xie Ping (vice manager and former CEO of Central Huijin Investment Company). In terms of institutional background, three board members have a background in the MoF,[3] three in the National Development and Reform Commission (NDRC),[4] four in the PBoC (one of whom, Hu Xiaolian, serves as head of SAFE), and three have a different background. In institutional terms, then, the composition of the CIC top management appears to be a careful compromise between the MoF, the PBoC and the NDRC (cf. Zhang and He 2009: 104). Although CIC has ministry status and thus outranks SAFE, SAFE is represented on the CIC Board.

Funding

The funding structure of CIC is quite complicated. On the surface, CIC was initially funded with a starting capital of US $200 billion. However,

CIC is neither a fund manager – simply managing the investment portfolio of the owner of the capital involved (the MoF) – nor is it owned by the MoF. Rather, through a complex financial structure, the CIC is a debtor to the MoF. The MoF issued RMB 1.5 trillion in bonds, bearing an interest rate of on average 4.5 per cent. The bonds were then sold to the PBoC, and the proceeds used to buy US $ 200 billion in foreign exchange reserves. The MoF then lent this sum to CIC, which is required to pay interest to the MoF (to the tune of some US $ 40 million per day, according to Lou Jiwei) (for details, see Cognato 2008: 15–16, 27; Martin 2008: 6–7; Zhang and He 2009: 104–105; Eaton and Zhang 2010: 495). Strictly speaking, one might say that CIC thus is not a real SWF, i.e., not *directly* funded from foreign exchange reserves, but from fiscal revenue (cf. Li Hong 2011: 410). Given the ultimate progeny of the funding, this is however a purely semantic distinction which need not deflect us from our purpose here.

By July of 2011, as a result of the value appreciation of its assets, the market value of CIC's portfolio was estimated at about $410 billion (www.swfinstitute.org, 27 July 2011). Some two-thirds of the funds were invested domestically (mostly in banks), and one-third abroad (increasingly in equities rather than securities) (for more details of the CIC's portfolio, see below).

Sovereign wealth funds and accumulation strategies

Sovereign wealth funds

Sovereign wealth funds are not a new phenomenon: Kuwait created the first SWF (the Kuwait Investment Authority) in 1953, followed by Singapore (1974), Abu Dhabi (1976) and Norway (1990), among others. A total of 17 SWFs were created before 1998. With the exception of Singapore, all these SWFs derive their assets from the proceeds of commodities exports, principally oil. Although some debate flared up in the West in the 1970s over the investment activities of the Kuwaitis and Libyans, with the onset of neoliberal globalization from the early 1980s onwards this discussion evaporated quickly. In the aftermath of the Asian financial crisis, a further 22 developing countries created their own SWFs in the years 1998–2006. In most cases that decision was informed by the desire to increase the rate of return on the growing currency reserves that these countries were accumulating as insurance against a repetition of the capital flight that sparked the Asian crisis in 1998 (Griffith-Jones and Ocampo 2008). More recently, however, with the decisions of China (2007), Russia (2008) and Brazil (2009) to create their own SWFs, the game changed: the entry of three of the four

BRICs (Brazil, Russia, India and China) on the scene was politicized and ideological and geopolitical considerations were raised among Western observers (Helleiner 2009).

Although SWFs are not new, academic literature on this phenomenon emerged only in the course of 2007. As a result, this literature is still heavily dominated by descriptive and classificatory studies, while attempts at theorization are still very scarce (for exceptions, see Clark and Monk 2010; Helleiner 2009; Helleiner and Lundblad 2008; Monk 2010; Shemirani 2011). Information regarding the organization and activities of SWFs, however, is readily available. Several financial institutions provide detailed information about SWF resources and how these are invested (e.g., various central banks, global private banks such as Morgan Stanley Research and Deutsche Bank Research, consultants such as McKinsey, and several specialized institutions such as the Sovereign Wealth Fund Institute, Opalesque Sovereign Wealth Funds Briefing and Roubini Global Economics (RGE) Monitor).

There is a large degree of consensus on the definition of an SWF, but certain definitional disagreements remain (e.g., Fernandez and Eschweiler 2008; Griffith-Jones and Ocampo 2008; IFSL 2009; Lyons 2007; Monitor Group 2009). For the purpose of this chapter, the definition of the Sovereign Wealth Fund Institute will be adopted:

> A sovereign wealth fund is a state-owned investment fund composed of financial assets such as stocks, bonds, real estate, or other financial instruments funded by foreign exchange assets.... The definition of sovereign wealth funds excludes, among other things, foreign currency reserve assets held by monetary authorities for the traditional balance of payments or monetary policy purposes, state-owned enterprises (SOEs) in the traditional sense, government-employee pension funds, or assets managed for the benefit of individuals. (www.swfinstitute.org)

At the beginning of 2008, total SWF assets were estimated at between US $3 trillion and US $3.7 trillion. This enormous sum exceeds the assets of the world's hedge funds (US $2.8 trillion). However, it trails total official reserves (over US $7 trillion), and it is dwarfed by the total assets of pension funds, insurance companies and mutual funds (US $75 trillion) or total global financial assets (estimated at US $190 trillion; Fernandez and Eschweiler 2008: 8). In early 2011, total assets of SWFs have expanded to more than US $4 trillion. (SWF Institute; see Table 7.1 for a list of the world's largest SWFs).

Table 7.1   Top 20 SWFs by assets, July 2011

Top 20 SWFs by assets (July 2011)		Assets in USD (billions)
Abu Dhabi Investment Authority (ADIA)	oil	627
Norway Government Pension Fund (GPF)	oil	572
China State Administration of Foreign Exchange (SAFE) Investment company*		568
Saudi Arabia Monetary Authority (SAMA) foreign holdings*	oil	473
China Investment Corporation (CIC)		410
Kuwait Investment Authority (KIA)	oil	296
Hong Kong Monetary Authority (HKMA) investment portfolio*		292
Government of Singapore Investment Corporation (GIC)		248
Temasek holdings of Singapore		157
China national social security fund		147
Russian national welfare fund**	oil	143
Qatar investment authority	oil	85
Australian future fund		73
Libyan investment authority	oil	70
UAE – Abu Dhabi international petroleum investment company	oil	58
Algeria regulation fund	oil	57
Alaska permanent fund (US)	oil	40
Kazakhstan national fund	oil	39
Korea investment corporation		37
Malaysia Khazanah Nasional	oil	37

Notes: * Some listings exclude these funds; they are, strictly speaking, part of the central bank/monetary authority, but they are managed independently as other SWFs.
** The Russian National Welfare Fund goes under several names, and it was part of the Stabilization Fund between 2004 and 2008. The assets given here include the assets of the Stabilization Fund.
Source: Sovereign wealth fund rankings, www.swfinstitute.org, accessed 26 July 2011.

Most observers expected that the assets of SWFs (especially those of oil exporting countries) were likely to grow rapidly (e.g., Jen 2007). However, expectations have been considerably lowered in the aftermath of the global crisis (Setser and Ziemba 2009). The financial weight of SWFs will thus remain incomparable to that of the established global institutional investors for a long time. What sets them apart is thus not so much their size but rather their being state-owned.

Motives

The available literature pays quite some attention to different types of SWFs in terms of origin of sources, motives for creation and investment strategy. Fairly refined typologies of SWFs have been proposed, for instance by Reisen (2008) and by Butt et al. (2008). Reisen distinguishes (like nearly all other sources) between SWFs based on commodity exports (especially oil and gas), and those based on what he calls 'structural saving surplus' (or, shorter, 'noncommodity' exports). Reisen further distinguishes four different primary motives: diversification of foreign exchange reserves, economic diversification, economic efficiency and intergenerational equity. Where intergenerational equity is often the most important motive for commodity exporters (Kuwait, Norway, Saudi Arabia), the leading motives for noncommodity exporters (China, Singapore) seem to be diversification of foreign exchange reserves, economic diversification and economic efficiency. Secondary possible motives are technology transfer, network benefits (Reisen 2008) and industrial, macroeconomic and foreign policy objectives (Butt et al. 2008). So, when looking at the motivations of governments in creating SWFs, we see that strict financial objectives and broader macroeconomic and strategic considerations coexist.

Further, there are numerous analyses of concrete investment projects by SWFs (e.g., Beck and Fidora 2008; Bernstein, Lerner and Schoar 2009; Farrell, Lund and Sadan 2008; Fernandez and Eschweiler 2008; IFSL 2009; Kern 2009; Monitor Group 2009). With regard to SWF investment behaviour, observers agree that until now SWFs have been guided almost exclusively by considerations of return: they seem to have been called into existence primarily to realize greater returns than the more traditional ways of investing currency reserves. Their investment decisions (although not always successful) cannot be shown to be determined by noneconomic considerations (Kirshner 2009). They do, however, differ substantially from other new players in the global financial markets such as private equity and hedge funds: SWFs have a much longer time horizon, which may have implications for the future (Butt et al. 2008). The conclusion from this literature would seem to be that, notwithstanding the broader range of motives that can be quoted in the abstract for the establishment of SWFs, in reality they are created for primarily financial reasons. This conclusion would be premature, however, which will be clarified below.

Responses

Host government responses do not reflect this presumed strictly 'rational' practice on the part of SWFs. The lack of transparency, combined with the key role of government officials, in the governance of most SWFs have given rise to a concern that ultimately SWFs may be guided by motives other than simply a better-than-average return. These motives might result in the destabilization of key financial markets, or even in control over key strategic sectors of Western economies by hostile states. This distrust of the longer-term motives of SWFs from China, Russia and the major oil exporting countries has led to investigations in the US and elsewhere by governmental and parliamentary bodies (cf. Cohen 2009; Helleiner 2009; Lavelle 2008; Truman 2008; Weiss 2008). Responses among host governments, global or regional economic and financial institutions and opinion makers, can in fact be situated on an axis running from highly protectionist to liberal. The protectionist reflex is strong among those guided by a realist/mercantilist orientation: these voices aim to tighten legislation on incoming foreign investment. This was first manifested in the blocking of the takeover of Unocal by CNOOC (China National Offshore Oil Company) in 2005 and the acquisition by Dubai Ports World of port facilities in the US in 2006 (Ziemba 2007; on CNOOC-Unocal see Shortgen 2006). More liberally oriented voices are equally concerned over the potential misuse of financial clout by SWFs. They argue that the best strategy is to stimulate transparency (Truman 2008); commit them to voluntary codes of conduct (such as the IMF-inspired 'Santiago Principles', which were pushed for by the Bush administration [Martin 2008: 4, 18]); or more generally make them (and their governments) share the responsibility for governing global (financial) markets (IWG 2008; also European Commission 2008; IMF 2008b; OECD 2008b).

Theorizing SWFs

This very brief general discussion on SWFs shows that to the extent that there are theoretically informed contributions, the theorization is very thin and it can mostly be situated on the one-dimensional axis between liberalism and mercantilism. These theoretical interpretations of the rise and agency of SWFs are marred by serious shortcomings. The liberal interpretation is based on the assumptions of neoclassical economic theory, and thus sees SWFs as 'rational' market actors whose behaviour can be steered through co-optation and self-regulation. Their long-term investment horizon may help in this respect (Butt et al. 2008). The liberal viewpoint is incapable of integrating the essential political dimension of the SWF phenomenon into its analysis. Conversely, the mercantilist approach – like the realist tradition in International Relations theory (IR) – is characterized by a state-centric ontology. It sees SWFs as instruments of state power, employed to challenge the status quo in the liberal global economic order. In this perspective, the economy is reduced to state interests. In addition, both the liberal and the mercantilist traditions tend to negate the determinative quality of dynamics at the level of the world political economy (state system plus global economy) as a whole. Rather, the world political economy is seen as constituted by international relations, i.e., by relations between (ontologically prior) national units.

This chapter in contrast adopts a global political economy approach which takes the global context as point of departure, and views political and economic logics as fundamentally intertwined and mutually constitutive (e.g., Cox 1987; Gill and Law 1988; Palan 2000; Schwartz 2000). One of the main themes in this GPE literature is the existence of different forms of state characterized by specific state-society relations linked to different models of economic development and different growth strategies for developing countries – lately called 'emerging markets'– as well as how these forms of state are at the same time determined by and constitutive of the global order (Cox 1987, Schwartz 2000). Our argument here is that the activities of SWFs must be understood against the background of the growth strategy pursued by the home state.[5] Two ideal-typical strategies[6] can be distinguished: a strategy maximizing income derived from the possession of natural resources (exploiting 'natural advantages'), and an investment-driven industrialization strategy that partly ignores 'natural (dis)advantages'. These two types of accumulation strategies have long ancestries in economic thought. The first type can be traced back to David Ricardo's theory of comparative advantage, and it may be called a Ricardian strategy (Schwartz 2000: 59–60). The second type finds its intellectual origins in the ideas on industrialization of Nicholas Kaldor, the Kaldorian strategy (ibid.: 60–62).

The most extreme form of a Ricardian strategy is the rentier strategy. Rent (income derived from the possession of natural resources such as land, strategic waterways, oil, or more generally any form of property) can to some extent be found in any economy. But when rent is the prime or even only source of income we may speak of a rentier economy. If the state is actively engaged in the organization of the rentier economy, we speak of a rentier state (Beblawi 1990). Obviously, most oil producing and exporting states fall within this category. In such states, the creation of SWFs seems to be primarily inspired by the desire to replace one source of rent (depleting oil reserves) by another (foreign portfolio investments).

A Kaldorian strategy is an industrialization strategy that ignores comparative disadvantages: 'by increasing skills, experience, and the division of labor, investment and production themselves change the nature of the factors available in the production mix' (Schwartz 2000: 61). Such Kaldorian industrialization strategies are often referred to as 'mercantilist' (Wallerstein 1984) and 'developmentalist' (Chong 2007). Prime examples are the East Asian states (e.g., Singapore, South Korea, and China). Here we will identify this type of strategy as a neo-mercantilist developmentalist strategy (cf. Cox 1987).

SWFs established in rentier states may be expected to focus on replacing one source of rent by another without much consideration of a domestic build up of productive capacity. Their capital originates from the exploitation of natural resources (oil and gas in particular) or geographic monopolies (e.g., the Suez Canal). They will support a national trade and currency strategy oriented towards deeper integration in the global economy, and contribute to the reproduction of the power and wealth of a small elite.

The typical neo-mercantilist-developmentalist state may be expected to create SWFs in order to support a national industrial strategy aimed at technological upgrading, capturing key nodes in the global value chain, aiding national (state-owned and parastatal) corporations and generally at upward mobility in the world economy.

The global context in which these strategies are pursued is a key to understanding how they work out both internally and externally. Externally, it is important to recognize that the rise of SWFs in the global order has both strategic and structural aspects. The strategic aspect can be studied by focusing on the behaviour of the SWFs themselves and their impact on other actors. The structural aspect must be approached from a systemic level: in what ways do the global order – in this case more specifically the governance structure of global financial markets – and SWFs mutually influence each other? Two answers are possible. It may be that SWFs (and the elites they represent) challenge the status quo and that their rise is a moment in the emergence of a fundamentally new power structure. Alternatively, they may simply aspire to a place at the table, and thus be perfectly willing to be co-opted into the existing power structure, a mode of integration called hegemonic integration (Pistor 2009a, 2009b; see also Van der Pijl 1998, 2006). This very question applies *a forteriori* in the case of China.

China's mercantilist-developmentalist strategy

China's accumulation strategy

China cannot serve, obviously, as a typical case. Simply by the size of its population and economy, and consequently by its impact on the global system, the Chinese case is in many ways atypical. Nevertheless, the heuristic framework outlined above can still be applied fruitfully to an analysis of China's sovereign wealth strategy, especially as China's foreign economic strategy has often been characterized as mercantilist.

The general story of China's economic ascent is familiar enough and it does not need to be recounted extensively here.[7] Since the announcement of Deng's Four Modernizations in 1978, and more in particular, after the suppression of the Tiananmen uprising in 1989, the Chinese leadership staked its political survival on the provision of stable and rapid growth in per capita income. The legitimacy of the regime is almost completely based on the regime's ability to maintain stability and raise the standard of living from year to year. In order to do that, and in order to ensure the growth of employment in the private sector to compensate for the gradual elimination of loss-making outdated state-owned industries (particularly in heavy industry), the target annual GDP growth has been around 8 per cent (Saich 2011: 67–107).

China has in fact realized an average annual growth rate of around 10%; the Chinese economy is now the second largest after the US, and China is the world's largest exporter. China's accumulation strategy is geared heavily towards export-led growth. The share of exports in GDP has grown steadily, from some 10 per cent in the early 1980s to a peak of more than 30 per cent in the early 2000s (Li Minqi 2008).[8] More than half of Chinese exports are produced by the subsidiaries of foreign firms (Sauvant and Davies 2010). This successful export strategy was underpinned by a 'managed' exchange rate (inspired to a great degree by the experience in the Asian financial crisis of 1997–1998), essentially keeping the yuan pegged to the dollar.[9] China's exchange rate policy, while indeed to some degree contributing to the global imbalances that some hold responsible for the outbreak of the global financial crisis, has served certain key functions for China's domestic economic policy. In particular, it has allowed the Chinese government to manage the gradual reduction of the state sector in the economy, and the gradual resolution of the problems of China's domestic banking system. Thus it avoids the mass layoffs and even greater social unrest (than what is already the reality) that would inevitably accompany a sort of 'shock therapy' such as many former Soviet republics including Russia underwent on the advice of the IMF.

Nevertheless, the success of this strategy has led to the accumulation of a huge mountain of currency reserves (surpassing $3 trillion early in 2011), mostly in US dollars. The majority of the dollar reserves (more than 1 trillion) are invested currently directly in US government bonds and related securities. It is very likely that this figure underestimates the total value of Chinese investments in US government bonds. They are probably partly routed through offshore investment vehicles, e.g., in London, so that some of the Chinese holdings appear in the statistics as British holdings. In 2009, the UK ran a substantial current account deficit but nevertheless increased its holdings of US debt from $130 billion to $300 billion, which may be a good indication of this (Johnson 2010). At the end of 2009, China held about half of all foreign-owned US debt, or one-seventh of the total (ibid.).

Notwithstanding repeated US demands that China appreciate the RMB (e.g., Cline 2010), China's purchase of US government securities has facilitated the continuation of the US double deficit. A turn away from the dollar by China would force the US to be more prudent in printing, borrowing and spending dollars (Steil 2010). In other words, the Chinese and US governments both have big stakes in the current mutual financial embrace (cf. Xiao 2010). As Martin Jacques puts it, 'a Faustian pact lies at the heart of the present relationship between the US and China, which in the longer run is neither economically nor politically sustainable' (Jacques 2009: 360). Such interdependence implies a strong *dependence* on both sides. Here, we are particularly concerned with China's dependence on the US. The Chinese are very heavily exposed to the US dollar, a currency whose long-term prospects are not very promising. In addition, the dollar peg and the continued accumulation of reserves produce inflationary pressure in China and for that reason gives the Chinese leadership a headache (*Financial Times* 18 January 2011). Premier Wen Jiabao recently and explicitly announced that RMB appreciation would be used as a weapon against inflation: the policy of gradual appreciation vis-à-vis the dollar was resumed in June 2010 (4.4 per cent since then) (*Financial Times* 16–17 April 2011; also see Wen's direct intervention in the *Financial Times* of 24 June 2011). However, the pace of appreciation is limited by domestic constraints. Full convertibility of the RMB would require the opening of China's capital markets (Wolf 2011). Given the immaturity of the banking sector and the structural need for a very high savings rate, however, this line of action would be very costly for China. For these reasons the Chinese will allow only a modest appreciation of the RMB, one that remains in balance with the 'underlying real exchange rate' (Tyers and Zhang 2011: 293). As a consequence, the pace of the reduction of the Chinese surplus will be dictated by the implementation of domestic reforms (regulation of large state-owned enterprises, introduction of systems of social security and health care) reducing the savings ratio (ibid.: 294).

Given that the Chinese surplus will not be sharply reduced any time soon, the Chinese regime is confronted with a pressing short- and medium-term dilemma: how to reduce China's exposure to the US dollar without in the process driving down the value of the dollar, and thus of a very large part of its own reserves (cf. World Bank 2011: 136).

Reducing the dependence on US government bonds and on the dollar

The Chinese have a number of options to deal with this situation. In principle, the simplest response to the dilemma, which would reduce the dependence on US government debt, would be to diversify into direct investment in the US, in the financial sector as well as in manufacturing and in the primary sector. This has, however, turned out to be fairly difficult. The acquisition of the personal computer division of IBM by Lenovo is one of the few major success stories. Other attempts by Chinese capital to acquire US firms or establish a new foothold in the US have stumbled on political opposition.[10] Notwithstanding these obstacles, Chinese foreign direct investment (FDI) in the US in recent years has doubled annually: the biggest category is industrial machinery, while investment in real estate (however risky) is also growing rapidly (*Financial Times* 5 May 2011 a).

However, diversifying into FDI in the US does not reduce China's dependence on the US dollar. There is truth to the simple solution suggested by Martin Wolf: '…if China wants to escape from the tyranny of that dreadful dollar, stop buying' (Wolf 2011). We can distinguish five different ways of doing that, i.e., of diversifying Chinese reserves into nondollar assets:

- diversify currency reserves into gold or other currencies (Euro, yen, SDRs)
- invest in global resource stocks (commodity hoarding)
- increase FDI globally (either in resource exploitation, manufacturing or finance)
- internationalize the use of the RMB so that an increasing proportion of China's foreign trade is settled in RMB rather than in dollars
- reduce the payments surplus by expanding domestic growth.

In recent years, each of these instruments has been employed to some extent; the policy mix has changed over time, but basically included all of these components to some degree at any time (Breslin 2003; Chin and Helleiner 2008; Hung 2009; RGE Monitor 2009b; Roxburgh et al. 2009; Steil 2010).

During the first four months of 2011, the Chinese exchange reserves grew by around $200 billion, and three-quarters of this new inflow was invested in non-US dollar assets (*Financial Times* 21 June 2011), providing a recent strong indication of a possible reversal of China's strategy in this respect. This tendency to reduce exposure to the US dollar is not unique to China. Over the past decade, the share of the US dollar in global currency reserves diminished from 71.1 per cent in 2000 to 62.1 per cent in 2009, while the Euro share increased from 18.5 per cent to 27.5 per cent. The move out of the dollar is mostly accounted for by the so-called emerging markets: the dollar share in their reserves fell from 78.4 per cent to 58.5 per cent, while the Euro share in their reserves increased from 18.1 per cent to 30.2 per cent (World Bank 2011: 131).[11] In addition, China, as well as other emerging economies, have in recent years bought large quantities of gold, which explains part of the huge rally of the gold price in recent times (*Financial Times*, 5 May 2011b).

Since the launch in 1999 of the Go Global campaign, Chinese companies (often state-owned) have been extremely active globally investing in exploration and exploitation of energy reserves, in acquiring agricultural land for the production of food and especially biofuel, and in taking over leading global mining companies (e.g., the ultimately failed attempt by Chinalco to acquire a large stake in Rio Tinto, *The Guardian* 4 June 2009). The stock of China's outward FDI reached $230 billion by the end of 2009 and it is expected to surpass the $1 trillion mark within a few years (*Financial Times* 5 May 2011a). The focus in Europe is on deals giving access to high value added activity (*Financial Times* 26 April 2011a). In Southeast Asia, Chinese FDI is primarily in the form of the relocation of labour-intensive industries from the coastal regions of China where wages are rising rapidly. In Vietnam alone there are more than 700 affiliates of Chinese companies (Sauvant and Davies 2010; for general overviews of Chinese FDI see Davies 2010; Nolan and Zhang 2010).

The growth of Chinese international trade and the global expansion of Chinese capital go hand-in-hand with slowly but surely growing moves towards the use of the RMB as an international currency. The move towards the internationalization of the RMB takes place in three different forms: (1) the settlement of bilateral trade, (2) using the RMB in bilateral currency swaps, and (3) the issuance of RMB securities to raise capital (World Bank 2011: 139–142; RGE Monitor 2009b; Blanchard

2011: 45–46). Cross-border trade settlement in RMB has taken off in the second half of 2009, and it reached a level of $18.7 billion in the third quarter of 2010 (Lardy and Douglass 2011: 12). Agreements are mostly with other emerging economies (Zhou 2009). In November of 2010, Russia and China concluded an agreement to use domestic currency in the settlement of bilateral trade (*Voice of Russia* 2010). Researchers in Hong Kong's Monetary Authority estimate that 20 per cent to 30 per cent of Chinese exports may potentially be invoiced in RMB if the RMB were made fully convertible (RGE Monitor 2009b), and Singapore is aiming to become the main hub for RMB clearance (*Financial Times* 20 April 2011). Finally, since the end of 2008, China concluded eight currency swap agreements for a total of some RMB 800 billion (World Bank 2011: 141). Now, few if any observers anticipate the RMB to challenge the dollar as the leading global currency. However, it is increasingly assumed that the world may be moving to a situation in which the dollar will lose its absolute primacy, and in which we in fact will see the emergence of a new monetary order characterized by three macro-regional currency blocs organized around the economies and currencies of the US, the Eurozone and China (World Bank 2011; see also Bergsten 2011 and Wu et al. 2010).

Finally, a reorientation of macro-policy priorities towards expanding domestic growth would reduce China's export surplus and thereby reduce its reliance on the dollar. Such a reorientation has been a part of the Chinese government's policy mix for several years, especially after Hu Jintao and Wen Jiabao came into office in 2003. Hu launched the concept of the harmonious society, one of the principal components of which was the stimulation of investment in the Western parts of China to counteract the tendency towards increasing social and regional inequalities (Saich 2011: 96 ff.). The policy to attract investment to the countryside was so successful that after the crisis of 2008 the supply of migrant labour dried up in the major eastern industrial centres, leading to successive hikes in the minimum wage rates in such cities as Beijing and Shanghai. Real wages have risen by more than 12 per cent annually in the past decade, pushing labour intensive industries to move west, or to move to countries in South and Southeast Asia offering cheaper labour. The effects of rising wages, however, have been mitigated substantially: labour productivity has increased by comparable figures (much more rapidly than in competing countries such as Brazil or Indonesia), while the quality of infrastructure equals that of a country like South Korea. In addition, value added created in China is only about 10 per cent to 15 per cent of the final price of exported goods (see various reports in the *Financial Times*). All these mitigating circumstances give the Chinese government time to adjust, however, at the price of a constant threat of inflation (which would fuel social unrest) and of speculative bubbles (e.g., in real estate) (Magnus 2011).

The creation of a separate state investment corporation, financed from the rapidly accumulating currency reserves, was intended to play a major role in the realization of the ambition to liberate China from its dependence on the dollar and to push China along on its trajectory towards becoming a truly leading economic power.

The China Investment Corporation

As recounted earlier, the CIC was endowed in 2007 with a working capital of $200 billion, with about two-thirds of this amount invested domestically (mostly in banks), and one-third invested abroad (increasingly in equities rather than securities). By July of 2011, the market value of its portfolio – grown considerably through asset appreciation – was estimated at about $410 billion (www.swfinstitute.org, accessed 27 July 2011; for more details of the CIC's portfolio, see a.o. Bernstein, Lerner and Schoar 2009; Clark and Monk 2009; Cognato 2008; Martin 2008; Roxburgh et al. 2009; Truman 2007; Ziemba 2010).

CIC demonstrates rather different strategies domestically and abroad. Domestically, the most eye-catching and strategically important investment has been its acquisition and incorporation of the Central Huijin Investment Company (Huijin), for approximately one-third of the $200 billion. Huijin had been created in 2003 as a subsidiary of the PBoC, and its role was 'to promote the restructuring and listing of state-owned financial institutions' (Zhang and He 2009: 108–109). The ownership of and capital injection into Huijin gave the CIC controlling stakes (in several cases majority stakes) in the former state banks Bank of China (BoC), China Construction Bank (CCB), Industrial and Commercial Bank of China (ICBC), the China Everbright Bank as well as stakes in several smaller financial companies. In addition, CIC was to use a third of its working capital (later reduced) to recapitalize the China Development Bank (CDB) and the Agricultural Bank of China (ABC). Altogether, these holdings give CIC control over nearly 60 per cent of all China's bank assets and outstanding loans (Blanchard 2011: 40; Cognato 2008: 23–25; Eaton and Zhang 2010: 496–497; Martin 2008: 7–10; Zhang and He 2009: 105–106). In this way, we can say that the Chinese government has established a key financial holding company under its own direct control (and apart from established strong institutions such as the MoF and the PBoC) as a foremost instrument with which to help the domestic banking sector deal with its large backlog of nonperforming loans and thus prepare for a successful internationalization offensive, as well (see Li Hong 2011: 428-9, for more details). As such, Huijin can be considered a strategic investor. This is the basis for Blanchard's claim that the CIC in fact largely has the function of bolstering domestic modernization and thus supports the regime's legitimacy (Blanchard 2011: 43). And in the shorter run, CIC's amalgamation of Huijin has enabled it to earn the kind of returns necessary to make its interest payments to the MoF; the successful IPOs of BoC, CCB and CICB have earned it huge profits (Zhang and He 2009: 105–106).

CIC's investments abroad have been more controversial and less successful, certainly in the early days of its existence. In the run up to its official establishment, it acquired, in May of 2007, at the very start of the US subprime crisis, a 9.4 per cent share in the Blackstone Group ($3 billion). This was followed in December by a 9.9 per cent stake in US investment bank Morgan Stanley ($5 billion) while acquiring 80 per cent of the US private equity fund JC Flowers ($3.2 billion) in April of 2008. Of course, the market value, particularly of Blackstone and Morgan Stanley, fell dramatically in 2007 and 2008. This exposed CIC to much public criticism in China (Zhang and He 2009: 106; Cognato 2008: 21; Eaton and Zhang 2010: 497). Contrary to the public statements of CIC claiming that these deals were strictly 'financial', closer scrutiny shows that personal networks were also keys to the conclusion of these agreements. Blackstone's chairman of Greater China operations (and former Hong Kong finance secretary) Antony Leung has close ties to the financial authorities in China (Shih 2009: 339; Cognato 2008: 21; Monk 2009: 15), while the deal with Morgan Stanley was no doubt made easier by the fact that Morgan Stanley's Wei Sun Christianson and CIC's Gao Xiqing studied together (Monk 2009: 15). Morgan Stanley and Huijin are joint-venture partners in the China International Capital Corporation (CICC), China's largest investment bank, headed by the son of Zhu Rongji (Cognato 2008: 21, 25; on the role of CICC, see also Li Hong 2011: 418). In 2008, thanks to what is considered its 'conservative asset allocation', CIC outperformed most other SWFs and pension funds, and returned to the international market earlier than other SWFs (RGE Monitor 2009a). As for CIC's more recent foreign activities, Ziemba (2010) has identified five main trends:

(1) A significant share of CIC's US investments is passive (about one-fourth of its US equity exposure);

(2) CIC diversifies both away from US assets (in Europe as well as Asia) as well as within US dollar denominated assets;
(3) CIC is heavily exposed to resources (especially mining and metals);
(4) CIC is still significantly involved in US financial companies;
(5) CIC's returns most likely increased in 2009.

According to press reports, CIC is making food security one of its priorities (*Financial Times* 23 September 2009), while it is committed to continue investing in Eurozone government bonds in spite of the recent debt crisis plaguing the Eurozone (*Financial Times* 28 May 2010). Repeated rumours that the Chinese government was considering increasing the capital entrusted to CIC were confirmed recently by the announcement that CIC will shortly receive between $100 billion and $200 billion in new funds (*Financial Times* 26 April 2011b).

Rivalry between CIC and SAFE

A final aspect of the CIC to be briefly touched upon is its relationship to SAFE. There is increasing rivalry between the CIC and other investment vehicles such as the China National Social Security Fund (CNSSF), but especially the State Administration of Foreign Exchange (SAFE), which manages the official reserves and in 1997 created its own sovereign wealth fund, the SAFE Investment Company (SAFE_IC) (Li Hong 2011: 408). In December of 2007, SAFE initiated its first activities in this area by buying small minority stakes in three Australian banks through a Hong Kong-based affiliate (Zhang and He 2009: 113). Since then, SAFE has expanded its foreign investment portfolio, which the Sovereign Wealth Institute estimated at US $347 billion in early 2011 (see Table 7.1 above). As indicated above, CIC has full ministerial status while SAFE is a subsidiary of the PBoC. To compensate for CIC's ministerial status, SAFE is represented on CIC's board of directors. It seems that the State Council has been very even-handed in distributing influence and power in the management of China's sovereign wealth. How is this state of affairs to be understood in the context of the discussion over China's accumulation strategy?

Three explanatory frameworks

The first answer basically sees the Chinese state as a unitary *rational actor* and interprets the creation of two rival agencies as a logical product of neo-mercantilist policies aimed at maximizing returns by encouraging competition between these investment funds (e.g., Clark and Monk 2009; Monk 2010; Roxburgh et al. 2009). This approach interprets

Chinese politics in terms of the rational (or irrational) behaviour of a monolithic actor, in which China, 'Beijing' or the Chinese Communist Party (the terms are often used interchangeably) is portrayed as a black box in which a fundamental unity of purpose defines its agency. This is characteristic for those inspired by a realist or neorealist theoretical predisposition.

The second answer approaches the phenomenon from a *bureaucratic politics* perspective: the creation of CIC and SAFE_IC is then interpreted as the product of rivalry between different parts of the Chinese state apparatus broadly defined. In this specific case, the main rivalry is said to be between the Ministry of Finance (MoF) on the one hand, which has partial control over CIC, and the central bank – the People's Bank of China (PBoC) – on the other hand, which has control over SAFE (Chin and Helleiner 2008; Eaton and Zhang 2008, 2010; Wright 2008; Zhang and He 2009). The creation of CIC in this perspective is a successful coup by the MoF to wrest control over part of the country's foreign exchange reserves from the central bank. As we know since Graham Allison's classic study (Allison 1971), the bureaucratic politics model in many cases provides a more forceful explanation of state behaviour than the rational actor model, because it allows us to open the black box and to recognize the importance of intra-state institutional dynamics. However, in a sense it reproduces the limitations of the rational actor model on a lower level of abstraction: it assumes that the behaviour of bureaucratic entities is governed by given and unchanging preferences, namely survival first and expansion second – just as realism assumes the preferences of the state to be given and unchanging.

A third answer may be called the *elite perspective*. It interprets Chinese politics as a struggle for power and influence between different groups or *factions* organized around key individuals. The studies of Victor Shih and of Li Cheng are representative of this approach.

In his landmark study of Chinese financial policy-making, Shih develops a theory of power in authoritarian regimes, or 'elite factional politics' (Shih 2008: 194–199). In his view, Chinese politics are characterized by a continuous struggle for power among a small number of 'generalist factions' and a larger number of 'specialist factions'. Generalist factions aim for power by constructing a winning coalition, while specialist factions seek to enrich their respective bureaucratic groupings (ibid.: 195). Although the specialist factions derive their identity from the particular segment of the state and/or party bureaucracy in which their leaders have their main position, the focus is very much on the individuals involved. According to Shih, the Chinese system owes its remarkable stability to the willingness of specialist factions to lend their support to whichever generalist faction succeeds in becoming (temporarily) the dominant one. In their rise to power, generalist factions reward specialist factions for (the promise of) their support by money and influence over policy (ibid.: 196). Again, as with the two earlier perspectives, something is missing: by implication, the behaviour of the factional leaders is assumed to be governed by invariable motives that are somehow inherent to their nature – in this case their nature as individuals guided by the motives of self-preservation and power maximization. There is little sensitivity to any underlying determinants of agency embedded in the evolving structure of socio-economic power.

The work of Li Cheng provides us with some insights that allow the analysis of power relations in China to begin to move beyond these limitations. Based on the meticulous excavation of the personal backgrounds of hundreds of power holders in China, Li has gradually developed the notion of 'two coalitions in one party' (Li Cheng 2008, 2009).[12] These two emerging coalitions are the *tuanpai* (consisting of leaders with a background in the Communist Youth League), and the *princelings* (known in Chinese as *taizidang*), consisting of the offspring of old revolutionary heroes or top party leaders (Li Cheng 2008, 2009, 2010).

The *tuanpai* dominate the current Hu Jintao/Wen Jiabao government. They are also identified as the 'populist coalition' (Li Cheng 2007, 2008) or the 'populist authoritarian' tendency (Saich 2011: 97–101). Their power base is disproportionately concentrated in the inland provinces (the 'red states': Li Cheng 2007: 24), and their politics are focused on reducing social inequality and promoting a 'harmonious society' (ibid.; Saich 2011: 98), and on propagating an international posture that is not biased by pro-US attitude (Saich 2011: 101). The accumulation strategy pursued by the *tuanpai* is geared towards promoting domestic growth and the elevation of the countryside and the agricultural sector (Hung 2009). They are politically more liberal (relatively speaking), and economically more conservative, i.e., cautious with respect to exposing China further to globalization (Li Cheng 2008: 90). Among the emerging fifth-generation of leaders born mostly in the 1950s expected to succeed to the top offices in 2012, the most prominent leader of the *tuanpai* is Li Keqiang, who is currently expected to succeed Wen Jiabao as Premier in 2012. Li Keqiang is said to be primarily motivated by a concern for the unemployed, and he favours a policy of improving housing and health care and creating a social safety net. He also favours improved relations with Japan and greater integration in East Asia (ibid.: 85–86).

The *princelings* base their claim to power on their descent from the first generation of revolutionary leaders. They do not form as coherent a faction in terms of policy preferences as the *tuanpai*, but they mostly know each other intimately from going to the same schools and moving in the same social circles (Li Cheng 2008; Shih 2008: 198–199). The *princelings* currently form the core faction in what Li Cheng calls the 'elitist coalition' (Li Cheng 2008: 77). In the late 1990s and early 2000s, the elitist coalition was led by Jiang Zemin and the Shanghai Gang. The *princelings* have been among the greatest beneficiaries of China's integration in the world market and the spread of capitalist development, and they are regionally concentrated in the coastal provinces (the 'blue states') (Li Cheng 2007, 2008; Hung 2009). The leading *princeling* currently is Xi Jinping (party secretary of Shanghai since 2006) who is poised to succeed President Hu Jintao in 2012. Xi's policy preferences can be summarized as 'promoting economic efficiency, attaining a high rate of GDP growth, and integrating China further into the world economy', boasting good relations with prominent US leaders such as Hank Paulson (Li Cheng 2008: 85–86). He is seen as friendly to business and he has served in several functions in the eastern provinces of Fujian and Zhejiang before being promoted to his Shanghai post in 2006 (Saich 2011: 104).

In sum, we may conclude that the creation of CIC cannot be seen as the deliberate choice on the part of a unitary power bloc to create internal competition for the PBoC and SAFE in order to stimulate more profitable management of the country's foreign exchange reserves. The detailed analyses by Zhang and He (2009) and by Eaton and Zhang (2010) in particular have made a convincing case against such an interpretation, and they have shown that rivalries between bureaucratic entities are a key component of what happened in 2007 and since then. However, the bureaucratic politics perspective remains marred by inherent limitations: it opens the 'black box' of the state, but only to replace it by the 'black boxes' of the various bureaucracies involved. A step forward in the understanding of the background is provided by the elitist perspective applied by Victor Shih, and particularly Li Cheng, who show that the struggles between various bureaucracies within the state and party apparatuses in China take place in the context of a struggle for influence and power between fairly stable and coherent coalitions (Shih speaks of 'generalist factions', Li of 'coalitions') whose preferences are beginning to assume broader contours than just those of the individual pursuit of wealth and power.

Conclusion

In this chapter, I have argued that sovereign wealth funds must be analysed against the background of the specific accumulation strategy pursued by the country in question. These accumulation strategies in turn express the dominant interests of the power bloc. In China, as the analysis of the China Investment Corporation has shown, these interests are shaped not just by the individual backgrounds and momentary political functions of their leaders, but arguably also by articulations with a much broader and deeper bifurcation between two configurations of societal interests and ideological convictions, each advocating a very distinct accumulation strategy for China (see also Kahn 2006). Perhaps we can argue (more extensive empirical research will need to be done to test this hypothesis) that the contours of this bifurcation are becoming clearer as the composition of the CCP widens and comes to encompass the full spectrum of social classes and layers in the emergent Chinese statist capitalist social formation (Bo and Chen 2009). There are arguably two emerging rival hegemonic projects, each expressing the specific interests of distinct configurations of social and ideological forces within the Chinese power structure. When looking at the impact of contemporary developments in China for the likely trajectory of global neoliberalism, it might be argued that the *princeling* coalition is more oriented towards deeper and faster integration of China in global markets, while the *tuanpai* programme implies a relative strengthening of mercantilist tendencies in China. However, due to the specific nature of the Chinese system and due to the absence of a dominant charismatic leader (such as Mao or Deng) to impose a particular direction, both 'coalitions' are represented fairly evenly in all the main organs of power (party and state). The actual accumulation strategy followed by the Chinese state is therefore the product of continuous compromise and renegotiation, rather than the wholesale execution of the integral programme of one of the rival coalitions. Barring any sudden and dramatic global developments (such as the collapse of the US dollar), changes in China's overall foreign economic strategy will be gradual and piecemeal.

Notes

1. I am grateful to Sarah Eaton, Herman Schwartz and Matthias Stepan for very useful comments on an earlier version of this chapter.
2. The State Council 'is the nation's highest executive and administrative body, consisting of Premier Wen Jiabao, four Vice Premiers, five State Councillors, Secretary General Hua Jianmin, and the heads of China's various ministries

and special commissions. There are approximately 50 members of China's State Council.' (Martin 2008: 5[fn])

3. According to Shih, the MoF is the powerbase of Prime Minister Wen Jiabao (Shih 2009: 334).

4. The NDRC, the successor to the powerful State Planning Commission, is considered a stronghold of former president Jiang Zemin (Shih 2009: 334).

5. As will be apparent by what follows, the approach chosen here is inspired by Herman Schwartz's work. He himself has very recently applied his framework to the study of SWFs, presenting a more refined typology than the simple one developed here (Schwartz 2011).

6. We will call these *accumulation strategies*. Following Jessop we define an accumulation strategy as a 'specific "growth model" complete with its extra-economic preconditions' (Jessop 1990: 198).

7. For some inspiring general introductions, see Amineh and Houweling 2010; Arrighi 2008; Harvey 2005, chapter 5; Henderson 2008; Jacques 2009.

8. That China is such a successful exporter should not necessarily lead to the conclusion that China's economic growth is exclusively the product of its export surplus. Estimating the contribution of exports (minus the part of imports used in the export sector) to economic growth is a complicated matter. Horn et al. (2010) conclude that in the period 2002–2008, exports explain roughly one-fifth to one-third of economic growth in China, meaning that during those years, when voices especially from the US to appreciate the RMB exchange rate significantly were very loud, at least two-thirds of China's economic growth was actually home grown. In 2009, the year of the huge economic stimulus, overall economic growth was 8.1 per cent, with a *negative* contribution by exports thus measured of 3.2 per cent.

9. The currency peg to the US dollar was introduced in 1994; it was revised and relaxed in 2005. Between 2005 and 2009 (when it was reintroduced in the face of the global financial crisis), the RMB underwent a 25.8 per cent revaluation in real terms (Blanchard 2011), without having much noticeable effect on the trade balance with the US.

10. In 2006, the China National Offshore Oil Corporation (CNOOC) attempted to take over Unocal, the California-based US oil company, but was blocked by political opposition in Congress (Shortgen 2006; for more general discussions, also see Cohen 2009; Kirshner 2009; Truman 2008; Weiss 2008; Wu and Seah 2008; Ziemba 2007).

11. Official data about the composition of China's currency reserves are not available.

12. Li speculates that the emerging pattern may be the upbeat to a proto-democratic bi-partisan political system in China (Li Cheng 2007). The speculations about the future political system in China will not be pursued here as they clearly reach beyond the more limited aims of this chapter.

8
The Rise of Non-Western National Oil Companies: Transformation of the Neoliberal Global Energy Order?

Naná de Graaff

Introduction

Some time before the financial crisis hit the global political economy, emanating from the very epicentre of the neoliberal heartland, a development had manifested itself within the global energy sector that was widely perceived to challenge its neoliberal structure. This development was mainly characterized by the re-emergence of resource nationalism in major producing regions of the world (e.g., Venezuela, Russia) and the outward expansion of non-Western state-owned major oil companies (such as Gazprom and several Chinese oil companies) (WIR 2007: 116–122; BCG 2007). As a result, and in combination with growing demand from the so called 'emerging economies', exponentially rising oil prices, the policitization of climate change and waning legitimacy of US power, energy security reappeared high on the political agenda (e.g., European Commission 2007b; CFR 2006; Cheney et al. 2001). Testifying to the threat that this was perceived to be to the industries' 'vested interests', waves of 'new protectionism' erupted within core neoliberal market economies, in spite of their prophesized belief in the beneficial imperatives of a global free and open market. A well-known example is the blocking by US Congress of the takeover of American oil corporation Unocal by CNOOC (Chinese National Offshore Oil Company), one of the major Chinese state-owned oil companies. More structural responses were legislative changes such as the US Foreign Investment and National Security Act 2007, strengthening the review of foreign acquisitions within 'strategic sectors', and the EU Commission's insertion of a reciprocity clause into its third energy liberalization package

(2008), aimed at protecting EU energy infrastructure from control by third countries (and state-owned companies). This clause, informally dubbed the 'Gazprom clause', would oblige foreign firms to 'unbundle' their production and transmission activities before they are allowed to obtain a controlling stake in European energy companies.

In stark contrast to the neoliberal restructuring of the 80s and 90s, in which the global energy sector was increasingly liberalized and priva-tized, some influential analysts hence predicted a return to state-gov-erned and increasingly nationalized energy sectors (e.g., Odell 2006). While the latter is not very likely to happen, at least not in the near future, the rise of the non-Western National Oil Companies (NOCs)[1] does seem to herald a transformation of the structure and existing power relations within the neoliberal global energy order. Whereas NOCs have played a key role in the contestation over energy resources at least since the establishment of OPEC, the key difference here is their more active and globalizing strategy, directly intervening outside their national borders and in the global energy market.[2]

In spite of a recent increase in studies on NOCs (Jaffe et al. 2007; Marcel 2006; Stevens 2008; Vivoda 2009; Wälde 2008), energy security (e.g., Correljé and Van der Linde 2006; Van der Linde 2005; Helm 2005; Yergin 2006) and 'resource wars' (Klare 2001, 2004; see also Stokes 2007), there is, as of yet, still little systematic empirical research done into the precise nature of this transformation: i.e., how it has been tak-ing place, with what (possible) effects and why (but see Marcel 2006). This chapter seeks to address these questions by showing how a selec-tion of the world's major state-owned oil companies from China, Russia and the Middle East, while in a process of autonomous global *expansion*, have simultaneously *integrated* into the global energy market through increased cooperation with the major private oil companies. In spite of the growth of these 'statist' actors, world energy markets thus seem to be getting increasingly interdependent, interconnected and *transnational*. But – as elaborated elsewhere (De Graaff, forthcoming) – the integration of the non-Western energy majors into the global energy market is not yet paralleled by integration of the non-Western oil elites into typical Western elite and business circles.

These phenomena, however, are analysed within the broader con-text of the enfolding process of capital accumulation, in particular the crisis of its latest phase, i.e., neoliberalism. As also argued in the introductory chapter of this volume, the rise of the non-Western NOCs has to be placed within a broader shift that is currently taking place within the global political economy, that is, the much commented rise of economic and political powers from outside the West shifting the centre of gravity of global power towards the Global South and East Asia in particular. These broader developments are seen as generated by the contradictions inherent in the capital accumulation process leading to successive crises. The particular focus here is on the expansionist character of capital accumulation and its spatial dimension, which in its endless search for new domains of expansion in order to avoid over-accumulation (i.e., surplus value that is not profitably invested into the production process), generates rival centres of accumulation that in turn become competitors to the originating source of (surplus) capital (Harvey 2006, 2003). This 'boomerang effect' and the ensuing power struggles generated by this contradictory dynamic inherent to capital accumulation mark the broader backdrop to the current transformation of the global energy order.

The chapter will be structured as follows: the next part will provide a brief historical backdrop to more recent developments as well as some theoretical viewpoints from which these are analysed. The third and main part of the chapter entails an empirical analysis of the corporate networks of five major non-Western NOCs. This analysis is performed with the use of Social Network Analysis. The findings will be discussed in the context of the results from another study (De Graaff, forthcoming) on the networks of the major oil companies' boards of directors. On the basis of these findings, some possible future scenarios will be outlined with a focus on the question of to what extent the transformation of the global energy order that is currently taking place is also a transformation that fundamentally challenges its neoliberal architecture.

Emergence of the neoliberal energy order and its crisis

Prior to the first wave of resource nationalism, the international energy order was dominated by a cartel of major Anglo-Saxon oil companies (called the 'Seven Sisters')[3] and characterized by administrative pricing.[4] In the subsequent transition period (mid-1950s until mid-1970s) the oil sector went through a significant reorganization in terms of state-industry cooperation and a concomitant redistribution of power between the resource-holding states outside the West and the Western resource-seeking states (see e.g., Yergin 1991; Bina 2006). During this first wave of resource nationalism many resource-holding states outside the West nationalized their industries, threw out foreign oil companies or renegotiated the terms of the contracts (i.e., the rent-split). In addition, there was the formation of OPEC (the Organization of Petroleum Exporting

Countries) in 1960, which allowed the main non-Western oil producing states to gain more control over volumes and prices of oil, as well as the direction of flows (but see Mabro 2005 on the effective power of the OPEC; also Nitzan and Bichler 2002; Bridge and Wood 2010).

In most mainstream accounts, the rise of resource nationalism is explained by forces of demand and supply and their supposedly neutral impact upon the price of oil (see e.g., Wälde 2008; Wilson 1987). While certainly forces of supply and demand played a role in this transition, as did the price of oil, these did not operate in a vacuum but they should be related to the prevailing global geopolitical order and the power relations within it. In addition, these developments should be analysed within the more general context of globalizing capitalism as the main economic and social organization of production (see also Bina 2006; Labban 2008, and on how oil prices are formed Mabro 2000, 2005). The global geopolitical order at the time was dominantly structured by the Cold War and its bi-polar constitution, which prevented Soviet resources from entering the international oil market (but see Labban 2008: 95–109) and which also instigated several 'hot wars' (e.g., Korea, Vietnam) (Yergin 1991). Supply from within the Anglo-Saxon countries was diminishing due to a slowdown in discovery and development. In fact during this period, the US turned from net-exporter to net-importer and as a consequence supply increasingly had to come from non-Western regions, in particular the Persian Gulf region, but also the South American region (in particular Venezuela) and parts of Africa (ibid.). In combination with the strong global demand for oil (in part due to the Cold War and its 'hot wars'), this led to a tight oil market. This process also coincided with a strong demand for independence and sovereignty from the previously colonized regions. In that sense, this first wave of resource nationalism was also a revolt against and liberation from Western dominance, in this case, in particular from the European powers – a process that was much encouraged by the US, but which, once the Mideastern oil producers had 'liberalized' themselves, inadvertently backfired for them in terms of loss of power over terms of access to crucial natural resources. It was thus the interrelation between these dynamics that provided for the empowerment of the state-owned NOCs. This power was, however, still constrained not only by the dependency on effective demand and the development of global competitive spot (oil) prices (see Bina 2004: 8),[5] but also by the dependency on technology and capital that could only be provided by the International Oil Companies (IOCs), as they are most commonly referred to, that is the major (Western) private oil companies. When subsequently in the mid-1980s there was a glut on the oil market with decreasing oil prices as a result, this gave more leverage to the holders of capital and technology (the IOCs) and put pressure on resource-holding states to liberalize their mineral investment regimes in order to attract capital and technology that was needed to keep up production (Bridge 2008; CIEP 2004). This then provided a fertile basis for the growth of the neoliberal energy order, as well as its inherent contradictions, which will be elaborated below.

Again, forces of supply and demand and a correlating oil price – although important determinants – should be analysed in relation to other dynamics such as the changing geopolitical arena and the US-led project of neoliberal globalization (see on the latter also the chapter by Van Apeldoorn and De Graaff in this volume). Another critical determinant which greatly influenced the geographical structure of supply and demand was, of course, the end of the Cold War and the disintegration of the Soviet Union. This enabled Russian exports to be released onto the world oil market at an ever larger scale (see Labban 2008: 95–122) and opened up the resource-rich territories of Central Asia that had previously been under Soviet control. Additionally, perhaps in a more indirect, but nonetheless highly influential sense, the end of the Cold War for many implied a sense of victory of the Western free market model. It was anticipated this model would now automatically envelop the remainder of the world into a peaceful and globally integrated unity of liberal-democratic market economies (e.g., Fukuyama 1992), at the same time gradually diminish the role of the state and its territorial borders and put an end to conflict between nation states.

In any case, the energy order now became dominantly shaped on a global basis by the neoliberal project of 'global commodification and marketization' (see the Introduction of this volume). Within the West, the IOCs had responded to their loss of access to resources not only by strategies to diversify supply, but also with a huge wave of mergers and acquisitions. This is an effective way of restoring and increasing profitability as well as enlarging the reserves (on the balance sheet) without the access to actual new resources or reserves (see e.g., Bridge and Wood 2010: 571–574). Outside the Anglo-American core, major resource-rich regions came under pressure to liberalize and privatize their industries for reasons outlined above, providing the IOCs with renewed power to expand and open up new domains for production. In particular, the Central Asian regions, the traditional geopolitical 'heartland' of the global political economy as identified by Mackinder (1904), became a focal point of interest and contestation. But also in Latin America (e.g., Sader

2008; Mommer 2002) and Russia (Labban 2008: 110–122) the neoliberal imperatives of privatization and liberalization were widely implemented – if necessary with various grades of coercion. In the Middle East, Iran fervently tried to attract foreign capital and technology, in spite of the persistent blocking of its attempts by US sanctions (see e.g., Labban 2008: 127–138).

However, all of this seemed to change rather drastically as the new millennium took its first unsteady steps, with the shocking events of 9/11 as both the first evident sign and a catalyst. Geopolitics and energy security moved centre stage again, and with rising oil prices, the resource holders regained both power and assertiveness, renationalized their energy industries and globally expanded the reach and influence of their state-owned firms (NOCs). This most recent transition, however, is a not simply a rerun from the one that took place in the 1960s and 1970s, but is intimately related to a crisis of the neoliberal energy order.

To be sure, similar dynamics are at work: a changing geographical structure of supply and demand, in particular the rapidly growing demand from the emerging economies (BRICs) and declining supply within the OECD region, leading to a tight oil market, increasing volatility and exponentially rising prices. This, in turn, has led to changing strategies, in first instance, on the part of the resource-holding states that used their growing power to set out a renewed independent and assertive course: re-nationalize their energy sectors and renegotiate the agreements that were made during the neoliberal 1990s to allow them to capture a much larger share of the rent. But also on the part of the resource-seeking states that increasingly reframed and redrafted their energy policies in a much more explicitly political and military way[6] and the 'new protectionism' erupting in the liberal market economies as mentioned in the introduction of this chapter.

Underlying these developments is the rise of big economies in the Global South, with China surfacing as a major economic contender of the US, which is drastically reshaping global geoeconomic and geopolitical power relations. There is an increasing resistance to US and Western dominance in what now has become a multipolar world order. With that comes an increasing awareness of and resistance towards the global inequalities produced by the neoliberal (free market) model that these powers advocated (and at times violently imposed upon the rest of the world). The 9/11 attacks were perhaps the most visible indicator of this trend, not only because they revealed the vulnerability of military superpower the US, but also because this attack came from forces within what had been considered America's most important energy ally in the Middle East (Saudi Arabia). This signalled a significant demise of US hegemonic power.[7] It is, hence, not only a crisis of Western dominance but also of the neoliberal model. Of course, with the ensuing global financial crisis emanating from Wall Street, which can be said to represent the very icon of the neoliberal model, these developments were only aggravated and accelerated. Below, I identify some of the 'contradictory' outcomes of the neoliberal growth model with respect to the oil sector. That is, certain dynamics that emerged from this growth model but to an extent undermined the perspective of continued capture of surplus value and or control over its distribution by the actors that most ferociously advocated the neoliberal model.

At the level of inter-company competition, some of the regained independence of the resource-holding states and their state-owned firms was actually facilitated by the organizational restructuring in the upstream part of the oil production chain that had been taking place in the previous era of low oil prices and neoliberal restructuring. The latter had driven many IOCs to outsource crucial exploration functions to oil service providers, resulting in a dramatic growth of the oil service market, with players such as Halliburton, Schlumberger and Baker Hughes assuming increasingly dominant roles and gradually extending their global reach. Contrary to the interests of the IOCs, however, this development helped the empowerment of the NOCs, which now could rely on these energy service companies (commonly abbreviated as ESCOs) to provide them with the technological knowledge and management expertise for which they had previously relied on the IOCs (e.g., Bridge 2008).

Another more general and fundamental contradictory outcome of the neoliberal growth model is the financialization of the oil market and the concomitant growth of financial speculation and speculators which has become increasingly influential on the price of oil, and hence on the whole power balance within the global oil order (see e.g., Mabro 2000, 2005; for more elaborate analyses of other aspects of financialization – one of the core parts of the neoliberal project – see the contributions of Hager and Perry and Lewis in this volume). While an issue of considerable debate (e.g., Kaufman and Ullman 2009; Commodity Future Trading Commission 2008), there is general acknowledgement that financial speculation has a major impact on the increasing volatility of oil prices (Mabro 2000, 2005; Engdahl 2008). Crude oil is the most actively traded commodity in the world and the NYMEX Division light sweet crude oil futures contract is the world's largest volume futures contract trading on a physical commodity (NYMEX 2008). Global benchmark prices for oil are decided at two international oil exchanges: NYMEX and ICE Trading (Engdahl 2008).[8] What the effective influence is of NYMEX and ICE Trading on the price of oil in relation to other dynamics that impact upon the oil price, such as the demand and supply balance (e.g., growing demand as the result of the rise of China); strategy and cooperation at the state-industry level (e.g., OPEC's decisions on output and price); and geopolitical relations and tensions (e.g., the influence of concomitant outbreaks of war and/or intrastate violence), is a complex and controversial question (see e.g., Engdahl 2008; Zadeh-Hossein 2008; Mabro 2000). This is not the place for a close investigation into that issue, but the important point to make here is that it is obviously an *additional* crucial dynamic of influence on the oil price and on the power distribution in the global oil market, but yet it *evades* both the power of the resource-holding states (and their firms) and the power of the resource-seeking states (and their firms). Financial speculation increases the volatility of oil prices and in that sense leads to increased instability of the global oil order and the power distribution within it – yet it remains unregulated and beyond the control of the main actors within the global oil production network, irrespective of whether they are producers or consumers. Given the centrality of oil to global capital accumulation in general, the impact of this yet uncontrolled dynamic due to financialization and speculation cannot be underestimated. In a broader perspective, the inherent contradiction here is that while the financialization of capital was a response typical of the neoliberal era from primarily the US (in particular leading segments of its corporate elites) to the limits encountered by its productive power, in order to stay in the lead of global capital accumulation processes, it dialectically created outcomes that are (potentially) detrimental to US (and) transnational capital interests.

Another 'boomerang effect' created by neoliberal capital accumulation processes is the emergence of the rapidly growing economies of the Global South – most significantly China – that are now seen to challenge the Western-dominated world order. The dynamic by which the expansion of capital takes place is most aptly captured by Harvey and are what he calls the 'spatio-temporal fix' (2006, 2003). His argument in brief is that the surplus value produced in the (capitalist) production process constantly needs to be profitably invested in order not to become devalued. When surplus value reaches the limits of profitable investment, a crisis of over-accumulation is imminent. In order prevent such a crisis, surpluses will seek either temporal displacements and/or geographical expansion (Harvey 2003:109–115). One way to do that is to export the surpluses and set in motion capital accumulation in new regional spaces. The latter, however, while in the first instance benefits the originating centre of surplus capital, eventually generates rival centres of accumulation because the new spaces of capital accumulation will generate surpluses of their own that they in turn will seek to absorb through geographical expansion. Hence, they will become competitors to the originating source of surplus capital (Harvey 2006, 2003). With respect to the global energy order, the rise of the non-Western contenders does not only heavily influence the geographical structure of demand and supply of hydrocarbon resources, but it also greatly influences the logics of competition over these (increasingly scarce) resources. One of the most visible expressions of this transition is the change in strategy on the part of many of the non-Western state-owned oil majors towards a more active and globalizing strategy, directly intervening outside their national borders and in the global energy market. Indeed, these processes are not only driven by structural forces of capital accumulation, but also – and importantly – by concrete agency. In fact, while structural forces both constrain and enable agency, they are also continuously shaped by it (e.g., Bhaskar 1979). It is therefore argued that in order to understand the transformation of the energy order and its implications, we need to look not only at the structural forces driving the contestation over hydrocarbon resources, but also at the social relations that underpin the energy order and the way by which agency shapes the latter.

The focus of the following empirical analysis will therefore be on the most important actors driving the particular development of the expansion of the state-owned oil majors: the oil companies themselves and the directors in charge of them. The next part of this chapter, which builds upon De Graaff (2011), will show how the expansion of these 'statist capitalists' has taken place by looking at the configuration and development of the corporate networks of five major non-Western NOCs in the period 1997–2007. These will be discussed in light of findings presented elsewhere (De Graaff, forthcoming) on the corporate elite networks of the directors in charge of these major oil companies in 2007.

Expansion of the NOCs and their integration into the global energy order

The rise of the National Oil Companies from outside the Western core, the alleged 'threat' that they might pose to neoliberal market mechanisms and those actors that abide by and benefit from those rules have generated a lot of debate within Western industry and policy circles. Whereas some analysts predicted a return to state-directed energy sectors in the West (e.g., Odell 2006) and others suggested that IOCs should take on some characteristics of their NOC competitors in order not to lose out in the game (Vivoda 2009), there is also well-grounded empirical research showing that many major NOCs are in fact increasingly *internationalizing* and becoming more like the IOCs (Marcel 2006; Stevens 2008). Within the bulk of new literature on NOCs, however, there have been no studies on the *relations between* NOCs and IOCs. Most often, these two groups of actors are pitched against each other, pictured as an 'IOC v. NOC' game, and when one group of actors loses power the other gains or vice versa (Jaffe et al. 2007; Stevens 2008; Vivoda 2009; Wälde 2008; Wilson 1987). This chapter, by contrast, looks at the *shared properties* of these actors and the *interdependencies* between them, instead of comparing their individual properties. That is, it takes a relational perspective. This is argued to reveal a dimension of change that otherwise remains obscured. As will be shown, the much-discussed global expansion of major non-Western NOCs in the period since the mid-1990s has been paralleled by their integration into the global oil sector due to increased *cooperation* between state-owned and private energy companies. The global oil market has hence become increasingly transnational and integrated. To underpin this claim, the results of a longitudinal social network analysis of the corporate relations of a selection of the world's major NOCs in the period 1997 to 2007 are outlined below (for an extensive analysis see De Graaff 2011: 265–278). There is also an explanatory argument underlying this approach: namely, that all important changes that impact upon the global oil sector such as price fluctuations, geopolitical tensions and changes in supply and demand are *mediated by the underlying relations* of its main actors.

For this analysis, the world's five largest NOCs from the most important regions in terms of hydrocarbon resources and geopolitical impact were selected from the widely recognized Petroleum Intelligence Weekly (PIW) annual ranking of the Top 50 oil companies (Energy Intelligence Group 2008).[9] They are Saudi Aramco (Saudi Arabia, 100 per cent state-owned), National Iranian Oil Company (NIOC) (Iran, 100 per cent state-owned), Gazprom (Russia, 50 per cent state-owned), China National Petroleum Company (China, 100 per cent state-owned) and PDVSA (Venezuela, 100 per cent state-owned).[10] The method of Social Network Analysis (SNA) is employed to analyse how the corporate networks of these companies (NOCs) have been changing over time. The advantage of SNA is that it enables analysis of social relations among actors instead of an analysis of their individual attributes (for more elaboration on SNA see Scott 1991; Wasserman and Faust 1994; Scott and Carrington 2011). The software programme UCINET (Borgatti et al. 2002) was used to perform the analyses.

Data were collected from annual reports of the companies and companies' websites (the latter being an increasingly rich and reliable source for energy-resource data, see Arnott 2004). Additional data sources were company databases (such as Hoover's and *BusinessWeek*); the energy statistical data bases of the US government's Energy Information Administration (EIA), the International Energy Agency (IEA); and Energy Intelligence Group reports (EIG 1997, 2002, 2008).

When we compare the corporate networks of the top five non-Western NOCs in 1997 and 2007, their expansion in terms of corporate relations[11] is clearly confirmed (see Figure 8.1 below).

However, what these graphs also show is that the *expansion* of the corporate networks of these NOCs has been paralleled by their *integration* with other core companies of the global oil sector (that is, companies ranked into the PIW Top 50). This is most clearly illustrated by the nodes (circles) on the right side of the graphs, representing the companies of the PIW Top 50 to which the five major non-Western NOCs are *not connected* (i.e., isolates). Whereas in 1997 30 out of the 45 PIW Top 50 companies were not yet connected to the non-Western NOCs and only 10 were connected to them, it turns out that in 2007 only 14 out of the PIW Top 50 companies were *not* connected to these five top non-Western NOCs. From the colours of the nodes it can be seen that these included both IOCs (white), NOCs (black) and Hybrids (i.e., partly state-owned) (grey).[12] It can be concluded that, although the largest non-Western NOCs have been part of the PIW Top 50 core for decades, they have become significantly more *interrelated* with the other PIW Top 50 companies since 1997.

That the expansion of these NOCs indeed has not yet led to the emergence of an NOC-dominated global oil market can be seen in Figure 8.2 below. Here, the corporate relations of the five top non-Western NOCs with other companies of the PIW Top 50 core are categorized according to whether this is a relation between NOCs only, or also including IOCs and/or Hybrids.

Comparing 1997 and 2007, we do see a significant increase in the relations between fully state-owned energy majors (NOC-NOC) over time. However, in this period the relations between fully state-owned energy companies and private companies (NOC-IOC) have also more

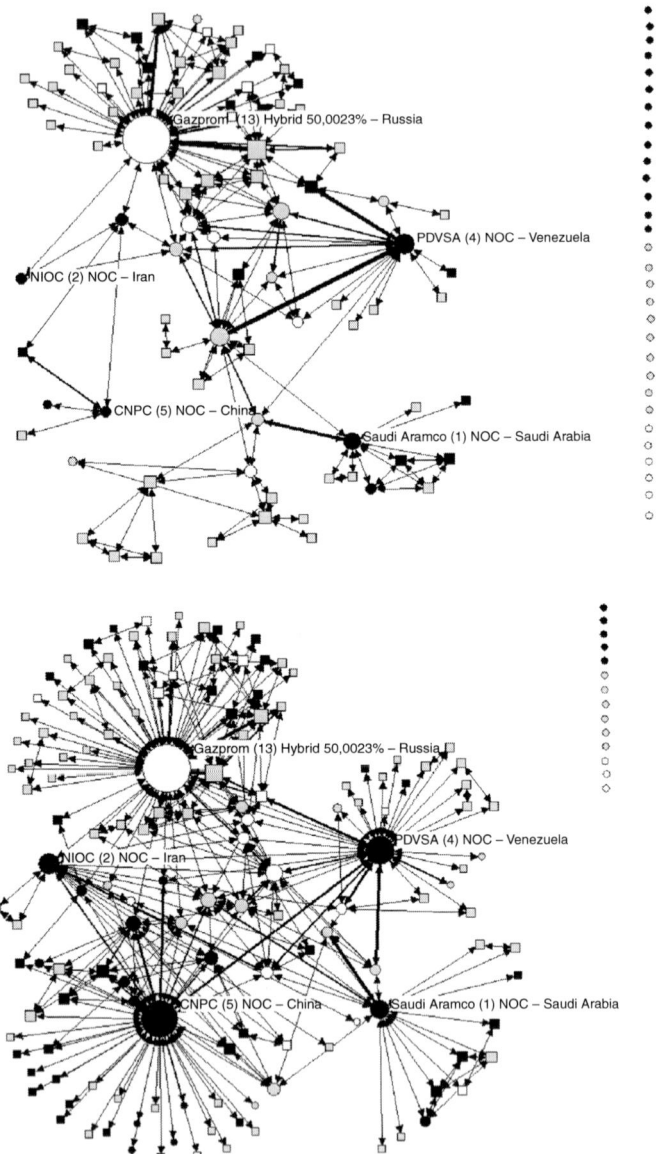

Figure 8.1   Corporate networks of five major NOCs in 1997 and 2007 compared*

Note: * Figures originally published in De Graaff (2011: 271).

Sources: Data collected by author, see page 172 above.

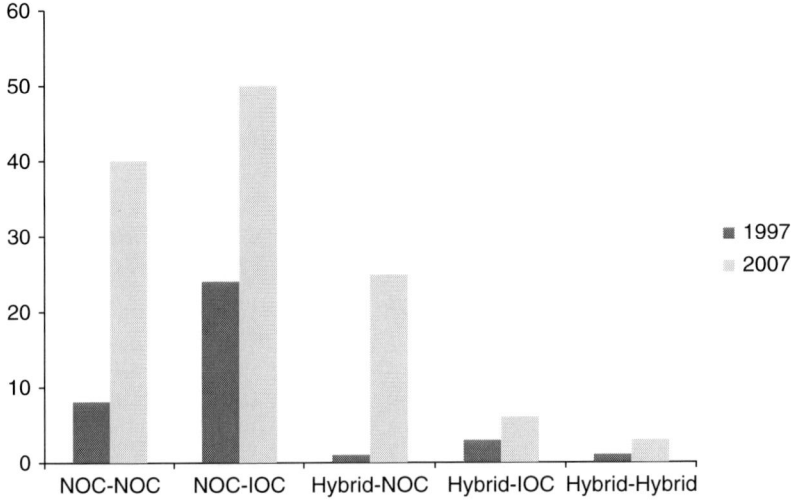

Figure 8.2   Changes in type of corporate relations of five top NOCs 1997 and 2007*

Note: *Figure originally published in De Graaff (2011: 277).

Sources: Data collected by author, see page 173 above.

than doubled, *and still exceed the NOC-NOC relations*. The largest increase can be seen to have taken place in relations between hybrid companies and fully state-owned companies (HYBR-NOC). This overview illustrates that the expansion of these NOCs is not a phenomenon of 'NOC growth' only, but it is also a process of increased *cooperation between* and hence *integration of* state-owned companies and private/hybrid companies, maybe best described as *a hybridization* of the relations between the major players in the global oil sector.

It thus seems that in spite of the resurgence of resource nationalism and the alleged challenge to the neoliberal foundations of the global oil order, the period since 1997 has been characterized by a persistent trend of *transnationalization* that has significantly transformed the structure of the core of the global oil sector. As the NOCs are progressively integrating into the global oil market, it becomes harder to frame the contestation over hydrocarbon resources as 'OPEC v. the West', or the 'IOCs v. the NOCs'; the distribution of power now might become increasingly diffused.[13] This new underlying configuration of relations will also mediate the effects of conjunctural forces, such as a plummeting or rising oil price, loss of revenues, financial crises and changes in supply and demand, in a different manner than when the NOCs were situated more outside the global oil market.

However, as elaborated elsewhere (De Graaff, forthcoming), the expansion and integration of the non-Western state-owned oil companies has not (yet) translated into more cooperation or integration between the corporate elite networks of the West and of the non-Western contenders. As shown, on the basis of extensive analysis of a selection of the world's major oil companies' board members (including both the NOCs analysed here and the five largest IOCs), the non-Western oil elites do not interlink with their Western counterparts through interlocking directorates. They also do not link with them through membership of transnational policy-planning networks crucial to the emergence and maintenance of the neoliberal project and globalizing capital (see introduction of this volume). The Western oil elites, or at least a part of them, by contrast, turned out to be closely linked to, on the one hand, transnational capital through a corporate network of interlocking directorates.[14] These directorates include the world's major TNCs in several key industries (extractive industries, car industry, defence, technology) and key players of global financial capital (such as Goldman Sachs, Royal Bank of Scotland, Societe Generale). On the other hand, they are connected to a network of key influential global and regional planning/coordinating bodies, with at its core the European Roundtable of Industrialists (ERT), the World Economic Forum (WEF) and the Bilderberg Group. Connected to these are e.g., the Trilateral Commission, the US-Russia Business Council, the International Accounting Standards Foundation (IASF) and some UN organizations. The fact that they are connected to and through these bodies suggests an exchange of views, ideas and information and a potential for coordination of interests. These might not be the particular interests of the oil companies that they represent, but rather – as is often suggested – a broader business community interest. This is confirmed by the fact that indeed, many of these 'institutional big linkers' are also 'corporate big linkers', most of them with brokerage positions within the corporate 'inner circle' (see De Graaff, forthcoming).

The non-Western oil elites, however, are nearly unconnected to these configurations of social (class) forces typical of and constitutive of the neoliberal project (e.g., Van der Pijl 1984, 1998; Van Apeldoorn 2002; Carroll 2010). The exception that should be mentioned in this respect is Saudi Aramco, which did have a few directors with ties to the transnational corporate network and the policy-planning network; however, these directors in most cases turned out to be Western directors.[15] These actors are potentially important brokers between the Western and non-Western oil elites.

Instead, the non-Western oil elites turned out to be heavily integrated with the state apparatus, even to the extent that in many cases, the state is not only the ultimate owner of the corporation, but the actors in charge of these majors are also themselves *state executives at often high level positions*. Indeed, these oil elites seem to be 'state capitalists' par excellence but of a different kind then previously conceived (e.g., the Soviet example). It should be noted that it was also found that the Western oil elites – in spite of their transnational ties and orientation – are still predominantly linked to national corporate networks and do display a persistent pattern of revolving-door careers with government and policy advising positions. The national and statist dimension thus by no means has become irrelevant or transcended by the Western oil elites. However, this is significantly different from the non-Western oil elites' relations to the state. Hence, the expansion of the latter into global energy markets, without significant integration in terms of elite formation might herald a transformation towards a more truly multipolar world in which the neoliberal Anglo-American heartland is indeed increasingly challenged by rival state capitalisms as suggested in the introduction. The outcome, however, as will be elaborated in the conclusion, remains necessarily uncertain.

Conclusion

The empirical findings discussed in this chapter elucidate that while the non-Western oil elites analysed here are increasingly active within the West in terms of business activity, directing a major expansion of their National Oil Companies, which at the same time generates increased cooperation with the Western private oil majors, this has not been accompanied by integration within Western corporate elite circles.

What does this imply in terms of future trajectories and to what extent does it indicate a movement beyond neoliberalism? It is, of course, an open question what direction these developments will take. History is a contingent phenomenon that does not follow any predetermined path even if there are structural forces shaping agency in both constraining and enabling ways and vice versa. The following is therefore necessarily an exercise of a rather speculative nature, but with that caveat in mind, some possible 'scenarios' can be discarded.

One possible scenario would be a continuation of the neoliberal energy order into which the rising non-Western powers and their companies will be gradually co-opted. The internationalization of many NOCs and the expansion and integration of the NOCs into the global oil market – as shown in this chapter – does seem to be an indication of this. This seems to be a more likely option than the scenario of a gradual transition towards a more 'statist' energy order, as some analysts have predicted and which was feared by some in the industry. Even if Western oil interests and their leading corporate elites were challenged by the rising powers of the Global South and Russia, with the resurgence of resource nationalism and expansion of their oil majors. However, although the neoliberal model they epitomized has revealed its limitations even to its most fervent advocates (e.g., Greenspan, see Andrews 2008) and although much of the world's most globalized capital had to be rescued by the state, a trajectory towards a state controlled and 'NOC dominated' energy order seems unlikely to happen.

If the trajectory would be one of gradual integration then this could indeed imply that the rising non-Western oil elites are incorporated into the existing power structures of the transnational corporate elite and the neoliberal fundaments on which these rest. In that case, this might indeed indicate their adaptation to the latter's rules of the game, i.e., the deepening of capitalist discipline and neoliberal market mechanisms (as for instance argued, but not empirically substantiated by Robinson 2004; and Harris 2009). However, integration does not necessarily imply adaptation on the part of the non-Western oil elites. It might as well imply a diffusion of corporate and elite power at the global level. In that case, this could herald a more fundamental transition towards a more multipolar and inclusive energy order, no longer structured by a Western 'core' dominating the Southern 'periphery'. This would include more hybrid forms of cooperation and coalitions of interests, different ways in which the organization of capital expansion are orchestrated and a redefinition of the role of the state and its relation to capital (see also Carroll 2010). The lack of elite integration seems to imply that the non-Western oil elites still have little access to and influence within the typical Western neoliberal elite and business circuits. Although this can be interpreted in several ways (i.e., are they not *allowed* access or do they perhaps not want access?) this might also lead to a scenario of inter-elite power conflicts between the established elites of the West and the contending elites of the emerging Global South.

In any of these scenarios, however, the centrality of the capital accumulation process remains unchanged, which makes any transition one of variation within a capitalist order, including its underpinning social relations and its imperative of endless capital accumulation. In that respect, it is questionable whether a transition towards a more multipolar energy order, with more hybrid forms of cooperation and coalitions of interests, would imply any improvement in terms of the challenges that beset the current energy order such as high energy prices, climate change, militarization and looming geopolitical conflicts over hydrocarbon resources.

Notes

1. National Oil Companies (NOCs) is the most commonly used label to refer to a quite diverse group of energy companies that have in common that they are at least partly state-owned. Although this label is not unproblematic – first of all because these companies are increasingly transnational in terms of their operations and organization; second, because most of them are not exclusively oil companies, but much more diversified (a company as Gazprom, for instance, is also labelled NOC) – the usage will be maintained in this chapter.

2. It should be noted that the focus here is on non-Western NOCs, while there are major Western NOCs as well, such as Statoil and ENI, which were already widely integrated within the global energy market and which were never seen as a 'threat' in the same way as the non-Western ones.

3. Referring to the eight Western private oil companies: Exxon (Jersey), Mobil (Socony-Vaccum), Chevron (Standard of California), Texaco, Gulf, Royal Dutch/Shell, BP, CFP (See Yergin 1991).

4. Quite instrumental in this respect is what is known as the 'As Is Agreement', or Achnacarry Agreement. The agreement is named after the Castle in Scotland in which the heads of the major oil companies of the cartel came together over a weekend of grouse shooting, while at the same time setting forth a set of principles aimed at maintaining their absolute cartel status and control over oil prices. This was in response to the price wars that were at the moment raging worldwide (see e.g., Bina 2006: 9 and Yergin 1991).

5. In fact, OPEC took over the administrative price system from the Seven Sisters cartel, but it could not sustain it in the context of the competition of non-OPEC supplies, stagnant world demand and surplus capacity within the OPEC region (see Mabro 2000).

6. Indicators of this 're-militarization' of energy security are, for instance, recent discussions within NATO to give it an explicit role in energy security (Van Gennip 2006); the Chinese military expansion into Africa (Klare 2004); US post-9/11 security strategy (Cheney et al. 2001).

7. Resistance against US dominance and the free market model is, however, not restricted to Islamic countries, but is manifesting itself in regions as diverse as South America and Russia, and also within the western world itself (e.g., the split between 'old' and 'new' Europe over the invasion in Iraq, the anti-globalist movement).

8. In addition, just about a year ago, the Dubai Mercantile Exchange opened. It is the first energy futures exchange in the Middle East.

9. The PIW ranking is based upon operational data from more than 130 firms and it uses six individual rankings (oil reserves and production, natural gas reserves and output, refinery capacity, and product sales volumes) that together determine the overall position of a firm. Therefore – in contrast to rankings based upon market capitalization or revenue only – this

provides a more evenly balanced ranking between private and state-owned companies.

10. In 2007, all of these companies were ranked in the top 10 of the PIW except for Gazprom, which was ranked twelfth.

11. When mapping the corporate networks of these five NOCs, all of their external corporate relations were included: joint ventures (domestic and abroad), wholly owned subsidiaries (abroad), consortia (domestic and abroad), equity interests/alliances (domestic and abroad), different forms of operating and service contract agreements and other relations such as lease contracts and memoranda of understandings. When applicable, the ownership structures of these relations were included in terms of the percentage of the different participating actors' stake in the relation.

12. The square nodes are oil companies outside the PIW Top 50 with which the five NOCs had corporate relations.

13. With respect to a power balance between IOCs and NOCs, it should, however, be noted that the latter have been owners of about 80 per cent to 90 per cent of the world's proven hydrocarbon resources for decades (see also Wolf 2008). The power that resides in owning the resource, and to a large extent the decision power of access to that resource, thus dominantly resides with the NOCs – at least when their ultimate owners (the state) are resource *holders*. But that 'power division' has remained rather unaltered for the past decades and it has thus not been the direct cause nor has it been altered by the last wave of resource nationalism and politicization of energy (security), i.e. the recent challenges to the neoliberal energy order.

14. An interlocking directorate means that one person sits at several corporate boards simultaneously.

15. For example, Sir Moody-Stuart, who in 2007 was director at Saudi Aramco and previously was a director at Shell, and the Italian business tycoon Bernabe who is director at CNPC/PetroChina.

9
Post-neoliberalism in Latin America?

Andreas Tsolakis

Introduction

The landslide elections in the mid-2000s of so-called 'pink' (or 'left-leaning') governments in Latin America constituted a milestone in the region's historical development. They occurred in a climate of intense social conflict, and apparently signalled the conclusion of a long crisis that had defined, for a quarter of a century, the interrelated developmental cycles of political and economic liberalization in the region. Not surprisingly, the 'pink tide' immediately attracted significant media and academic interest across the political spectrum. Hugo Chavez's landmark victory in Venezuela's 1998 presidential election was followed by the successive elections of presidential candidates in Venezuela, Brazil, Argentina, Panama, Uruguay, Bolivia, Ecuador, Chile, Paraguay, Costa Rica, Nicaragua, Guatemala and Honduras who characterized themselves and have generally been characterized as 'left-leaning', 'anti-neoliberal' and 'anti-imperialist' (Cameron 2009; Robinson 2008; Lievesley and Ludlam 2009).[1]

All pink governments 'have made bold claims about their determination to promote equality and to transform how power is exercised in Latin America' and their electoral success is a manifestation of an 'underlying trend toward the emergence and mobilization of social and political currents variously protesting against the current political order, affirming or seeking recognition for subaltern groups, and demanding social and cultural change as well as political citizenship' (Cameron and Herschbert 2009: 1). The unprecedented concurrence of governments tied (to varying degrees) to subaltern social forces,[2] advocating the rolling back of neoliberalism and proclaiming their abhorrence of the Monroe doctrine signalled potentially far-reaching change in the region's production and power relations (Robinson 2008; Lievesley and Ludlam 2009; Petras and Veltmeyer 2009).

This chapter assesses, from a historical materialist perspective, the extent of these changes through a comparative analysis (Skocpol 1984) of three distinct cases: Brazil, Venezuela and Bolivia. The choice of these cases is not arbitrary. The Lula, Chávez and Morales governments are emblematic manifestations of the pink tide, often portrayed as representing distinct and contradictory facets of the 'left'. Perhaps simplifying to the extreme a rich variety of interpretations, problem-solving accounts (Cox 1981) have tended to distinguish between good, bad and ugly lefts. The 'moderation' of the Luiz Inácio Lula da Silva government embodies a good, social democratic left, which also includes Lagos and Bachelet in Chile and, less decisively due to their more 'erratic' economic decisions, the Kirchners in Argentina, Vazquéz in Uruguay and Lugo in Paraguay. The Hugo Chávez government embodies the bad left par excellence: populist,[3] statist and taking advantage of high oil prices to push through an authoritarian and aggressively internationalist agenda of 'twenty-first century socialism' (in the disquieting shadow of the Castro brothers) (Castañeda 2006; Gratius and Tedesco 2009; Cameron 2009). On its side, the Evo Morales government, (along with Correa in Ecuador, Ortega in Nicaragua, perhaps even Colóm in Guatemala and Zelaya in Honduras, recently overthrown by a military coup), seems more difficult to grasp. It is often portrayed as an ugly left that has articulated vociferously anti-neoliberal and anti-US discourses (with shades of indigenism) and that has pushed through nationalizations and land reform while actively cooperating with Venezuela and Cuba through bilateral agreements and multilateral initiatives such as the regional organization Bolivarian Alliance for the Peoples of Our America Alianza Bolivariana para los Pueblos de Nuestra América (ALBA). At the same time, while regularly contending that 'capitalism is the worst enemy of humanity', it has demonstrated greater cautiousness in its foreign relations, greater respect for private property and for the 'checks and balances' of liberal democracy, and it implemented a more 'responsible' fiscal and monetary policy than the Chávez regime (Castañeda 2006; Lievesley and Ludlam 2009). Critical scholars, on their side, have tended to invert these qualifications (Petras and Veltmeyer 2009; Ellner 2008; Wilpert 2007; Dominguez 2009; Buxton 2009; Branford 2009).

The literature, sometimes imbued with external-internal and state-market dichotomies, has tended to exaggerate national divergences and to overlook common structural mechanisms of capital globalization. From a historical materialist perspective, global production relations are greater than the sum of the internal/domestic political struggles and hegemonies defining national formations (Van der Pijl 1998; Van Apeldoorn 2004; Overbeek 2000b, 2004).[4] This allows for the correlation of apparently 'independent' domestic processes through a set of internally related and historically grounded concepts (production, capital, value, class), and reveals that the historical trajectories and social formations of Bolivia, Brazil and Venezuela share structural mechanisms rooted in the continuities and changes produced by European colonization and the globalization of capital relations (Robinson 2008).

Structural commonality helps to question the idea of an essential 'exceptionalism' characterizing each Latin American state-society complex. Take, for example, the persistence of noncapitalist organizational forms in Bolivia's *Altiplano*, Brazil's particular history of black slavery, Venezuela's relatively long era of 'democratic' governance since 1958, its rentier form of state capitalism and Dutch disease (Buxton and Phillips 1999; Ellner and Tinker Salas 2005; Lievesley and Ludlam 2009).[5] Beyond inevitable national idiosyncrasies, the political struggles (between elite and subaltern forces, between elite forces, between subaltern forces) over ownership rights and wealth redistribution, and over developmental and governance models, are common to all cases and are correlated with developments in their direct vicinity and beyond. In all cases, a confluence of racial and class domination, expressed in economic, institutional and ideological forms, has produced complex hierarchical social formations (at the apex of which *criollo* [white-skinned] elites have maintained themselves primarily through coercion) in constant process of transformation accelerated by the globalization of capital. In all cases, the violence of slavery, serfdom and capital accumulation generated extreme degrees of inequality and systematic social instability. As such, all three cases offer important lessons for the structure-agency problématique and the dialectical process of structural continuity and change (Bieler and Morton 2001). The implications of this comparative analysis are therefore of broader relevance than the cases themselves.

Is Latin America embarking on a 'post-neoliberal' developmental trajectory? The story of the implementation of neoliberal reforms in Latin America has already been told many times.[6] In our cases, neoliberal restructuring typically commenced with the design and implementation of comprehensive stabilization and structural adjustment packages in consultation with MDIs (Bolivia's New Economic Policy [NEP] in 1985; Venezuela's *paquete* in 1989 consolidated by the *Agenda Venezuela* in 1996; and Brazil's first *Collor* Plan in 1990 consolidated by the *Real* Plan in 1994), although ad hoc stabilization plans had regularly been implemented in preceding decades (Foxley and Whitehead 1980). These respective social and political 'bangs' opened national cycles of protracted struggles, within and beyond states, for and against reforms that were aimed essentially at accelerating capitalist development by further disciplining labour while achieving consent through poverty-reduction targeting and polyarchy (minimal forms of political representation) (Robinson 1996: 49).

Neoliberal restructuring fostered an acceleration of capital globalization through trade and price liberalization, monetarism and fiscal austerity. It also fostered a shift from state capitalism (characterized by import-substitution strategies [ISS] and state-led industrialization) to the privatization of accumulation, the intensification of primitive accumulation in both 'formal' and 'informal' economies – the latter of which had expanded in the wake of the debt crisis and privatizations (estimated in the late 1990s at 60 per cent of GDP, encompassing 70 per cent of firms and 67 per cent of the labour force in Bolivia, 49 per cent of GDP in Venezuela and 40 per cent of GDP in Brazil). These historical processes effectively capture the history of the rise of capitalism in neoliberal form in the region (Buxton and Philips 1999; Robinson 2008).

The social costs of the debt crisis of the 1980s (in all cases) and hyperinflation through the first half of the 1990s (Brazil and Venezuela) were extremely high. In fact, most of the social damage had occurred prior to the launching of comprehensive neoliberal packages, although restructuring marginally improved (Brazil), perpetuated (Venezuela) or intensified (Bolivia) prior negative trends in terms of income distribution, poverty and real wages. The poverty rate for the region, having risen during the 'lost decade' (40.5 per cent or 135.9 million persons in 1980 to 48.3 per cent or 200.2 million persons in 1990), marginally declined in relative but not absolute terms thanks to targeted WB-funded social and employment programmes (Emergency Social Fund in Bolivia in the late 1980s, *Bolsa Escola* and *Programa Alvorada* under the Cardoso administration in Brazil). The rate declined to 44.3 per cent or 226 million in 2002, while the region's GDP per capita, having averaged 1.4 per cent annual growth between 1970 and 1990 (–1.1 per cent in the case of Bolivia) and 1.3 per cent in the following decade (thus failing to keep pace with inflation), did not sustain subaltern consent to the intensification of capital accumulation.

Furthermore, the marginal improvements that occurred in the mid-1990s in key social indicators were either shaven off or stalled during the 1998–2001 regional crisis (for instance, GNI per capita plunged from $5060 to $3050 in that period in Brazil). Dwindling accumulation and a recrudescence of inequality and poverty accelerated the unravelling of neoliberal hegemony, while polyarchy and decentralization paradoxically opened up new spaces for the reorganization and projection of subaltern power, fuelling the pink tide of the 2000s.

Mass mobilizations against neoliberalism targeted price liberalization and the restructuring, privatization or liquidation of state-owned corporations and banks, as well as utilities. It is all too often forgotten in critical research that the organizational 'vanguard' of social resistance to stabilization measures was invariably state employees, in part because, unlike 50 per cent to 70 per cent of workers confined to the informal sector, they enjoyed permanent contracts and retained their membership in trade unions.

Although collective agency in the state allowed the persistence of a labour power bloc through the 1980s and 1990s, the reconstitution of subaltern organizations in civil society in the mid-1990s was what really fuelled the pink tide. In Bolivia, the military repression of *cocaleros* (coca farmers) with USAID technical, financial and military assistance fuelled the projection of the Movement Towards Socialism's (Movimiento Al Socialismo – MAS) organizational power beyond the department of Cochabamba and its subsequent electoral success at the national level. In Venezuela, social mobility in the army allowed individuals with a poor background, such as Chávez, to assume positions of authority and power and thereafter lead mass movements based in the *barrios* of major cities. In Brazil, the effective alignment of three subaltern organizations, the Landless Rural Labourers (Movimiento Sin Tierra – MST), the United Workers' Central (CUT) and the Workers' Party (PT), provided a mighty platform for the projection of subaltern power beyond their bastions in the so-called ABC region (industrial cities in the Greater Sao Paulo area). At the same time, the aftershocks of the 1998–1999 financial crisis aggravated social resentment and facilitated the landslide election of Lula at the head of the PT in 2002 and the second place of Morales in Bolivia's 2002 presidential election.

Some policy elements of the neoliberal restructuring efforts were thus implemented successfully, while others remained in limbo or had to be rolled back; some institutions were transformed, eliminated or created while others remained bastions of continuity. It is therefore in the dialectical process of capital accumulation, rising inequality and impoverishment since the 1980s, the reconstitution of subaltern organizations in civil society, continued resistance to restructuring in the state, economic crisis in the late 1990s and in some cases US military intervention, that left parties achieved the successive electoral victories contributing to the regional pink tide.

It is against this background that the chapter investigates the extent to which new forms of capital accumulation and new forms of governance and rule are rising out of these contradictions and struggles. Five central attributes of neoliberalism allow us to assess comparatively the 'post-neoliberalism' hypothesis: austere fiscal policy (including welfare cuts), monetary stability, trade and price liberalization, the privatization of accumulation, and perhaps less perceptibly, 'lean' state building.[7] Each of these attributes contributes to forming and sustaining an ideological whole aimed at achieving subaltern consent to an ever-greater transfer of wealth from labour to capital. Their 'purity' is questionable, but they indicate tendencies rather than fixed absolutes and the absence of one of them does not invalidate the concept of neoliberalism itself, which is treated here as of the 'family resemblance' type (Collier and Mahon 1993).

Few observers would contend that Chávez and Morales (not to mention Lula) have led a popular capture of the state to revolutionize production relations. The weight of the past is manifestly too heavy, and the voluntarism of leaders such as Chávez immediately confronts the strict limits of the possible in global capitalism (Robinson 2008; Lievesley and Ludlam 2009). The orientation of pink governments towards state capitalism or a 'state developmental' model legitimized by the articulation of nationalist and anti-imperialist discourses, has had to adapt to a world market characterized by increasingly complex transnational production networks, financialization and growing international and domestic imbalances expressed in varying levels of class inequalities and uneven development. Increasing competition *through* state-owned enterprises (SOEs) in the hydrocarbons, mining and a few high-tech sectors (such as telecommunications and aeronautics), often through joint ventures with private capital, has intensified the integration of state-society complexes in the global capitalist production structure and consolidated the capitalist form of the state.

The management, by 'pink' governments, of capitalist relations of production has taken place against the background of geo-political shifts and of continued transnational capitalist elite formation. Profound social changes are taking place within and beyond the Latin American space, including at one level the shifting centre of economic gravity towards East Asia, European stagnation and US imperial overstretch, and at a deeper and less transparent level, the temporary frailty and rapid reconsolidation of transnational capital (in part through interlocking directorates and cross-shareholder structures involving SOEs) and MDIs. The chapter concludes by assessing the structural effects of the struggles that have defined the implementation of reforms in these cases and questioning the validity of the concept of 'post-neoliberalism'.

Post-neoliberalism in Latin America?

Structural revolution is not taking place in any of the cases under study (Webber 2008; Lievesley and Ludlam 2009; Ellner 2008; Tsolakis 2010b). However, have pink governments undermined any of the attributes of neoliberalism and engineered a robust state capitalist alternative? Have they deepened 'grassroots' participatory democracy? To what extent have inequality reduction policies affected capital circuits? The implementation of pink governments' respective political and economic programmes has been conditioned by the fluid interface of internal and external balances of power between the governments and subaltern, domestic and transnational capitalist forces. These relationships of forces have manifested themselves both in 'civil society' and in the institutions of the state, have either accelerated or hindered structural transformations and are shaping the pink tide's differentiated forms.

World rankings based on a series of variables related to the 'ease of doing business' (WB) or 'economic freedoms' (Heritage Foundation) are relevant indicators of the degree of continuity and change in each country. Unsurprisingly, and in line with the portrayal that business elites make of the 'left', the former survey ranked Bolivia 149 (29 in regional ranking) and Venezuela 172 (32 and last in regional ranking) of the 183 countries surveyed, while Brazil, despite the positive image projected in liberal media and MDI reports, remains an environment insufficiently conducive to private business, struggling at the 26 position in the regional ranking and 127 worldwide.[8] In turn, the latter currently ranks Brazil 113, Bolivia 147 and Venezuela 175.[9] Except for recent re-nationalizations in Bolivia and Venezuela and the re-establishment of various price controls in the latter case, the 'imperfections' of 'business freedoms' persisted through the neoliberal era and they are rarely the product of explicit policy redirections by pink governments (IMF 1998; WB 1997, 1998, 2003).

From the very moment anti-systemic political parties in Bolivia, Brazil and Venezuela achieved electoral victories and took control of the government, they immediately faced, to various extents and in ways not dissimilar to the early 1980s, the disciplining wrath of global markets through capital strikes and inflationary pressures. Morales, Lula and Chávez were all structurally constrained to consolidate the functional relationship between capital and the state by maintaining fiscal and monetary stability, pursuing trade liberalization, upholding 'state-building' efforts by undertaking legal actions towards increased transparency and accountability in the state and wage restraints in the public sector, while sustaining polyarchy. The nationalizations implemented by the Morales and Chávez governments paradoxically entrenched the hegemony of capital – in a nationalist-developmental form underpinned by neoliberal tenets – in their respective social spaces.

In all cases the MVR, PT and MAS leaderships assured MDIs prior to their election that they would protect private property (except in strategic sectors, and distinguishing between nationalizations and expropriations), pursue tight monetary and fiscal policies and control excessive labour demands. They all had to tread carefully in order to avoid being portrayed by 'markets' as a group of socialists bent on full-on expropriations (leading invariably to capital flight and hyperinflation), and to avoid being seen as mild reformists by a majority enraged by the violence of restructuring and repression and with high expectations and proliferating demands. They therefore sustained the depoliticized (rules-based) management of Central Banks, allowing monetarism to prevent excessive money circulation and to condition austere fiscal policies while containing real wage increases and public employment. They accumulated foreign reserves as a buffer against world recessions, although low capital inflows beyond capital-intensive extractive sectors since the late 1990s alleviated the impact of any foreign capital strike in the overall economy, especially in the Bolivian and Venezuelan cases, where diversification is more limited than in Brazil.

The entrenchment of capital has thus perpetuated the class constitution of the state, while the investiture of 'anti-systemic' parties opened the floodgates of wage and other demands, which have been contained through Constitutional changes, wage increases, universal pension reform and a battery of welfare programmes (*Bolsa Familia* and *Fame Zero* in Brazil, various schemes in Bolivia, the Missions in Venezuela) financed primarily by increased taxes on corporate profits (boosted by high market prices).

Of the three cases, and despite radical policies such as land reform and the defence of 'indigenous zones' in Bolivia, only the Chávez government has actively sought to break or undermine capital circuits through creative exchange and production structures, while fostering participatory democracy at the 'grassroots' level and recently rebuilding alliances with trade unions. Indeed, 'The combination of policies with transformational potential and a discourse that empowers people was particularly evident in the case of the Chávez government and explains why it faced open resistance from the business sector and the US government' (Ellner 2008: 4). Yet the attacks on private capital, caricatured in the information media, must be qualified. It is crucial to emphasize the continued preponderance of private capital in banking and production, and many of the expropriations and price and foreign exchange controls are very recent as a consequence of the world crisis and as ideological attacks by MDIs, media and conservative parties have been intensifying.

I agree with seasoned students of Latin America that, in the Venezuelan case, the Chávez government was radicalized by systematic US and business attacks during its first term (Buxton 2009). The president, at the head of a loose coalition of various parties (the Patriotic Pole), immediately set out to enact a new Constitution which would lay the foundation of new Bolivarian Fifth Republic and break the institutional power of the 'traditional' AD and COPEI parties. 'Socialism' was not, at the time, elemental to the *chavista* discourse, and the government initially distanced itself from trade unions and rather galvanized support in the poor *barrios* by attacking *puntofijistas* and the 'oligarchy' responsible for the impoverishment of the majority. Chávez, like Morales, reclaimed national myths and figures to legitimize their reform project. Interestingly however, a central reference point in the Venezuelan government's discourse was Simón Bolivar, who led the continent's liberation from Spanish colonial rule and who had seen his ambitions to form a Spanish American state frustrated by parochialisms and internecine feuds. The Bolivarian internationalism of Chávez informing the vision of a multi-polar world order complemented his appeals to a post-*puntofijo* nation.

On his side, Morales was elected on the political platform of rolling back neoliberalism and decolonizing Bolivia's society and state. The electoral programme of the MAS, couched in nationalist rhetoric, with sometimes inconsistent classist, indigenist and internationalist undertones, reasserted Bolivia's sovereignty in the international system, founding the 'movement towards socialism' upon seven pillars:

(1) Above all, and as a way to ground legally the MAS's 'revolutionary' and 'democratic' struggle, the election of a Constituent Assembly following the chavista example.

(2) An 'agrarian revolution' to redistribute unproductive state-owned and privately owned landholdings to indigenous communities – a policy also implemented in Venezuela.

(3) The Venezuela-style re-nationalization of privatized corporations in strategic sectors (in particular hydrocarbons and mining) as a pivot for industrialization in other sectors.

(4) An ambitious social welfare programme to redistribute the income generated by gas and mineral exports, including an increase in the legal minimum wage (see below), the implementation of a *Renta Dignidad* (universal pension scheme involving a monthly payment of bol.200, or $26 for pensioners, financed by gas receipts, at an annual cost of $260 million for the Treasury), the *Bono Madre-Niño*, which provides for free health care to pregnant women and bol.1800 over two years for the child, expected to cost $100 million per year, and which recently secured WB financing, and the *Bono Juancito Pinto*, which allocates bol.200 to parents per child in primary school in order to stimulate child schooling.

(5) A creative administrative and fiscal decentralization articulating various forms of 'autonomy' – departmental, municipal, indigenous – to channel the demands of contradictory elite and indigenous forces.

(6) The submission of two laws ('Tijera' and 'Marcelo Quiroga Santa Cruz', approved by Congress in August 2007) to generate government accountability, fight corruption, reduce waste in state administration and bring to trial Gonzalo Sánchez de Lozada and his Government Ministers, responsible for massacres in the Gas War of October 2003.

(7) Support the alternative regionalist movement promoted by Venezuelan President Hugo Chávez, enshrined in the ALBA.

In order to address popular demands for the radical overhaul of the social and institutional structure of Bolivia, the MAS followed the Venezuelan example by taking a legalist approach, whereby the creation of a new Constitution would synthesize various social interests and create a new ('refound') Bolivia (Crabtree 2009; Tsolakis 2010b).

In the cases of Bolivia and Venezuela, the violent attempts of elite opposition forces to derail their progressive reform projects and undermine the legitimacy of pink governments through production cuts to intensify inflation, conditioned quite different responses. In Bolivia, the projection of financial, organizational and ideological power (primarily through private television media) by elites has counterbalanced the momentum of labour and indigenist forces, while bastions of the opposition in the state – the senate, the prefectures, municipalities – have hindered and redirected social and institutional change and the form of the Constitution itself. Yet since the attempt of the opposition to trigger a full-fledged war of movement in the *Oriente* in the wake of Morales' resounding victory in the revocatory referendum of August

2008, the MAS has demonstrated its political acumen by retaking the initiative and by consolidating a hegemonic bloc formed by indigenist and nationalist movements within the confines of Bolivian power relations.

The Chávez government, in contrast, taking advantage of growing oil rents, has actively mobilized the collective agency within and beyond Venezuela's frontiers, to break capital circuits through creative forms of economic and political organization under the banner of a Bolivarian 'Socialism of the Twenty-First Century' (Buxton 2009; Petras and Veltmeyer 2009). The social forms of economic development (cooperatives, social production companies) and political organization (communal councils) have developed on the back of Chávez's perpetuation of rentier state capitalism. Nevertheless, while experiments in the socialization of the means of production in Venezuela have opened new spaces of resistance to capital, these are scarcely expanding islands in a sea of market and capitalist relations.

The capacity of the Morales government to mobilize resources for structural change has proved more limited, while the Lula government was effectively subdued prior to its investiture in 2002. The Lula government has more explicitly articulated a nationalist, neoliberal project that consolidates and actively furthers, in 'close collaboration' with the WB (WB 2006b: iii), the latter's Private Sector Development Strategy, despite enhancing state participation in production and finance and intensifying transnational capital investments (inwards and outwards through equity investments by Brazilian firms in Latin America and beyond), while expanding welfare spending and increasing minimum wages.

There are few indications that the promotion of cooperatives, the protection of indigenous communities and the development of the ALBA are denting the appropriation of labour power by capital in the region. The resurgence of state capitalism and anti-liberal discourses concurrent to the disciplinary effects of capital strikes and inflationary pressures are stringently hindering the revolutionary potential of Chávez's Bolivarian 'Socialism of the Twenty-First Century' and Morales's promotion of 'indigenous zones' in Bolivia's *Altiplano* (highlands), as the intensification of primitive accumulation in both rural and urban areas is profoundly transforming pre-capitalist 'communitarian' production forms.

Let us now assess in more detail the attributes of neoliberalism in pink government's management of capital relations. Of the five proposed attributes of neoliberalism, only the privatization of accumulation has been affected in all cases, and only in sectors considered strategic by pink governments (chiefly extractive industries, telecommunications, energy and water utilities), although the list of strategic sectors has increased in the Venezuelan case. The persistence of neoliberal principles such as monetary and fiscal stability, free trade and the promotion of private capital development (including FDI) under pink administrations are not antithetical to enhanced state participation in capitalist production, especially as the latter has been complemented by the continued depoliticization of monetary policy and public–private partnerships.

In Brazil, the state continues to control 40 per cent of the financial system's total assets (25 per cent are controlled by the two largest state-owned banks), although three of the largest ten banks are foreign-owned. The Lula government either privatized or did not affect prior privatizations of public services such as railways, telecommunications and electricity, although regulatory agencies oversee prices. Dilma Rousseff, the protégée of Lula elected to Brazil's presidency in October of 2010, recently argued that 'during the crisis, after the failure of Lehman Brothers, it was [state-controlled] institutions like the Banco do Brasil, Caixa Econômica Federal and the National Development Bank (BNDES) that prevented the economy from being shipwrecked'. Furthermore, the government actively strengthened Petrobras, the state-owned energy giant. 'In other words, Brazil's state capitalism succeeded where the private sector failed' (*The Economist* 2010b). Although the Lula government created eight new state companies (including the revival of state telecommunication monopoly Telebrás, or electricity company Eletrobrás), the government continues to rely heavily on FDI and public–private partnerships, particularly for infrastructural developments. In fact, the line between private and public capital is becoming increasingly blurry, as for example, Petrobras recently purchased a $1.4 billion share in Braskem, a large private chemical corporation. At the same time, 'private' national champions such as Vale (mining) and Embraer (aeronautics) have received active government support to compete and invest abroad.

In Bolivia, although Article 308 of the new Constitution states that 'the private accumulation of economic power' will not be allowed to 'endanger the economic sovereignty of the State' and that the 'the right to own private property either individually or collectively [must] fulfil a social function' and 'not harm the collective interest', this is directed primarily at landownership and unproductive latifundios, although progress in land reform remains slow. Although the government re-nationalized companies in the hydrocarbons, mining, telecommunications and energy sectors, it has not undermined property rights, and nationalizations, as in the Venezuelan case, have involved a majority shareholding by the state or the obligation for TNCs to engage in joint ventures with SOEs rather than full-on expropriations. Bolivia's financial sector, although vulnerable to state interference and poorly developed, has remained in private transnational capitalist hands.

In contrast to Morales and Lula's 'moderation' in relation to private ownership of the means of production, the radicalization of the Chávez government following the 2002 coup attempt against his government has manifested itself in nationalizations, expropriations and the maintenance of price controls. The failed coup produced not only a traumatic shift in the social balance of power by undermining the hegemonic capacity of business elites and conservative factions of the army and galvanizing socialists in the Movimiento Quinta República (MVR), it also produced a radicalization of the government's posture in its relationship with capitalist forces, the US and Colombian governments, and a rearticulation of its hegemonic strategy towards 'socialism for the twenty-first century'. The latest phase of the government's trajectory, concurrent to the global economic crisis and declining electoral support for the MVR, has witnessed attacks on private property of the means of production that caused vitriolic critiques in the media. Following nationalizations in the cement, dairy, steel and banking industries in 2008 and in the petroleum, tourism, agribusiness and banking industries in 2009, the government intensified nationalizations in 2010 of both domestic and foreign private businesses. It nationalized all ports and outsourced them to Cuba's state port authority, seized several private banks and brokerage firms. It also took control of several food retailers in a bid to extend its reach over the food supply and to control inflationary pressures. As in Bolivia, recent land reforms have allowed the government to seize unproductive cultivable land and some urban properties. Financial assets are heavily concentrated in the four largest banks, while foreign presence in the financial sector has diminished rapidly. Yet interestingly, state-owned banks only hold about 30 per cent of all banking assets. As 'business confidence' was further undermined by nationalizations, land reform and exchange controls, Venezuela has faced rising capital flight in 2008 and 2009. A capital outflow of US \$3.1 billion in FDI was recorded in 2009, up from US \$349 million in 2008 (Economist Intelligence Unit 2010).

Control of the price of fuel has been maintained through the neoliberal era, and remains in all cases, although the Bolivian government recently made an attempt to liberalize it (implying a 73 per cent increase in fuel prices) in December of 2010, before retracting it in the face of widespread and intensifying popular protests (Chávez 2010). Chávez, possibly mindful of the *Caracazo* of 1989, has criticized the most generous fuel subsidy in the world, especially for gasoline, but maintained gasoline prices below 3 cents per litre over his nearly 12 years in office. However, the government controls almost all prices through regulation and subsidies, while nationalizations have been accompanied by the re-establishment of a series of price controls for public services and utilities and the government is using a non-legislated system of guaranteed minimum prices to protect agricultural producers.

With regard to fiscal and monetary policy, the two central pillars of neoliberalism, budgetary 'austerity'– albeit accompanied by a 'careful' expansion of welfare spending fuelled by commodity price growth – remains prevalent even in Venezuela. Total government expenditures, including consumption and transfer payments, decreased slightly to 34 per cent of GDP in 2010, in part to fight against the recrudescence of inflationary pressures in recent years and as a consequence of the global downturn and declining oil prices in 2009. Monetary stability has remained the cornerstone of all government policies, as government officials remain mindful of the political consequences of hyperinflation. The independence of Central Banks was sustained by the continued governorship of orthodox Henrique Meirelles in Brazil and Juan Antonio Morales in Bolivia. It is enshrined in the 2009 Bolivian Constitution.[10] In Venezuela however, monetary decisions are increasingly controlled by the president, severely undermining the central bank's independence and the depoliticized management of money. Although tight monetary policy between 1998 and 2002 had produced a significant decline of inflation rates, presidential control, in addition to recurrent capital strikes, has caused skyrocketing inflationary rates, in contrast to their effective containment in the other cases: while official statistics have it averaging 27.1 per cent between 2007 and 2009, the actual rate is probably much higher.

Lean state building was never successfully achieved in Bolivia, Brazil and Venezuela, and the WB and IMF systematically complained of the lack of advances in streamlining and civil service reform prior to and during the pink tide (IMF 1997, 2009; WB 2003). However, both the Lula and Morales governments have explicitly fought against state 'fat' to generate government accountability, fight corruption and reduce waste in state administration. The Lula government explicitly requested the intensification of financial and technical assistance by the WB to 'improve the quality of expenditure' and thereby enhance administrative effectiveness, especially in municipal and regional governments, by containing the wage bill and undermining patronage below the federal level (WB 2010: 1). The Morales administration, in turn, forced a reduction of the wages of high-ranking officials in 2006 and passed anticorruption legislation while successfully isolating corrupt MAS officials (including, in recent months, the head of Bolivia's drug enforcement agency). Depoliticized state agencies, chief among them the Bolivian Central Bank (BCB), have remained relatively unscathed, as the incumbency of Juan Antonio Morales until mid-2006 perpetuated a monetarist economic management that persists to this day. The exchange system remains free of restrictions on current international payments and transfers, and no significant controls on capital flows have been imposed (IMF 2009: 1). Interestingly, one of the pillars of the MAS's programme has become macroeconomic stability, in stark contrast with its more radical electoral rhetoric. Not incidentally, the IMF (2007, 2009) has lauded repeatedly the MAS leadership's fight against corruption and waste in the institutions of the state and the increased efficiency of tax collection agencies, although the government has not been able to prevent persistent patronage. The Chávez government, on its side, has tended to perpetuate rentier state capitalism, and rather fostered the formation of alternative power centres beyond the state (see below), and it has only marginally affected the endemic patronage and corruption that characterized preceding governments (WB 2002; Ellner 2008; Buxton 2009).

Concerning trade, the fortunes of all three governments are in large part conditioned by global demand for raw commodities, especially hydrocarbons and minerals, and in general by the terms of trade. The cash lifeline that the US thirst for oil provides to the Chávez government does go a long way towards explaining the ability of the government to remain in power despite capital strikes. Skyrocketing oil prices and an increase in exported oil volumes continue to boost export earnings, which totalled US $32.5 billion during the first half of 2010, up from the US $24.4 billion recorded in the same period a year earlier. These windfall profits from hydrocarbon exports have undoubtedly alleviated the substantial capital flight mentioned previously. The level of imports, however, declined amid a fall in domestic demand and tightened foreign exchange controls.

Despite attempts to diversify production, Venezuela's capital accumulation process remains overwhelmingly dependent on the oil and gas sectors, which constituted, in the former's case, 94 per cent of the country's export earnings, more than 30 per cent of GDP, and almost

50 per cent of government revenues in 2008 (31.5 per cent in 2009). In Bolivia, even without significant private domestic capital formation – a situation prevalent before Morales's election and not caused by the MAS government (Tsolakis 2010b), GDP growth has been more robust (circa 4.5 per cent in 2006 and 2007, 6 per cent in 2008, 4 per cent in 2010). The value of exports increased from $1.6 billion in 2003 to $6.4 billion in 2008 (50 per cent of their value being constituted by hydrocarbons and 30 per cent by minerals and metals), generating an unprecedented positive trade balance of $1.409 billion, just as corporate taxation was increasing significantly, allowing foreign exchange reserves to grow to $8.317 billion by late 2009. Brazil has achieved greater export diversification (transportation equipment, iron ore, soybeans, footwear and coffee) in tandem with the tremendous growth and expansion of SOEs, and it stimulated the quadrupling of inward FDI since 2003 to US $38.5 billion in 2010 (increasing its share of worldwide FDI to 3 per cent as FDI was plummeting worldwide in 2009 and 2010). This includes heavy state participation (shareholding, joint ventures and other capital investments), and in spite of a 42 per cent decline of inward FDI in 2009. The financial uncertainty caused by the crisis affected disproportionally outward FDI by so called 'Brazilian trans-latins', which recalled more than US $10 billion intra-firm loans from their overseas subsidiaries in order to inject funds into parent companies in 2009 (from US $21 billion in outward FDI the preceding year), although foreign equity holdings by Brazilian firms concurrently rose by $4.5 billion, indicating the intensification of transnational portfolio diversification by Brazilian capital.[11] Yet FDI and capital formation in general remains confined primarily to sectors characterized by low-and medium-low technology intensity and high labour intensity. The peripheral character of Latin America is manifest in the fact that total FDI in Latin America constituted a mere 7.6 per cent of the US $1.04 trillion in total FDI worldwide for 2009 (ECLAC 2010).

Trade restrictions remain almost absent in all cases (although non-tariff barriers proliferate, a continuation of the state of play in the 'neoliberal era'), underpinned by the three states' continued membership in the WTO. Brazil's average tariff rate was 7.6 per cent in 2009, Venezuela's 9.4 per cent, and Bolivia's 3.7 per cent. In all three cases, certain import restrictions (for example, sugar in Bolivia), market access barriers in services, complex customs procedures and customs corruption, restrictive regulatory and licensing rules, export subsidies and insufficient protection of intellectual property rights continue to increase the real cost of trade, although it remains exceptionally low by world standards.

In Bolivia, more than one-third of total imports are smuggled into the country to avoid taxation, while Venezuela has intensified its import bans and restrictions in the past year to contain the fiscal deficit and inflation.

With regard to capital and labour 'freedoms', all MDIs continue to criticize the lack of flexibility of labour markets, which hinder business formation and fuel informality. The problem persisted and intensified during the recurrent fiscal and monetary crises of the 1980s and 1990s. All pink governments have successfully struggled to contain organized labour demands for substantial increases in minimum wages, with a view to controlling, yet again, excessive demand and inflationary pressures. Surprisingly, income and corporate taxes remain very low. In Bolivia, the top income tax rate is 13 per cent, the corporate tax rate 25 per cent, and overall tax revenue as a percentage of GDP was 28.5 per cent in 2010. Venezuela's top income and corporate tax rates are 34 per cent and overall tax revenue as a percentage of GDP was only 13.6 per cent last year, demonstrating the centrality of oil rent to its accumulation of capital. However, although Venezuela's 1999 Constitution generally provides equal treatment for foreign and domestic investors, the government restricts investment in certain sectors. Furthermore, it controls foreign exchange and fixes the exchange rate, while the repatriation of capital, dividends or profits at the official rate requires authorization.

Despite the continuation of neoliberal tenets, substantial achievements are observable in all cases, albeit with varying degrees of redistribution and capital controls. Raw data demonstrates the pink tide's quite unprecedented material improvements for the majority of the population, combined with high levels of capital accumulation fuelled by the worldwide economic boom of the mid-2000s. In all three countries, poverty rates have declined substantially (by 30 per cent in the Bolivian and Brazilian cases, by more than 50 per cent in Venezuela), GDP per capita and minimum and real wages increased considerably, despite high inflationary pressures. Material inequality, however, has only decreased marginally except in the Venezuelan case, while real wages in all cases remain lower than in the early 1980s. It is not incidental that, despite numerous management (in the oil sector) and capital strikes (various production cuts in the oil and agribusiness sectors, and significant capital flight) since 2002, the Chávez government achieved the greatest progress in terms of redistribution and poverty reduction, using windfall oil rents to expand the financing of health, housing and other welfare services and to increase wages.[12] While FDI and public–private partnerships in the form of joint ventures and technology transfers have been actively promoted by the Brazilian and Bolivian governments, including in those sectors in which nationalizations have taken place (and which historically attracted foreign capital), constraints on private capital accumulation remain, chief among them the assertiveness of organized labour, of which state restrictions are a reflection. The transnational capitalist bloc articulating business associations, TNCs, conservative party elites entrenched in key state agencies and MDIs have averted structural change in all cases, but at the cost of unwillingly accepting some resource redistribution to subaltern forces.

'Anti-imperialism'?

Domestic developments, traversed by foreign collaboration with domestic forces to oppose reforms, must be placed within worldwide and macro-regional processes of social and institutional change. The Bolivian, Brazilian and Venezuelan spaces are torn by the contradictory initiatives of Bolivarian allies, other neighbouring states, the US State Department, TNCs and MDIs. It appears that the dialectical result has been the protection of private property (which has been dented to a greater extent in Venezuela) as well as fiscal and monetary discipline, the persistence of depoliticized economic management, but also restrictions on private accumulation in sectors considered as strategic. One could superficially refer to more of the same by finding parallels with prior revolutionary situations in all three cases. Yet this would overlook profound social changes within and beyond these national spaces, including at one level the shifting centre of economic gravity towards East Asia, European stagnation and US imperial overstretch, and at a deeper and less transparent level, the temporary frailty and reconsolidation of the transnational historic bloc and MDIs through the re-disciplining of labour and the elimination of unfit domestically-oriented capitalists since the collapse of the financial system in September 2008 in the absence of an existing alternative social model and power bloc. The process of internationalization of the state seems to be persisting in the cases of Brazil and Bolivia (in Venezuela the presence of MDIs was more limited during neoliberal reform and only partially produced internationalization), and it is manifestly redirecting Morales- and Lula-sponsored reforms. Yet internationalization is also distorted by the development of alternative forms of multilateral cooperation and the penetration of subaltern forces in the executive and legislative institutions of the state. Concurrent internal and external institutional struggles are thus placing states on unpredictable *capitalist* developmental paths.

The overarching aims of free trade, fiscal and monetary stability point to a consolidation of existing forms of governance. At the same time, the active promotion of macro-regional integration projects and of FDI by East Asian powers and by Latin American SOEs are indicating that governments have been taking advantage of geoeconomic transformations to promote a multi-polar balance by constructing a new power bloc. The alternative macro-regional projects built by pink governments enter in contradiction with the continued integration of Latin American states into global governance institutions (IMF, WB, WTO). The reconfiguration of the region's geo-political balance became increasingly manifest as pink governments, having rejected the US's continental market integration project, the Free Trade Area of the Americas (FTAA), thereafter restricted to different degrees their collaboration with US's 'imperial instruments' (IMF, WB, USAID, DEA and US military). At the same time it actively participated in the creation of new (UNASUR, ALBA, Banco del Sur, IIRSA) and consolidation of existing (Mercosur) regional institutions, all of which explicitly excluded the US government.[13] Taken to the letter, the discourses of charismatic presidents (Chávez, Morales, Kirchner, Lula, Correa, Lugo, Colom) have indeed pointed to the emergence of a new era of regional development counterpoised against US (and in its shadow, European) imperialism (García 2006; Robinson 2008; Lievesley and Ludlam 2009). The Chávez government has gone furthest in reconfiguring its relationship with the WB and IMF by pre-paying all outstanding debt in 2007, interrupting existing projects and reducing the physical presence of the WB to a Liaisons Bureau, thereby severely curtailing the capacity of influence of the latter in Venezuela, although the WB had been scaling back its financial and technical assistance since the arrival in power of Chávez (WB 2002). In contrast, MDIs' investment portfolio remains significant in both Bolivia and Brazil (WB 2006, 2009, 2010, 2011).

These international realignments and their potential to challenge neoliberal hegemony must be taken with caution. Many of the electoral victories of the left were pyrrhic, as conservative and liberal parties reversed the tide in the majority of the cases. Several left-leaning presidents were forced to form liberal-conservative coalition governments (Chile, Panama) while several bastions of conservatism resisted the pink tide, in the cases of Peru and Mexico, by a whisker.[14]

Furthermore, in almost every Latin American country, MDIs and US and European development agencies have maintained their physical presence and pursued their close collaboration with key government agencies: central banks, finance ministries, corporate and financial regulatory agencies, but also regional and local levels of the administration. In other words, the pink tide is not a flood.

The continued integration of national states into global governance institutions, then, enters in contradiction with the alternative macroregional project built by the Venezuelan, Cuban, Bolivian, Nicaraguan, Dominican and Ecuadorian governments. Hugo Chavez's alternative to the FTAA, the ALBA,[15] is founded on a creative approach to regional integration that aims to dissolve the cash nexus binding the world market through the creation of alternative, de-monetized and expanding circuits of international exchange based on solidarity and welfare provision (the exchange of oil for medical services is the conventional example) (Harris and Azzi 2006; Lievesley and Ludlam 2009). The ALBA system of integration purposely prioritizes social needs and poverty reduction above private accumulation and private ownership. Its guiding principles are solidarity, complementarity and the reduction of asymmetries through compensatory financing. Its principal lines of activity have been direct support for projects directly benefitting the poorest social strata, nonreciprocal and compensated trade arrangements (i.e., direct product exchanges), and concessional financing for the reduction of energy import bills for state-owned enterprises and for social and physical infrastructural projects (Girvan 2008).

ALBA's expansion has signified the dissolution of the FTAA, and it is an indication of a profound reconfiguration of bilateral relationships between the US and Latin America. However, four fundamental constraints have undermined this project. Firstly, ALBA's exchanges of services continue to intersect with established circuits of capital, and they are quantitatively too limited to undermine money discipline. They constitute drops of water in a sea of market relations. Secondly, the other regionalist Chavez-Morales initiative, the *Banco del Sur*, which seeks to provide an alternative to IMF lending, unwittingly undermines the ALBA by incorporating a notoriously Conservative government (Colombia) and by offering micro-credit to small entrepreneurs. This is a striking example of the expansion of capital through a process of primitive accumulation into rural areas, including indigenous communities, hence undermining communitarian production purportedly defended by the MAS in Bolivia. More importantly, its capital of $20 billion is dwarfed by that of conventional development institutions and its political impact is likely to be minimal. Third, the ALBA is a top-down initiative that has no roots in labour and indigenous movements, affecting both the depth and breadth of its impact on transnational production relations. Fourth, the Bolivarian bloc intersects with a multilevel regional and global governance complex which dwarfs its size and potential success, and a multitude of bilateral integration projects (ranging from joint ventures, military cooperation, infrastructure development, commercial agreements, to the fight against cocaine production and narco-trafficking),[16] which legally constrain government policies. Crucially, most Latin American governments have refused to join ALBA and instead worked towards the consolidation of Mercosur and continental energy integration (the construction of a pipeline from Venezuela to Argentina, for instance).[17] An unprecedented movement towards interstate cooperation and peaceful conflict resolution fostering a macro-regional transnational network of interest, despite conflicts among new Latin American government officials, may potentially sustain the formation of a macro-regional bloc with enhanced power in the global appropriation of social surplus. Nonetheless, ALBA is manifestly not the prominent institutional crystallization of regional integration drives.

Participatory democracy?

A lot has been made of the centralization of power in the executive organs of the state, especially under Chávez and to a lesser extent Morales. The evidence shows that the portrayals of the Bolivarian movement merely as a manifestation of authoritarian attempts to centralize power in the person of Chávez and his direct entourage, through populist discourses and the reproduction of pre-existing clientelistic practices, are severely distorted and historically myopic (Ellner 2008; Lievesley and Ludlam 2009; Petras and Veltmeyer 2009). Highly centralized executive power is a hallmark of these countries' constitutional orders. Centralization, facilitated by existing presidential systems, was profoundly intensified through the depoliticization of economic management and state internationalization during the era of 'democracy-cum-neoliberalism'. In all cases, forms of 'hybrid' or 'coalitional' presidentialism continue to define the workings of these governments, although the transient hegemony achieved by the MAS, the MVR's offshoot (United Socialist Party of Venezuela – PSUV, created in 2007) and PT have tended to marginalize minor parties and to considerably reduce, if not eliminate, the need to form government coalitions. The consequences may be positive indeed, as the patronage, corruption and high levels of rotation that characterize the executive agencies of the state in Brazil may be partially alleviated in the Bolivian and Venezuelan cases by reducing the number of 'players' in the patronage game.

The Chavista movement is also far more heterogenous, as a new capitalist faction benefitting from state largesse, bureaucrats, careerists and professional sectors continue to actively support the government and act as a conservative force, advocating a slower, more defensive and conservative pace to the Revolution. The creation of institutions of political participation parallel to the state, such as the *consejos comunales* (neighbourhood-based legislative, cultural and budgetary bodies), and the *misiones sociales* (educational, nutritional, health, collective-entrepreneurial and cultural projects), was precisely aimed at building direct democracy, diffusing political power and kick starting the socialization of production. However, with the steady radicalization of the Chávez government, these parallel organizations were seen increasingly as capable of replacing the traditional and alienating bodies of liberal democracy, although the recent electoral defeats of the PSUV have induced observers to question the revolutionary potential of these new organizational and productive forms.

The democratic shortcomings of the PSUV, but also of the MAS and PT, however, are also rooted in their historical development — their internal authoritarianism and strong-man *caudillismo*, the need to accommodate a vast number of parochial and arguably anti-progressive organizations on their flanks (including some indigenous groups in the Bolivian case) and the consequent blurriness of their long-term social projects. The perpetuation of undemocratic controls inherent to most 'leftist' social organizations (trade unions, political parties and emerging 'plebeian' organizational forms) are historically conditioned elements, located in the *longue durée* of Latin America's social relations.

The central legitimizing instrument for pink government rule, including the consolidation of polyarchy, the expansion of social welfare investment, mandated increases in minimum wages, temporary price controls for foodstuffs and land reform have proven effective, for the time being, in satisfying or reining in the demands of the governments' grassroots (including those 'thin' transnational movements generated by the World and regional Social Forums, for instance). These initiatives have expectably antagonized transnational and domestically- oriented business forces, which had benefitted from and often governed the neoliberal restructuring of social relations in Latin America. The latter's entrenchment in state institutions (senates – except in Venezuela, where the senate was constitutionally abolished – prefectures, municipalities and Central Banks) and their alliances with US and European governments, MDIs and foreign capital (including those conservative forces dominating administrations in Colombia, Peru and other conservative bastions in the region) in favour of the status quo, have hindered social and institutional change although at the cost of heightened welfare spending and capital income taxes.

Contemporary institutional struggles validate conceptualization of the state as a fluid, contradictory organization of subjection. As a social relation constituting and constituted by broader – including 'domestic' and 'foreign' – production relations, the state is a terrain of incessant intra-elite and class struggles (Poulantzas 1978; Tsolakis 2010a), which have regularly threatened to overwhelm the Morales government in Bolivia. They are beginning to severely undermine the hegemonic power of the Chavez government in Venezuela, and they have ensured a mild reformism and imperialistic tendencies underpinned by nationalist discourses in the Brazilian case.

Yet, in the case of Venezuela, the onslaught of capital flight and inflationary pressures caused by domestic capital (especially in food production) is beginning to bear fruits, and the radicalization of the government is undermining its dominance despite growing oil rents. There are serious indices that the PSUV's hegemony is losing steam, as its (admittedly close) defeat in the 2007 referendum on Constitutional reform, due to the abstention of many *chavistas*, has been followed by the loss of regional governorships and advances made by the opposition in the 2010 parliamentary elections. The ideological and economic crisis affecting the Chávez government's ability to generate order and change explains to a large extent its decision in April 2011 to increase the minimum wage by 26.5 per cent and public sector wages by 40 per cent. These changes were made in order to contain the substantial declines in the purchasing power of workers due to inflation, while Chávez realistically urged workers to use their increased incomes responsibly, in the 'fight against speculation, since every time we raise wages the capitalists raise prices', and demanded that people steer clear from 'the very consumerism that capitalism itself promotes' (Reardon 2011). Whereas the PT has achieved unprecedented hegemony in Brazil, the MAS in Bolivia has unwittingly initiated a new cycle of upheavals by seeking to improve its fiscal position and fight against trafficking by liberalizing fuel prices before retracting this decision in the face of mass upheavals.

Conclusion

Following the rich tradition of historical materialist scholarship, I have approached neoliberal restructuring and the pink tide dialectically and holistically. I traced the capacity of pink governments to articulate effectively state capitalist and anti-liberal discourses as 'grassroots' political parties and to consolidate their hegemonic power within their respective social spaces, to the unsustainable social contradictions that underlay neoliberal governance in the region.

The trajectory of Latin America in the latest phase of capital globalization has been shaped by the confrontation between transnational elites, domestically-oriented elites and labour forces in 'civil society' but also within the institutions of states. The radical programmes of social and state restructuring engineered by transnational forces from the mid-1980s were regularly undermined by social resistance. Democratization in the late 1970s faced the disciplining effects of capital strikes, fiscal and inflationary crises, which in turn allowed capitalist elites to take the initiative in the mid-1980s and 'lead' democratization processes by articulating neoliberal discourses forging 'necessary' linkages between economic and political liberalization. In the case of Venezuela, the attempts of the AD-COPEI leaderships to maintain a veneer of representation by silencing and marginalizing left factions in their respective parties and to repress 'anti-systemic' mobilizations were rapidly frustrated by the violence of the Caracazo and subsequent attempts by leftist military officers with links in the poor neighbourhoods of major cities to eventually take power through the urns.

Struggles for and against neoliberal restructuring and for the production of a new social model of development in all three cases were a manifestation of common structural processes, although the divergences observed during and since the so-called 'neoliberal era' are reflections of the internal and external balance of social forces in these countries and the ability of governments to muster collective agency in order to shape production patterns in the context of capital globalization.

The pink governments themselves are reflections of the intensity of struggle and the structural power of subaltern forces in the region. While in most cases governments have sought to give social mobilizations a 'state form' that would alleviate class struggles, only in the case of Venezuela has there been 'a genuine attempt to push the state form to the limit, to open it out into real forms of popular control' (Holloway 2007:1). This explains the extraordinary animosity of media and mainstream academia towards the *Chavista* movement and its 'imperialistic' use of oil rents to finance socialism abroad.

Protracted struggles by conservative forces, including within the MAS, PT and PSUV, have ensured the protection of private property as well as fiscal and monetary discipline, thereby severely undermining any revolutionary potential of the policies designed by the Morales and Chavez governments in Bolivia and Venezuela, and limiting the impact of welfare investments in Brazil. In cases in which the assertiveness of governments against capitalist forces has been excessive (for example, in Venezuela), rampant inflationary pressures and recurrent capital strikes have sustained the discipline of money.

I have therefore emphasized structural continuity in emergent forms of accumulation and governance. Directly prior to (Brazil, Venezuela) or immediately after (Bolivia) the electoral victories of the MAS, the MVR and PT on the back of widespread mobilizations, they immediately faced the discipline of capital. The historical trauma of the debt and inflationary crises of the 1980s and 1990s has taken its toll on government intransigence towards capital. Lula, faced with a run on deposits and capital flight prior to his investiture, assured 'markets' of his commitment to pursuing his predecessor's restructuring efforts – a promise he made good on. The expansion of state participation in transnational capital accumulation – through outward FDI and the promotion of joint ventures between SOEs and private capital – has intensified the capitalist form of the Brazilian state. In the cases of Venezuela and Bolivia, neither governments have abolished private property of the means of production, nor have they taken a radical anti-imperialist stance by outlawing FDI, foreign ownership and profit repatriation, although the Chávez government has intensified its confrontation against capitalist forces in the past couple of years just as the hegemony of his Bolivarian movement is beginning to wane. Indeed, 'what they are doing is normalizing regulatory relations in the face of exceptional profits' (Lievesley 2009: 24). Hence, pink governments have paradoxically been consolidating the functional relationship between capital and the state by maintaining fiscal and monetary stability.

Labour co-optation through welfare spending and wage increases has been facilitated by a favourable geoeconomic context characterized by the insatiable demand for natural resources of East and South Asian state- society complexes, a partial disengagement of the US, the unprecedented 'generosity' of MDIs (especially towards the Morales administration) and heightened investments by TNCs, especially in extractive industries and despite higher taxes on capital income.

These advances, in a favourable global context up to 2008, have all improved the material conditions of the majority in all three cases, and explain the extraordinary popularity and continued electoral success of pink leaders. Yet elite struggles against the redistributive reforms implemented by the Venezuelan and Bolivian governments have regularly threatened to overwhelm them (a coup attempt and management strike in the oil sector in Venezuela in 2002, opposition-led upheavals, including illegal referenda on autonomy statutes in hydrocarbon-rich regions through 2008 in Bolivia). On its side, the Lula administration has achieved quite unprecedented social stability, benefitting from the economic boom of the mid-2000s, alliances with transnational capital and MDIs, a 'reconstituted' 'middle-class', and crucially, the co-optation of dominant factions of the CUT and the MST. It has manoeuvred expertly the labyrinthine coalitional presidentialist system founded on proportional representation (based on a d'Hondt system that fosters the proliferation of small parties) and a highly decentralized governance form, by effectively co-opting, controlling or marginalizing minority parties and revolutionary forces.

The rhythms and the forms taken by accumulation, class struggles and hegemony vary across the globe, and within regions. The hegemonic movement of neoliberal concepts of control is a case in point: the crisis of neoliberal hegemony in Latin America preceded the worldwide economic crisis that followed the bankruptcy of Lehman Brothers in 2008. The economic crisis itself has tended to affect Latin American governments positively: the deep recessions affecting the US and the EU have given them breathing space to further regional integration (ALBA, UNASUR) and allowed them to build capacity to project both capital and power abroad. At the same time, rising raw commodity prices, especially minerals, metals and hydrocarbons, have allowed governments to pursue the expansion of welfare programmes sustaining their misnamed 'post-neoliberal' hegemonic blocs. They have also allowed geo-strategic realignments with Chinese and Indian TNCs. Whereas the temporary crisis of neoliberal hegemony in Europe and the US has paradoxically reinvigorated neoliberal restructuring efforts (radical labour and pension reforms, anti-welfarist discourses), in the case of Latin America, the crisis has reinvigorated state capitalism.

Although it is too early to predict the medium- and long-term social and political impact of these aforementioned struggles, of the incumbency of the Obama administration in the US, and of the worldwide economic crisis in the region, in view of the fact that pink governments have not erased capitalist social forms and that the Latin American space is undergoing an intensification of its integration into worldwide market relations, incessant elite resistance and class struggles, including within state institutions, will most likely continue to imperil their transient hegemony.

Notes

1. Imperialism is conventionally defined in two ways, which are not inconsistent but rather perceived to have historically sustained each other: (1)

imperialism as an over-accumulative need by metropolitan capital to appropriate resources and labour on its periphery – through portfolio capital or, increasingly, FDI – in order to expand the market for commodities produced in the metropolis and thereby alleviate structural crises of over-production; and (2) as political-military domination in international relations (Clarke 2001; Halliday 2002; Sutcliffe 2002).

Neoliberalism and the left are contested concepts. So is their validity with regard to the pink tide. There is unfortunately no space to produce a more elaborate discussion of their conceptualizations. It is generally accepted that the left consists in the constellation of organized social forces that profess a commitment to egalitarianism (the reduction of material disparities through wealth redistribution), participatory democracy (the effective diffusion of decision-making power to subaltern forces) and some form (and different degrees) of labour decommodification and/or structural change (Panizza 2005; Cameron and Hershberg 2009; Ellner 1993: 15; Cleary 2006: 36; Tsolakis 2011).

Neoliberalism, in turn, is conceived here as ideology, a set of concepts of control articulated to reproduce and project the hegemonic power of transnational capitalist forces, i.e., a transnational hegemonic project (Van der Pijl 1998; Overbeek 2004; Harvey 2007).

2. Subalternity is understood here in the context of counter-hegemonic practices and forces, including the working class – waged labour in the dialectical movement of capital accumulation – and those social forces at the margins of expanding capital circuits, which tend towards integration into the world market through a process of primitive accumulation and labour commodification (Van der Pijl 1998).

3. Populism is presented as a perverted expression of the left, a 'politics of antipolitics' that rests on the instrumentalization and galvanizing of subaltern movements by populist leaders, 'privileg[ing] majoritarianism over the checks and balances of liberal politics' (Panizza 2005: 721–722).

4. In contrast to Realist understandings of 'hegemony' as dominance in inter-state relations, neo-Gramscian approaches define it as the ideological power of ruling over subaltern classes within a given 'national' social formation but also globally, which generates and sustains social cohesion and order (Gramsci 1971: 169–170; Van der Pijl 1998: 51).

5. As in Mexico and Colombia, Venezuela was exempt from the repressive wave of authoritarian military-civil historic blocs that scarred the rest of the region in the 1960s and 1970s. Yet it was never incorporated in the 'Lockean' space characterized by the consensual or hegemonic dominance of capital (Robinson 1996; Van der Pijl 1998). The Venezuelan social formation was governed by a bicephalous 'democratic' pact, the so-called *puntofijismo*, between the two dominant parties Acción Democrática (AD) and Partido Social Cristiano de Venezuela (COPEI), which alternated in office and, unable to legitimize high poverty rates and rising inequality levels, resorted systematically to coercion to maintain order (Ellner 2008).

6. Authoritative accounts, from various perspectives, include Pastor (1987); Williamson (1990); Sachs (1989, 1990); Dunkerley (2007); Conaghan and Malloy (1995); Robinson (1996, 2008); Whitehead (2002); Buxton and Phillips (1999a, 1999b); Kohl and Farthing (2005).

7. Considering the systematic emphasis on 'state', in particular 'government-building' in internal documents produced by neoliberal multilateral institutions (IBRD 1993: 12; DAC 1989: 31), understandings of neoliberalism as a 'retreat of the state' are rejected here (Strange 1996).
8. http://www.doingbusiness.org/rankings
9. http://www.heritage.org/Index/Country/Venezuela
10. Article 327 of the new Constitution enshrines the depoliticization of the BCB (*Asamblea Constituyente de Bolivia* 2007).
11. Outward FDI by Bolivian firms are unsurprisingly insignificant, while 98 per cent of Venezuela's US $1.8 billion in Outward FDI in 2009 is in the hydrocarbon sector, reflecting the extreme concentration of Venezuela's transnational production networks.
12. http://oit.org.pe/WDMS/bib/publ/documentos/salarios-latinoamerica_1995-2006.pdf
13. IMF: International Monetary Fund
    DEA: Drug enforcement agency.
    USAID: United States Agency for International Development
    UNASUR: *Unión de Naciones Suramericanas* (Union of South American Nations)
    IIRSA: *Iniciativa para la Integración de la Infraestructura Regional Suramericana* (Initiative for the Integration of the Regional Infrastructure of South America)
    Mercosur: *Mercado Común del Sur* (Southern Common Market)
14. It is too early to assess the consequences of the recent election of Ollanta Humala to the presidency in Peru.
15. See official website of ALBA at http://www.alternativabolivariana.org accessed 16 January 2009.
16. Recently, the Bolivia-Brazil Action Plan was established by the Morales and Roussef governments to fight against cocaine production and replace the DEA, which was expelled from Bolivia in 2008 for political interference.
17. Morales antagonized the Brazilian administration in 2006 by achieving a substantial increase in the price of gas exported to Brazil as well as Argentina (from $3.40–$3.60 to $5 per million Btu) and by forcing Petrobras to sell Bolivia's two biggest refineries (operating in Santa Cruz and Cochabamba) to YPFB in June 2007. YPFB took over all the shares, assets and liabilities, including oil derivative supply in Bolivia.

10
Beyond Neoliberal Imperialism? The Crisis of American Empire

Bastiaan van Apeldoorn and Naná de Graaff

A cursory reading of the confidential US diplomatic cables thus far released by Wikileaks appears to confirm two notions about the nature of US power in the current world order that we also find in some of the recent literature. First, that after the end of the Cold War the US has succeeded in creating a truly global empire, which it proactively seeks to maintain through the exercise of both hard and soft power in all corners of the world (on the contemporary US empire see, e.g., Johnson 2001; Bacevich 2002; Wood 2003 and Harvey 2003). Second, that in spite of these efforts, the US finds it increasingly hard to maintain the global order it has created, to actually make other states comply and effectively carry out its agenda, and to control events and shape outcomes – a fact subsequently even more dramatically illustrated by the unexpected 'Arab Spring'.

Whether terminal – as the late Giovanni Arrighi (2005) argued – or not, few would dispute that currently we observe a crisis of US hegemony, one that has not been caused, but certainly has been aggravated by the global financial and economic crisis that started at the very centre of the Empire (Konings 2010). The theme of US hegemonic decline has thus made a comeback and the limits of the American empire have once more become visible (cf. Colás 2008; Layne 2009a). Arguably more aware of these limits than its predecessor, the current Obama administration knows that sustainable economic growth is essential in restoring US power and leadership. The question, however, is on what kind of growth model or accumulation strategy such a sustained recovery is going to be based, since the neoliberal accumulation strategy, centred on the interests of the most transnationally oriented sections of US capital, has been shown to suffer from deep internal contradictions.

In this chapter, we will argue that it has been on the basis of such an accumulation strategy that since the end of the Cold War the US has pursued an imperial geopolitical strategy aimed at creating and maintaining a US-centred neoliberal world order. Although they became more visible in the aftermath of the 2008 'great crash', the contradictions of this strategy were in fact already coming to the surface earlier on. Indeed, US *neoliberal* imperialism – as a particular variety of American imperialism – already had entered into a crisis at the end of the 1990s and was then transformed into what we with David Harvey (2003) call *neoconservative* imperialism. This new geopolitical strategy, however, still rested upon the same neoliberal accumulation strategy. In that sense, neoliberalism was not fully transcended but only modified. Arguably, then, it has been only with the current financial and economic crisis that the crisis of neoliberal American imperialism more broadly understood has become fully manifest. This then raises the question of whether and how yet the US may be able to transform its project of global empire. In order to assess this we must go beyond a structural analysis and recognize that geopolitical strategy is always made by particular actors (in our case US state managers) *within their particular social context*. Adopting this perspective, we will analyse the corporate affiliations of key foreign policy-makers in both the current and the previous administration. The analysis indicates that the strong underlying continuities in US geopolitical strategy that we observe, and in particular the continuing adherence to a neoliberal accumulation strategy, can to a large extent be explained in terms of the strong ties between US geopolitical strategy-makers and US transnational capital.

After having briefly described the origins of US capitalist imperialism in the middle of the nineteenth century and its evolution into the post-war era, the next section will analyse the rise of the neoliberal form of this imperialism, its culmination into Clinton's neoliberal globalization strategy and within the context of its rising contradictions, its transformation into a neoconservative strategy under Bush, which, however, continued to be premised on a neoliberal growth model. The final section analyses how the crisis of the latter has formed the context in which Obama is now formulating 'his own' geopolitical strategy. We will conclude that this strategy, though containing some new elements and emphases, not only continues Bush's emphasis on coercion, but also for now continues to bear a strong neoliberal imprint.

The origins and evolution of US imperialism from the civil war to the Cold War

With the end of the American civil war in 1865, and hence the victory of the industrial capitalism of the North over the slave plantation economy of the South, US expansionism turned from territorial expansion (across the American continent) to economic, non-territorial, i.e., capitalist expansion (LaFeber 1998). The US thus became, as Ellen Wood argues, the first capitalist empire, ruling primarily through 'the economic mechanisms of capitalism' (Wood 2003: x; see also Colás 2008). Since, then, the overarching goal of American imperialism has been, in the thesis developed by historian William Appleman Williams (2009), to ensure and maintain around the world an 'Open Door' to US capital.

The material basis for this Open Door imperialism lay in America's growing economic power as the US became the world's largest economy in the period between 1870 and 1913 (Madisson 2003: 261). This was accompanied by a growing expansionism of American capital as the domestic market became saturated and new opportunities to reinvest accumulated capital were increasingly difficult to find internally. Enabling this expansion of American capital, helping, in the words of President Woodrow Wilson (quoted in Williams 2009: 58) 'American industries... to find a free outlet to the markets of the world' has since become a primary objective of American foreign policy. The class basis of this capitalist imperialism lay in the rise of a corporate capitalist class that came to exercise its hegemony over the US state, including its foreign policy-making apparatus. Although the Open Door is about a decisively 'non-colonial imperial expansion' (Williams 2009: 50), forcing and keeping the doors open to American capital also involves – next to the use of all kinds of diplomatic and financial sticks and carrots – the use of America's preponderant military to put in place and prop up US (investor)-friendly, 'free market' regimes and generally to defend the 'open door world' from any ideological, political or military force that could threaten it with closure (Layne 2006). These more general and enduring characteristics of US imperialism, which originated in the nineteenth century, were consolidated and projected on a much larger scale in the post-war era.

The making of the post-war liberal world order

Whereas the notion of US isolationism during the interbellum must be regarded as a myth (LaFeber 1994: ch. 11; Williams 2009: ch. 4), it is true that only with the development of a new accumulation strategy – which first took shape with Roosevelt's New Deal – that the US could create a sustainable material basis for a project of global hegemony (Van der Pijl 1984). The creation of the *Pax Americana* after 1945 is a story that does not need to be rehearsed here. Suffice it to say that through a combination of on the one hand, its productive power – in particular the development and subsequent internationalization of its Fordist growth model – as well as its financial power – in particular the hegemony of the dollar – and, on the other hand its military and geopolitical supremacy, the US was able to create the kind of US-centred and 'institutionalized' liberal world order in which global capital – US capital in particular – could thrive.[1] It thus came to achieve the goals of the Open Door in the major regions of the world, in particular in Europe and in East Asia (Layne 2006).

But the Open Door was first of all an open door to US Fordist industrial capital, with the rise of US multinationals and their expansion into Western Europe (aided by the Marshall Plan) and the rest of the globe. As such, the social purpose served by US imperialism at the time reflected the Fordist class compromise between organized labour and big capital (Van der Pijl 1984), forming the basis of a social power bloc that moreover, and critically, reined in the power of finance. This class configuration was reflected internationally in the Bretton Woods regime that combined liberal internationalism and trade openness with domestic embeddedness (that is, national policy-making autonomy protected by capital controls, see Ruggie 1982; Helleiner 1993; cf. Panitch and Gindin 2008). The leading class fraction within this configuration here emanated from Fordist industrial capital and associated bank capital. It was this leading section of US capital that expanded outwardly, and, in establishing links with Western European capital as a junior partner, entered into a process of what Kees van der Pijl (1984) called the formation of an Atlantic ruling class. The American core of this class formed the corporate elite that dominated America's foreign policy establishments and that through elite think tanks such as the Council on Foreign Relations (Shoup and Minter 2004), and through direct personal ties with policy-makers (Domhoff 1979) came to shape US geopolitical strategy. This strategy, although in the context of the Cold War ostensibly aimed at containing the Soviet Union – was in fact primarily driven by the Open Door objective of expanding open markets that US capital could dominate (Layne 2006).

While within the capitalist core US power rested on a large degree of consent – as reflected in the application of the Gramscian concept of hegemony to this form of imperialism (Cox 1987, Gill 1990, Rupert 1995), more coercive strategies were often in the foreground vis-à-vis the periphery (Westad 2005). That is, the US sought to force open the door to US capital not only by promoting decolonization but also, once the European powers had left (which of course in Latin America had already happened in the previous century), using both its financial and its military muscle to bring to and keep in power the right regimes, that is, the ones welcoming and protecting US investment, or to topple the wrong ones. It was in the context of the world economic crisis of the 1970s that the *Pax Americana* thus created came under pressure but was ultimately renewed and reinvigorated after the end of the Cold War. However, in the meantime, and as a response to the crisis, which was also a crisis of the Fordist accumulation strategy, it had taken on a new, neoliberal form that reproduced the imperialism of the Open Door in a hyper-liberal fashion, promoting the global widening and deepening of commodification.

The post-Cold War era: from neoliberal to neoconservative imperialism

As convincingly argued by a broad literature, neoliberalism can be understood as a concerted response on the part of Western capitalist classes (and arguably an emergent transnational capitalist class) to the crisis conditions affecting global capitalism in the 1970s (e.g., Overbeek 1993; Van Apeldoorn 2002; Harvey 2005). Throughout advanced capitalism, capital was confronted with a crisis of profitability as the Fordist production regime had exhausted itself, and the need arose to restore capitalist class hegemony. Although this project took different shapes and forms, depending on the historical-geographical context, its essence, as also argued in the Introduction of this book, can be captured as advancing dominant capitalist class interests, in particular as tied to global transnational corporations and global financial institutions, through a global project of both deepening and widening marketization and commodification (Overbeek 1993; Harvey 2005). This involved a process of intense capitalist restructuring, re-subordinating labour and restoring capitalist growth and profitability that also had a clearly spatial dimension as production was relocated especially to East Asia. In addition, neoliberalism has been premised on the rise of finance as a hegemonic capital fraction, siphoning off profits from production (cf. Perry and Lewis, and Hager in this volume). As an accumulation strategy, neoliberalism has thus been bound up with the processes of globalization and above all financialization, constituting a clear break with the Bretton Woods era.

In the construction of what became a neoliberal world order, US imperialism has played a crucial role as America's Open Door imperialism came to take on a neoliberal form. We will now examine in more detail the geopolitical strategy through which this neoliberal imperialism came to be pursued, especially in the 1990s.

Neoliberal imperialism and US geopolitical strategy

The neoliberal project originates with the Reagan administration (e.g., Harvey 2005), at which time it was combined with a geopolitical strategy that involved an aggressive stance against the Soviet Union, and a conscious attempt to defeat communism and win the Cold War, both through stepping up the arms race (Van der Pijl 2006: 234), and through an intensification of military interventionism in the Third World (LaFeber 1994: ch. 19; Westad: ch. 9). At the same time, the so-called Volcker shock (the interest rate hike by the new chairman of the Federal Reserve) signalled a new offensive against the Global South by precipitating a debt crisis (McNally 2009: 33–37). This heralded the new neoliberal era in which the South was subordinated to US-centred finance through the operations of the US treasury and the IMF (Soederberg 2004; Felder 2008; Sarai 2008; cf. Hager in this volume). Once the 'evil empire' was defeated, a context had been created in which neoliberalism could be consolidated and turned into a global strategy. Freed from the geopolitical constraints imposed by the Soviet Union, the neoliberal project in the 1990s was thus not only deepened but also came to be reflected in a new American geopolitical strategy during the Clinton Presidency.

The primary focus of this strategy was to promote a US-centred and US-led 'globalization' premised upon and propagating a neoliberal agenda of opening and expanding markets. This indeed is what the real essence of the Clinton Doctrine became: 'to batter down barriers to US trade and especially investment' (LaFeber 2002: 543; cf. Dumbrell 2002: 50). No US president before or after Clinton extolled the virtues of globalization the way he did. Thus in a major foreign policy speech toward the end of his second term, Clinton (1999) stressed that 'we must embrace the inexorable logic of globalization'. He praised the 'giant steps [taken] in opening the global trading system' and identified the continued creation of 'a world trading and financial system that will lift the lives of ordinary people on every continent' and the integration of 'former adversaries' Russia and China into the liberal international system as key objectives of US foreign policy.

Clinton thus translated traditional objectives of 'free trade and … open and equal US access to foreign markets' (White House 1995: 7) into a neoliberal globalization offensive (cf. Van der Pijl 2006) that entailed a renewed drive for not only free trade but also freedom of (US) investment and enterprise. At the discursive heart of this strategy we find the goal of promoting '*market* democracies', a notion that while following the longstanding tradition of the Open Door also clearly reflects neoliberal ideology:

> Our national security strategy is based on enlarging the community of market democracies … The more that democracy and political and economic liberalization take hold in the world, particularly in countries of geostrategic importance to us, the safer our nation is likely to be. (White House 1995: 2)

This global marketization project critically included the liberalization of financial markets, enabling 'capital to flow freely and safely to where it can be used most efficiently to promote growth' (ibid. 1998: 27). The IMF and the World Bank played a key role in enforcing the structural adjustment of the Global South to the exigencies of this new financialized global capitalism. Furthermore, (global) free trade was boosted through the creation of the World Trade Organization (WTO) in 1995 – celebrated by the Clinton administration as a major foreign policy success (ibid.: 34), and regionally through the creation of the North American Free Trade Association as part of the US strategy to 'advance the goal of an integrated hemisphere of free market democracies' (ibid.: 50). In sum, US imperialism came to operate, to a large extent, through neoliberal global governance.

This, however, does not mean that military power was not an integral part of neoliberal imperialism as well. Indeed, military power became a key instrument for the US as an enforcer of the new global neoliberal order, and as such, it was applied regularly, from Somalia to Sudan and Serbia. Yet, the military interventions that the Clinton administration carried out were relatively limited, using air power (rather than ground troops with all the risks of American casualties) as America's weapon of choice in its 'coercive diplomacy' (Bacevich 2002: 155). America's supreme military machine was thus above all given the task of policing globalization. Beyond punishing the miscreants – what came to be called the 'rogue states', a key concept in Clinton's foreign policy (Dumbrell 2002), meaning any regime not willing to follow the rules of US-imposed neoliberal order – the emphasis of neoliberal imperialism generally lay on consent above coercion. Furthermore, although uni-lateralist tendencies were growing, especially towards the end of the millennium, 'multilateralism' was still a favoured concept and foreign policy instrument during the neoliberal imperialism of the 1990s (Dumbrell 2002: 49, 53; cf. Skidmore 2005).[2] Below we will now analyse how this neoliberal strategy ran into its own contradictions and limits and thus gave way to a neoconservative imperialism.

Hegemonic crisis and the neoconservative response

With the benefit of hindsight we can say that the 1990s were the hey-day of neoliberal globalization and unrivalled US power. As such, it was also the highpoint of an American neoliberal imperialism resting upon a measure of transnational consent, i.e., expressing US hegemony. Those days are now over. In fact, we argue that what we view as the intersecting crises of neoliberalism and of US hegemony did not start with the 2008 global financial crash but rather around the turn of the millennium at which point many of the inherent contradictions of neoliberal globalization were already becoming increasingly manifest.

First, internally, that is, within different national state-society complexes (and thus also *transnationally*) neoliberalism produced growing centrifugal tendencies that tended to unravel the social order upon which also neoliberal accumulation is by necessity dependent. This process of disintegration had reached a point at which, according to Harvey (2003: 17), quoting Hannah Arendt, (civil) society appeared to be 'in the process of collapsing back into the aimless senseless chaos of private interests'. Second and related to this fundamental social contradiction, since the end of the 1990s the political limits of neoliberalism had increasingly manifested themselves globally. What increasingly amounted to a transnational revolt against the discipline imposed by neoliberal globalization took on many different shapes and identities: from Hugo Chavez' Bolivarian revolution, to the alter-globalization movement and to some forms of radical political Islam. Third, neoliberal globalization produced new geopolitical tensions as the dynamics of global capital accumulation shifted the centre of gravity of the global economy towards East Asia. This historic shift may be seen as the dialectical outcome of the very project of neoliberal globalization and how it has spread capitalist growth beyond the capitalist heartland. These growth processes, while in the first instance only serving the interests of the US and of US capital with American FDI into China helping to fix its problem of over-accumulation at home (Harvey 2003; McNally 2009), arguably slowly started to challenge American primacy as they have since allowed the emergence of rival centres of accumulation (Arrighi 2005; Van der Pijl 2006).

Together these developments constituted an emergent crisis of US neoliberal hegemony. We contend that it has been in this structural context that a shift from neoliberal to neoconservative imperialism took place (Harvey 2003; see also Arrighi 2005). The neoconservative strategy, we maintain, is not incompatible with neoliberalism but it involves a change with respect to the geopolitical strategy with which the US promotes what is still a project of US-centred neoliberal accumulation. In fact, neoconservatism shares with neoliberalism the central aim of preserving capitalist class power through strengthening the market as the arbiter of social life. Where it goes beyond neoliberalism is in its explicit recognition that the price mechanism alone cannot sufficiently provide order in society. As Harvey (2005: 85) writes, it is this overriding concern with order and the willingness to back up that order through coercion in the face of perceived 'internal and external dangers' that distinguishes neoconservative from neoliberal imperialism. The most crucial part of the neoconservative 'answer' to the political and geopolitical contradictions of the neoliberal project, we would argue, is about how to deal with the 'external dangers'. We will here outline what can be regarded as the key elements of this neoconservative response, i.e., a particular geopolitical strategy (extensively described elsewhere, e.g., Kagan and Kristol 2000; Dueck 2004; Stelzer 2004, and for the most important policy document in which this policy was officially laid out see the *National Security Strategy* of 2002, White House 2002).

First, an unequivocal commitment to maintain the US global primacy, and in particular its military supremacy 'beyond challenge' (White House 2002: 29). Second, a rejection of what was at least a partial postwar commitment to multilateralism and a turn towards an explicitly unilateralist imperialism (cf. Skidmore 2005). Third, what later came to be known as the pre-emptive strike doctrine: the *explicit* claim that the US cannot be constrained by international law in preventing so-called threats to its national security. Finally, the translation of the familiar goal of exporting America's model of liberal democracy (always part of the Open Door ideology; Williams 2009; cf. Monten 2005) into the objective of 'regime change' by military means, if necessary, through full-scale war. These elements subsequently were brought together under and legitimated by the concept of the *war on terror*, which enabled a redefinition of the security environment and the construction of a new and ubiquitous enemy of 'global reach' (White House 2002: 5). In sum, it is the relative shift from consent to coercion that distinguishes neoconservative from neoliberal imperialism.

Neoconservative geopolitical strategy and capitalist class networks

As argued in more detail elsewhere (De Graaff and Van Apeldoorn 2011), in order to understand the neoconservative turn in US imperialism it is insufficient to analyse merely the structural limits of neoliberalism. Rather we should integrate a structural account with an analysis of the agency of so-called neoconservative intellectuals who throughout the 1990s had been articulating a political project that sought to formulate an answer to some of these contradictions and limits of neoliberalism, in particular by outlining and propagating a more coercive US imperial strategy. Instrumental to the spread of these neoconservative ideas in the 1990s has been a dense network of think tanks and policy advocacy groups (with most of the key intellectuals concerned associated with the Project for the New American Century [PNAC], see De Graaff and Van Apeldoorn 2011). While the blueprint for the new strategy thus had been devised by and through this network in the decade before, it was only when George W. Bush took office, an administration that contained a total of 29 of the 52 original signatories of the PNAC, and after the window of opportunity offered by 9/11 – the neoconservatives' own 'Pearl Harbor', that is, the 'catastrophic and catalysing event' that they a year earlier had argued to be required for the desired 'revolutionary change' (PNAC 2000: 51) – that this new geopolitical strategy came to be implemented (on this, and on the role played by 9/11 see e.g., Halper and Clarke 2004: 129–131; Dorrien 2004: ch. 4; Parmar 2005).

As we have shown in previous work (De Graaff and Van Apeldoorn 2011), the people who were part of the original PNAC indeed formed a dense and cohesive neoconservative network as they were heavily connected through (present and past) government affiliations, corporate affiliations and institutional affiliations. Within the last category, we find both established think tanks and policy-planning bodies such as the American Enterprise Institute as well as ad hoc organizations that in the 1990s had been created to further a neoconservative geopolitical strategy such as the Committee for Peace and Security in the Gulf and the Committee for the Liberation of Iraq.

Critically, the neoconservative intellectuals and policy advisors that were thus linked to the second Bush presidency and formed a key set of actors shaping its geopolitical strategy, were no 'free floating intellectuals' but rather organically linked to dominant class interests, in particular those bound up with transnational capital. In fact, having carried out a

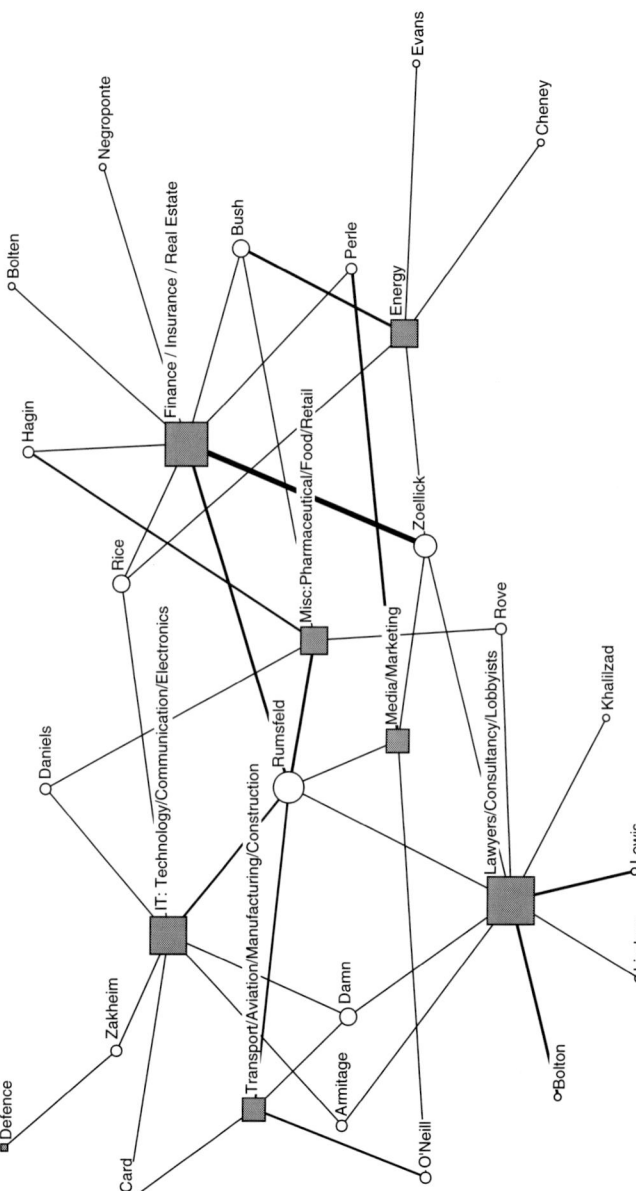

Figure 10.1 Corporate affiliations Bush network 2001 (sectoral composition)

Sources: US government (White House, Pentagon); annual reports; *BusinessWeek*, *Who's Who*; International Relations Center (http://www.irc-online.org/).

Social Network Analysis of what can be regarded as the 30 most important cabinet-ranking officials and senior advisors involved in the making of US foreign policy at the start of the Bush presidency (next to the
president, the secretaries of state and defence and their deputies, and the
national security advisor, this for instance also includes the secretary of
the treasury, and other key foreign *economic* policy-makers) we find that
of these 30 officials, 22 had a total of 89 corporate affiliations before
entering government.[3] It has to be noted that in all cases corporate affiliations here mean top-level positions at the level of the board or equiva-
lent. Below we show the sectoral composition of these corporate ties.

What is striking here is the relative dominance of law and consultancy firms and of finance, or more precisely, finance, insurance and
real estate (FIRE, cf. Hager in this volume). This can be taken as an
indication of the dominance of the more transnationally oriented sections of the American corporate community. Whereas financial institutions evidently represent transnational capital, this in fact also often
applies for the law and consultancy sector because the global business
consultancy and international law firms, which are overrepresented
within this sector, sell their services predominantly to big transnational (industrial and financial) corporations. With regard to finance,
the corporate affiliations include links to Goldman Sachs, Fannie Mae
(inter alia through US trade representative Robert Zoelick), and the then
prominent investment bank Solomon Smith Barney (through the 'big
linker' – with a total of 16 corporate affiliations before 2001 Secretary of
Defense Donald Rumsfeld). In the nonfinancial sector – with in this case
the IT/Communication sector in particular prominently represented –
we again find a dominance of transnational corporations including
Fortune 500 giants such as Chevron, Hewlett Packard (both affiliations
of National Security Advisor Condoleezza Rice), Eastman Kodak and
the notorious Enron, among others. In sum, we can observe how under
Bush the US's geopolitical strategy-makers were closely integrated into a
corporate elite network dominated by US transnational capital.

The continuing close ties to these interests thus help us to explain
the strong continuities – in terms of underlying goals – within the neoconservative geopolitical strategy, in spite of the above noted shifts in
means and emphasis with respect to the neoliberal geopolitical strategy
of the 1990s. The neoconservative project, we argue, while seeking to
compensate for the erosion of consent for neoliberal globalization by
emphasizing coercion in the geopolitical realm, in fact remained firmly
committed to the accumulation strategy that had previously underpinned the neoliberal globalization project (cf. Nederveen Pieterse

2004). The National Security Strategy from 2002 did indeed not just emphasize the coercive powers of US empire, but it also made it clear that this is still about a liberal capitalist empire first and foremost, observing that '[t]he great struggles of the twentieth century between liberty and totalitarianism ended with a decisive victory for the forces of freedom – and a single sustainable model for national success: freedom, democracy, and free enterprise' (White House 2002: preface). Bush's foreign economic policies clearly continued, and in some respects even heightened, the neoliberalism of the Clinton era. So next to a much-discussed 'political freedom agenda' (e.g., Monten 2005), the security strategy from 2002 also contained an extensive agenda for economic freedom, seeking to promote inter alia policies encouraging business investment, low taxation and 'financial systems that allow capital to be put to its most efficient use'(White House 2002: 17–20). It also contained an agenda for generally strengthening 'market incentives and market institutions', including a continuing strong commitment to institutions such as the WTO (ibid. 2006: 25–27).

Leading capitalist interests have moreover at times expressed key vocal support for Bush's policies, including the neoconservative post-9/11 geopolitical strategy. For instance, the US Chamber of Commerce, one of America's most prominent and powerful business lobbies, in its 2002 annual report stated that it 'fully support[s] President Bush's war against terrorism on all fronts' (US Chamber of Commerce 2002: 24). In the process of 'bringing war to the enemy' (ibid.) it moreover envisaged an important role for itself and the corporate community: 'the Chamber is providing the tools necessary to establish democracy, freedom, rule of law, and free market principles in undeveloped and unstable countries – most recently in Afghanistan and Iraq' (ibid.: 23). As Paul Bremer declared shortly after he had been appointed as governor: 'Iraq is open for business'.

In sum, the neoconservative project, as espoused by specific networks of intellectuals and linked to leading capitalist class interests, represented less a fundamental break with the neoliberal project as a specific variety of it. It signalled a shift in above all the geopolitical realm, while in the economic realm neoliberal accumulation increasingly came to take the form of a debt-fuelled, finance-driven expansion of the economy (McNally 2009). When this new bubble, however, burst in 2008, the unfolding crisis came to challenge not only the neoconservative project but also the neoliberal growth model to which it was still tied. It was in this context that Obama assumed office and US imperialism entered into a new phase.

The crisis hits home: the limits of neoliberal accumulation and the deepening contradictions of America's imperial strategy under Obama

Neoconservative imperialism, then, can be seen as a continuation of neoliberal imperialism by different means – that is, a political project for its continuation in the context of its rising contradictions. Though formulating an answer to these contradictions, the neoconservative project has not been able to transcend them, precisely as it was holding on to neoliberalism as an accumulation strategy and a class project. As a geopolitical strategy, the contradictions and limits of the neoconservative project became increasingly apparent in the second term of the Bush presidency.

First, the deliberate choice for a more coercive and openly unilateralist strategy, spurning allies, further eroded the legitimacy of American power in those areas where it still had some. Here the Iraq war has of course been particularly damaging, while this enormously (e.g., Stiglitz and Bilmes 2008) costly war arguably also has not been very effective in furthering (as intended) America's strategic objectives in the Middle East (Layne 2009b). Second, although the neoconservatives recognized the rise of China as one emerging danger for US primacy (Kagan and Kristol 2000), and although according to some analysts the Iraq War was partly intended to gain a strategic advantage vis-a-vis China by controlling the 'global oil spigot' (Harvey 2003: 25), Bush's geopolitical strategy in fact now appears only to have accelerated the arrival of a multi-polar world order in which the US is still the primary power but in which others are narrowing the gap. It has accelerated this structural power shift not only by undermining the legitimacy of American power but also by – through its blatant assertion of US primacy – provoking, in realist terms, a more proactive (even if still 'soft') balancing against the US on the part of emerging rival powers (Layne 2009a; see also Arrighi 2005). Third, and arguably most importantly, by failing to recognize the limits of the neoliberal accumulation strategy that continued to be followed by those transnational sections of US capital to which the neoconservative project was also closely tied, the US continued on the path that would bring it to the great crash of 2008. This in turn has further reinforced the other two trends.

The global financial and economic crisis that erupted towards the end of the Bush presidency thus brought the contradictions and limits of neoliberal accumulation out in the open, also from the perspective of the general capitalist interest. The crisis not only struck the US economy first, its effects also continue to remain more severe in the US than in many other advanced economies. Although the massive bailouts, stimulus packages and money creation by the Fed, have together averted a depression, growth remains sluggish and fragile, while the unemployment rate continues to hover around 9 per cent (excluding a much bigger hidden unemployment), and wages remain depressed. Next to continuingly high levels of private indebtedness – a proximate cause of the crisis – public debt continues to soar as the US is incurring record budget deficits. Adding to America's vulnerabilities (cf. Drezner 2009), nearly half of this public debt is externally financed, with in particular the Chinese buying massive quantities of US treasury bills.[4] Meanwhile, the crisis has been an obvious blow to global policies the US pursued through the Washington-based international institutions. In sum, and especially in light of the still continuing high growth path of the Chinese economy, the crisis has further weakened US power and further accelerated the aforementioned power shift in the global political economy.

It was in this context that Obama won the presidency on a platform of 'change'. Nevertheless, and in spite of the huge bailout first initiated by Bush and the subsequent public anger at Wall Street, and in spite of 'liberal' democrats calling for a reversal of financial deregulation, Obama was not elected on the basis of any project seeking to counter the neoliberalization of the past decades. Furthermore, while Obama had campaigned against the Iraq War, as well as a number of other of Bush's foreign policies, calling for a new kind of American leadership, he had in no way called for any kind of retreat from America's imperialist drive as such (Obama 2007). Yet it was clear, to Obama and his team, that given the above outlined problems into which the neoconservative strategy had run, both in terms of economic policies and in terms of foreign policy, some changes had to be made.

In spite of the 'objective' need for change, however, the most striking feature of the foreign policy conducted by Obama thus far is its continuity, not only with respect to its overall *objectives*, which remain in line with the kind of 'Open Door' capitalist imperialism that has been the hallmark of American grand strategy since the late nineteenth century, but also with respect to his predecessor in terms of the *means* employed, retaining many elements of the neoconservative imperialism outlined above. Thus, while maintaining an 'open international economic system' remains an 'enduring' American interest (White House 2010: 5, 7), the geopolitical strategy pursued by the Obama administration also reveals a continued relative emphasis on coercion in achieving this continued openness. Thus, the most important change with regard to the 'war on terror' is that the name has been dropped. Though employing a partially different rhetoric, Obama has, in fact, in line with what he had announced in his campaign (Obama 2008), expanded the war in both Afghanistan (more than trebling the number of US troops) and in Pakistan (through increased 'drone attacks'), while also expanding America's covert warfare around the world, with US Special Forces active in around 75 countries in 2010, up from 60 in 2009 (DeYoung and Jaffe: 2010). The recent Libya intervention and its justification by what some have dubbed the Obama doctrine (Obama 2011), also underlines that the US, under its current president, is no less inclined to use force.

Nevertheless, there are at least two significant differences with Bush's geopolitical strategy that may point to yet a new variety of US imperialism, and both of these elements can be read as a direct response to the limits and contradictions of neoconservative imperialism that became manifest in the final Bush years. First, the Obama administration somewhat better recognizes the limits of US power in a world arguably shifting towards multipolarity. This leads to a call for more representative international institutions, 'giving a broader voice – and greater responsibilities – for emerging powers' and for more diplomacy and *engagement* with both allies and hostile powers (White House 2010: 3). Although the latter has thus far not proven to be very successful, the renewed emphasis on diplomacy does signal a partial return to at least the rhetoric of multilateralism.

The second and arguably more important new element is the recognition of the importance of the economy and the need for a renewed strategy to sustain the recovery from the 2008–2009 deep recession: 'At the center of our efforts is a commitment to renew our economy, which serves as the wellspring of American power' (ibid.: 2). Indeed, it is striking how much attention Obama's National Security Strategy (NSS) pays to economic issues and policies, including sections devoted to education, science and technology, deemed key ingredients for enhancing US 'competitiveness' (ibid.: 28–34). Yet, what is equally striking, given the depth of the global crisis and how this continues to affect above all the US, is that nowhere is there any indication, either in the NSS, or in other policy documents or indeed in actual policies, of a clear *break with the neoliberal growth model*. The NSS does not go much further than arguing that the US should 'lead international efforts to prevent a recurrence of economic imbalances and financial excesses' (ibid.: 31). Yet, these efforts, e.g., via the G-20, have thus far, not borne much fruit, while global imbalances are currently only growing again.

Internationally, Obama's growth strategy appears to amount to not much more than promoting exports, which it strives to double by 2014 (ibid.: 24). This in fact is likely to imply nothing but a continuation of Open Door imperialism in which solutions to America's economic problems have always been sought externally (LaFeber 1998; Williams 2009; cf. Harvey 2003). In any case, the notion of exporting its way out of the crisis hardly amounts to anything even resembling an alternative accumulation strategy.

It is clear that any viable alternative would have to break with the power of financial capital (and hence with financialization as a source of capital accumulation), and arguably in the case of the US, substitute the current imperialist strategy in which US surplus capital is exported to overcome chronic crises of over-accumulation with one focusing on domestic reform and redistribution (reinvestment) through social expenditures and state investment in new technologies (Harvey 2003: 180–182). On neither front, however, does Obama show any significant movement. Regarding the reform of the financial sector, we cannot entirely dismiss the so-called Wall Street reform package (Dodd-Frank act). What has been dubbed the most radical regulatory overhaul of the US financial sector since the Great Depression has met the fierce opposition of Wall Street and other business lobbies. Yet, these were also successful inasmuch as the new law was ultimately much watered down before it was finally enacted (Dasch and Schwartz 2010). According to Robert Reich, Labour Secretary under Clinton and a prominent 'liberal', the bill 'creates regulatory loopholes big enough for bankers to drive their Jaguars through', neither effectively regulating the derivatives sector nor tackling bonuses (Reich 2010; see also Hager in this volume). In the meantime, as Sandy Hager shows in this volume, the US financial sector (or FIRE) has rapidly recovered from its crisis losses. Regarding the possibility of more *state-led* efforts to enhance the productivity of the US economy, in spite of some talk about stimulating green energy technologies (e.g., White House 2010: 34), the fact of the matter is that without any radical reform, the capitalist US state is practically broke and therefore will not be able to afford such policies. Any social, redistributive reform is also not in the cards. Indeed, Obama has not even succeeded in reversing Bush's tax break for the richest Americans. In the meantime, as we have seen, US foreign policy continues its imperialist outlook.

Colin Hay's notion that the current crisis may be better seen as a set of persistent pathologies as there is simply no viable alternative whereas a proper crisis always carries within it the beginning of something new

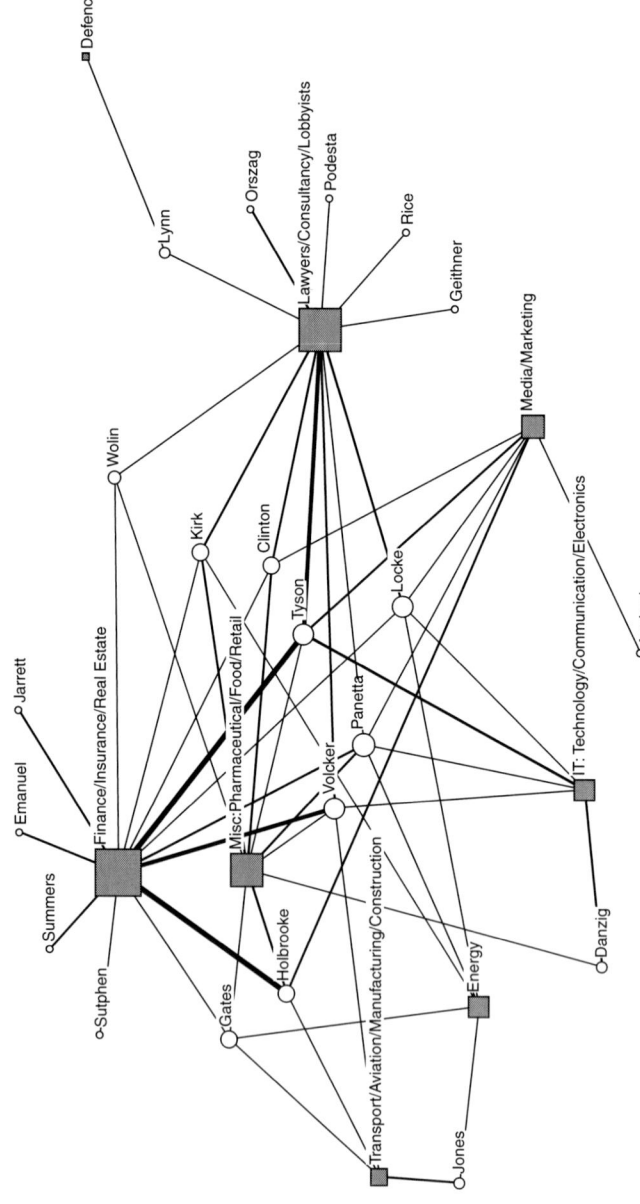

Figure 10.2 Corporate affiliations Obama network 2009 (sectoral composition)

Sources: US government (White House, Pentagon); corporate websites; annual reports; *BusinessWeek*, *Who's Who*; International Relations Center (http://www.irc-online.org/).

(Hay 2011), arguably then also applies to American neoliberal imperialism. But, crucially, such an alternative is also not to be expected as long as those in office are still tied to the same capitalist class interests and concomitant outlook bound up with the old model. This is clearly also the case with the economic and foreign policy team of Obama as we shall see below.

Obama's network of neoliberal grand strategy-makers

Having carried out for the Obama administration the same social network analysis with regard to the corporate affiliations of 30 key officials and advisors as we did for Bush, we indeed find a strong degree of continuity. As with the network of Obama's predecessor, we see strong ties to America's corporate elite, with a total of 22 out of 30 having had a total of 113 corporate affiliations before entering government. Moreover, as Figure 10.2 below indicates, this network is again dominated by the more transnationally oriented 'fraction' of US capital, with again the predominance of the sectors of finance and law firms and consultancies. Prominent corporate affiliations include (former) Wall Street investment banks Merrill Lynch and Morgan Stanley; insurance giants AIG and Prudential and leading transnational corporations such as AT&T, Boeing, Chevron, Coca-Cola, Honeywell, Raytheon and Wal-Mart, as well as international law firms such as McKinsey and Kissinger Associates. Given this continued dominance of US transnational capital within the networks linking Obama's foreign (and economic) policymakers to the corporate community, it seems indeed unlikely that this administration will help to move the US beyond neoliberalism.

What Patrick Bond (2009) has called the Obama neoliberals are in fact partly the same people that were among the main architects of the neoliberal policies pursued under Reagan and Clinton. Most notably among these in the team that came into office in 2009 were Paul Volcker and Larry Summers who respectively became the Chair of the President's Economic Recovery Advisory Board and Director of the White House's National Economic Council. Volcker, a former Chase Manhattan director and later director of inter alia Deutsche Bank, Nestlé and Prudential, was the Chairman of the Fed during the Reagan years (and, as indicated, instrumental in the unleashing of neoliberalism through the Volcker shock). Summers, who after leaving the Clinton administration and serving a stint as chief economist of the World Bank became managing director of hedge fund D.E. Shaw, was as (deputy) Treasury Secretary a key member of Clinton's economic team and in particular tasked with international economic policies focusing on privatization and liberalization. Also, the rest of Obama's economic team, including Timothy Geithner, Treasury Secretary and former Chairman of the Federal Reserve Bank of New York and an important architect of financial deregulation at the time, and Austan Goolsbee, a Chicago School economics professor who now heads another economic policy-making unit in the White House, the President's Council of Economic Advisors, can all be safely identified as neoliberals or what in the US mainstream are called 'centrists' (Bond 2009; Luce 2010).

Both Volcker and Summers have now stepped down from their positions of advising the President, but both have been replaced by men that if anything will only strengthen the ties of Obama to the corporate elite. Directly recruited from that elite is Jeffrey Immelt, CEO of global giant General Electric, and according to *The Washington Post* (Bacon Jr. and Goldfarb 2011) 'one of the most prominent corporate chiefs in the country', who will be the head of the new President's Council on Jobs and Competitiveness (replacing the earlier Recovery Advisory Board). The new Director of the National Economic Council is Gene Sperling, who held the same position during the second term of Clinton, and before joining the Obama administration earned more than a million a year working for Goldman Sachs and via a number of other consultancy jobs and board seats.[5] Obama has moreover further strengthened his business credentials by appointing William Daley, former advisor of President Clinton and later his Secretary of Commerce and in recent years top executive of JP Morgan Chase as well as director at inter alia Boeing and Merck, as his new Chief of Staff (after the departure of Rahm Emmanuel). The appointment, as earlier those of Volcker and especially Summers, provoked howls of protest from the liberal flank of the Democratic Party but was very much welcomed by corporate America, in particular by the US Chamber of Commerce (Rowland 2011).

In sum, also in terms of the actors in place, and the social networks in which they are embedded, we should indeed expect a continuation of neoliberal imperialism rather than any substantive chance. As interests of transnational capital still clearly predominate over the US policy-planning process and beyond their structural power are well represented in the White House itself, social reform at home is not on the agenda and the solution to the crisis will be sought in continuing to prise open and keep open the door to American capital and 'to capitalize on the opportunities presented by globalization' (White House 2010: 32).

Conclusion

In this chapter, we have seen how US imperialism evolved from a neo-liberal to a neoconservative form and currently continues under Obama in what appears to be a strategy that combines elements of both. More important than these variations are in fact the strong underlying continuities, not only in terms of pursuing what broadly may be defined as an Open Door to US capital, but also since the end of the Cold War the reproduction of a neoliberal growth model. These continuities must, above all, be seen in relation to the continued strong embeddedness of US grand strategy-makers in corporate elite networks dominated by US transnational capital. As we have seen, under Obama this has also meant that a break with neoliberalism, in spite of the crisis, is not yet in the cards. The course of American imperialism in this regard hence does not seem to be undergoing a radical change of direction any time soon.

The remaining question, however, is whether in the longer run there is in fact still a future for US imperialism, or rather for American empire, as such. As we have noted in the introduction, there is a case to make that US hegemony is in structural decline, and although that case has been made many times before, there are indeed reasons to believe that, as *Financial Times* commentator Gideon Rachman (2011) has put it, 'this time it is for real'. But although there may be a secular trend of a power shift away from the US, this does not spell an immediate end to American primacy. Indeed, given its still huge military superiority, the fact that it is still the largest economy with many of its transnational corporations still dominant in the global economy, that the dollar, to date at least, is still the international reserve currency (even if that position is under threat) and given that the rules of 'global governance' are still more set in Washington than in Beijing, it will still be quite some time before the US will lose its position of pre-eminence.

In the meantime, the US will continue to stay its imperialist course, and for now, so it seems, in neoliberal mould. If and when the pressures of US decline will further aggravate, and in particular when the (neoliberal) globalization process of which the US has been the main architect and beneficiary will increasingly seem to turn against it, this may surely lead to American imperialism taking on a different form, maybe even beyond the Open Door strategy that it has thus far followed. Indeed, it could take on a less liberal form, aggressively seeking to defend its crumbling empire with forms of violence that would also take us beyond anything the neoconservatives have practiced. In that case, neoliberal imperialism would be replaced by something more frightening and destructive, rather than with a strategy moving us towards a more progressive and equitable world order. For the latter to happen, the political system in the US itself (and arguably also in other countries) would have to fundamentally change – that is, in such a way that it is no longer dominated by the capitalist class interests that we have argued in this chapter have also continued to shape US geopolitical strategy in the post-Cold War era.

Notes

1. On US Fordism as a basis for US hegemony see Rupert 1995, and on how it was internationalized through a 'transatlantic' class project Van der Pijl 1984. On US financial power see e.g., Konings 2008.
2. That the Clinton administration favoured the concept of multilateralism does not mean it fully practiced it. Skidmore (2005: 208–209) clarifies a common misunderstanding regarding US multilateralism by defining the latter as consisting of two elements, one investing 'in the creation and maintenance of international institutions' and two, complying 'with the rules, norms, principles, and decision-making processes of these institutions on an equal basis'. Skidmore argues that US Cold War hegemony was characterized by its commitment to the former but that it never met the second criterion. After the end of the Cold War, Skidmore argues, US commitment to the first element has also been in decline – a decline that set in during (especially the second term of) Clinton but also, as we shall argue below, accelerated and sharpened under George W. Bush.
3. This social network analysis is part of a larger research project. The most comprehensive analysis of these data, which will also cover the Clinton and Obama administrations, will be found in Van Apeldoorn and De Graaff forthcoming.
4. As of May 2011, of the more than 47 per cent of public debt (excluding intra-governmental debt) that is foreign owned, 26.7 per cent, or more than US $1.1. trillion, is owned by mainland China (http://www.treasury.gov/resource-center/data-chart-center/tic/Documents/mfh.txt, retrieved 16 July 2011).
5. See http://www.bloomberg.com/apps/news?pid=newsarchive&sid=abo3ZoOi fzJg, retrieved 16 July 2011.

Bibliography

Abu-el-Haj, J. (2007). 'From Interdependence to Neo-Mercantilism: Brazilian Capitalism in the Age of Globalization', *Latin American Perspectives* 34(5): 92–114.

Aglietta, M. and R. Breton (2001). 'Financial Systems, Corporate Control and Capital Accumulation', *Economy and Society* 30(4): 433–466.

Aglietta, M. and A. Reberioux (2005). *Corporate Governance Adrift: A Critique of Shareholder Value* (Cheltenham: Edward Elgar).

Albert, M. (1993). *Capitalism Against Capitalism* (London: Whurr Publishers).

Albo, G. (2009). 'The crisis of Neoliberalism and the Impasse of the Union Movement', *Development Dialogue* 51 (January): 119–131.

Albo, G., S. Gindin, and L. Panitch (eds) (2010). *In and Out of Crisis: The Global Financial Meltdown and Left Alternatives* (Spectre).

Alchian (1987). 'Rent Theory in Eatwell' in J. Eatwell, Milgate, M. and Newman, P. (eds) *The New Palgrave: A Dictionary of Economics* (London, Macmillan).

Allen, F., R. Chakrabarti, S. De, J. Qian and M. Qian (2006). Financing Firms in India, *European Finance Association*, Zurich Meetings, Zürich.

Allison, Graham (1971). *The Essence of Decision. Explaining the Cuban Missile Crisis.* (Boston: Little, Brown).

ALTER-EU (2008). *Secrecy and corporate dominance: a study on the composition and transparency of European Commission expert groups*, Report by the Alliance for Lobbying Transparency and Ethics Regulation, available at http://www.corporatejustice.org/IMG/pdf/expertgroupsreport.pdf (last accessed 29 July 2011).

Altvater, E. (2009). 'Postneoliberalism or Postcapitalism? The Failure of Neoliberalism in the Financial Market Crisis', *Development Dialogue* 51 (January): 73–86.

Amable, B. (2003). *The Diversity of Modern Capitalism* (Oxford: Oxford University Press).

Amineh, M.P. and H. Houweling (2010). 'China and the Transformation of the Post-Cold War Geopolitical Orde' in M.P. Amineh (ed.) *State, Society and International Relations in Asia. Reality and Challenges* (Amsterdam: Amsterdam University Press), pp. 215–271.

Andrews (2008). 'Greenspan Concedes Error on Regulation', *New York Times*, 28 October, p. B1, http://www.nytimes.com/2008/10/24/business/economy/24panel.html (accessed on 13 May 2011).

Anonymous (1987). 'A Survey of Wall Street; Bustle, Bustle', *The Economist* 304(7506): 1–18.

Anonymous (2007). 'Black Boxes', *The Economist* 383(8529): 11.

Appelbaum, E. and Schettkat, R. (1995). 'Employment and Productivity in Industrialised Economies', *International Labour Review* 134: 605–623.

Arbix, G. (2010). 'Innovation and the Development Agenda', *Economic Sociology: The European Electronic Newsletter* 11(2): 16–23.

Arnott, R. (2004) 'National Oil Company Websites as Primary Sources of Oil and Gas Information', *Journal of Energy Literature* 10(1) (Oxford Institute for Energy Studies).

Arrighi, G. (2005). 'Hegemony Unravelling I', *New Left Review* 32 (March): 23–80.

Arrighi, G. (2008). *Adam Smith in Beijing. Lineages of the Twenty-First Century* (London: Verso Books).

Authers, J. (2009). On the Competing Ideologies behind the Regulatory Debate, *The Financial Times – Future of Finance Supplement, Part two: Regulation and Governance*, 26 October. Available at: http://econpapers.repec.org/paper/cdlissres/1023553.htm (accessed 21 November 2010).

Bacevich, A.J. (2002). *American Empire: The Realities and Consequences of U.S. Diplomacy* (Cambridge, MA: Harvard University Press).

Bacon Jr., P. and Z.A. Goldfarb (2011). 'Immelt to head new advisory board on job creation; Volcker to step down', *Washington Post*, 21 January.

Baran, P. and P.M. Sweezy (1966). *Monopoly Capital: An Essay on the American Economic and Social Order* (New York: Monthly Review Press).

Barnier, M. (2010). *Acting without delay to clean up financial markets*, Speech at the Ecofin Brussels Council, 16 February 2010.

Barrell, R. and Davies, P.E. (2008). 'The Evolution of the Financial Crisis 2007–8', *National Institute Economic Review* 206: 5–14.

BCG Report (2007). 'The 2008 BCG 100 New Global Challengers. How Top Companies from Rapidly Developing Economies Are Changing the World' (Boston: Boston Consulting Group).

Beblawi, H. (1990). 'The Rentier State in the Arab World', in Luciani, G. (ed.) *The Arab State* (London: Routledge), pp. 85–98.

Beck, R. and M. Fidora (July 2008). *The Impact of Sovereign Wealth Funds on Global Financial Markets*, Occasional Paper No. 91, European Central Bank, Frankfurt.

Bellamy Foster, J. and Magdoff, F. (2009). 'The Explosion of Debt and Speculation', *The Great Financial Crisis* (New York, Monthly Review Press).

Bello, W. (2006). 'The Capitalist Conjuncture: Over-Accumulation, Financial Crises, and the Retreat From Globalisation', *Third World Quarterly* 27(8): 1345–1367.

Bellofiore, R., F. Garibaldo and J. Halevi (2010). 'The Global Crisis and the Crisis of European Neomercantilism', in Leo Panitch, Greg Albo and Vivek Chibber (eds), *The Crisis This Time*, Socialist Register 2011, pp. 120–146.

Bennett, R.A. (1982). 'Nervous Bankers Start Striking Back', *The New York Times*, 10 January: 12.

Bergsten, C. Fred (2011). 'Why the World Needs Three Global Currencies', *Financial Times* 15 February.

Berle, A. A. and Means, G. C. (1991 [1932]). *The Modern Corporation and Private Property* (New York: Transaction Publishers).

Bernstein, S., J. Lerner and A. Schoar (2009). *The Investment Strategies of Sovereign Wealth Funds*, Fondazione Eni Enrico Mattei, Nota di Lavoro 25.

Bhaskar R (1979). *The Possibility of Naturalism* (London: Routledge).

Bichler, S. and J. Nitzan (2010). 'Capital as Power: Towards a New Cosmology of Capitalism', *Paper Presented at the 2010 Eastern Economic Association Conference*, 26–28 February, Philadelphia, USA. Available at: www.bnarchives.net/277 (accessed 21 November 2010).

Bieler, A. (2008). 'Co-option or Resistance? Trade Unions and Neoliberal Restructuring in Europe', *Capital and Class* 93: 111–124.

Bieler, A. and A. Morton (2001). 'The Gordian Knot of Agency-Structure in International Relations', *European Journal of International Relations* 7 (1): 5–35.

Bieling, Hans-Juergen (2001) 'European Constitutionalism and Industrial Relations', in Andreas Bieler and Adam D. Morton (eds) *Social Forces in the Making of the New Europe: The Restructuring of European Social Relations in the Global Political Economy* (Basingstoke: Palgrave Macmillan), pp. 93–114.

Bieling, H.J. and Schulten, T. (2003). 'Competitive Restructuring and Industrial Relations within the European Union: Corporatist Involvement and Beyond' in Cafruny, A.W. and Ryner, M. (eds) *A Ruined Fortress? Neoliberal Hegemony and Transformation in Europe* (Lanhan: Rowman & Littefield), pp. 231–260.

Bina, C. (2004). 'The American Tragedy: The Quagmire of War, Rhetoric of Oil, and the Conundrum of Hegemony', *Journal of Iranian Research and Analysis* 20(2): 7–22.

Bina, C. (2006). 'The Globalization of Oil. A Prelude to Critical Political Economy', *International Journal of Political Economy* 35(2): 4–34.

Birch, Kean, and Vlad Mykhnenko (eds) (2010). *The Rise and Fall of Neoliberalism. The Collapse of an Economic Order?* (London: Zed Books).

BIS (2009). *Consultative Document Strengthening the resilience of the banking sector*, December 2009, Basel Committee on Banking Supervision, Bank for International Settlements.

Blanchard, Jean-Marc F. (2011). 'China's Grand Strategy and Money Muscle: The Potentialities and Pratfalls of China's Sovereign Wealth Fund and Renminbi Policies', *The Chinese Journal of International Politics* 4: 31–53.

Bleakley, Fred. R. (1984). 'Bankers Trust Seeks Fed Backing for Commercial Paper Unit', *The New York Times*, 29 December: 1.

Blyth, M. (2003). 'Same as it Never Was: Temporality and Typology in the Varieties of Capitalism', *Comparative European Politics* 1: 215–225.

Bo Zhiyue and Chen Gang (2009). Global financial crisis and the voice of the New Left in China, *EAI Background Brief* 443. Singapore: East Asia Institute of the National University of Singapore.

Böhm-Bawerk, E.V. (1890). *Capital and Interest: A Critical History of Economical Theory* [S.l.], Macmillan.

Bond, P. (2009). 'Realistic Postneoliberalism – a View from South Africa', *Development Dialogue* 51 (January): 193–211.

Borgatti A.M., M.G. Everett and L.V. Freeman (2002). *Ucinet for Windows: Software for Social Network Analysis* (Harvard, MA: Analytic Technologies).

Boyer, R. (2000a). 'The Political in the Era of Globalization and Finance: Focus on Some *Regulation* School Research', *International Journal of Urban and Regional Research* 24(2): 274–322.

Boyer, R. (2000b). 'Is a Finance-led Growth Regime a Viable Alternative to Fordism? A Preliminary Analysis', *Economy and Society* 29(1): 111–145.

Braithwaite, T. (2010). 'Regulators Warned on New Bank Legislation', *Financial Times* 4 November: 15.

Brand, U. and N. Sekler (2009). 'Postneoliberalism: Catch-all Word or Valuable Analytical and Political Concept?', *Development Dialogue* 51: 5–13.

Branford, S. (2009). 'The Lula Government in Brazil: The End of a Dream' in Geraldine Lievesley and Steve Ludlam (eds) *Reclaiming Latin America. Experiments in Radical Social Democracy* (London: Zed Books).

Bremmer, I. (2008). 'The Return of State Capitalism, Survival', *Global Politics and Strategy* 50(3): 55–64.

Bremmer, I. (2010). *The End of the Free Market: Who Wins the War Between States and Corporations?* (Penguin Group USA).

Brenner, N., Peck, J. and Theodore, N. (2010a). 'Variegated Neoliberalization: Geographies, Modalities, Pathways', *Global Networks* 10: 182–222.

Brenner, N., J. Peck, and N. Theodore, (2010b). 'After Neoliberalization?', *Globalizations* 7(3): 327–345.

Brenner, R. (2002). *The Boom and the Bubble: The US in the World Economy* (London: Verso).

Brenner, R. (2004). 'New Boom or New Bubble? The Trajectory of the US Economy', *New Left Review*, 25 January/February: 57–100.

Brenner, R. (2006). *The Economics of Global Turbulence* (London and New York: Verso).

Brenner, R. (2009). 'What is Good for Goldman Sachs is Good for America: The Origins of the Current Crisis', *Institute for Social Science Working Paper Series* UCLA.

Breslin, S. (2003). 'Paradigm Shifts and Time-lags? The Politics of Financial reform in the People's Republic of China', *Asian Business & Management* 2(1): 143–166.

Bridge, G. (2008). 'Global Production Networks and the Extractive Sector: Governing Resource-Based Development', *Journal of Economic Geography* 8: 389–419.

Bridge, G. and A. Wood (2010). 'Less is more: Spectres of Scarcity and the Politics of Resource Access in the Upstream Oil Sector', *Geoforum* 41: 565–576.

Brooks, M. (2007). The Marxist Theory of Crisis. *Socialist Appeal,* available at http://www.socialist.net/marxist-theory-crisis.htm

Bryan, D. and Rafferty, M. (2006). *Capitalism with Derivatives* (Basingstoke: Palgrave Macmillan).

Buch-Hansen, H. (2008). *Rethinking the History of European Level Merger Control. A Critical Political Economy Perspective*, Copenhagen Business School, PhD Series 26/2008.

Buch-Hansen, H. and Wigger, A. (2010). 'Revisiting Fifty Years of Market-Making: The Neoliberal Transformation of European Competition Policy', *Review of International Political Economy* 17(1): 20–44.

Buch-Hansen, H. and Wigger, A. (2011). *The Politics of European Competition Regulation. A Critical Political Economy Perspective* (London and New York: Routledge).

Burnham, Peter (2000). 'Globalization, Depoliticization and "Modern" Economic Management' in Werner Bonefeld and Kosmas Psychopedis (eds) *The Politics of Change: Globalization, Ideology and Critique* (Basingstoke: Palgrave).

Bush, Janet (1989). 'Wall Street: SIA Chips Back into the Fairway', *Financial Times*, 11 December: 16.

BusinessEurope (2010). 'Europe at a Crossroads: Reform or Decline', Madrid, June.

Butt, S., A. Shivdasani, C. Stendevat, A. Wyman (2008). 'Sovereign Wealth Funds: A Growing Global Force in Corporate Finance', *Journal of Applied Corporate Finance* 20(1): 73–83.

Buxton, Julia (1999). 'Venezuela' in Julia Buxton and Nicola Phillips (eds) *Case Studies in Latin American Political Economy* (Manchester: Manchester University Press).

Buxton, Julia (2009). 'Venezuela: The Political Evolution of Bolivarianism' in Geraldine Lievesley and Steve Ludlam (eds) *Reclaiming Latin America. Experiments in Radical Social Democracy* (London: Zed Books).

Buxton, J. and N. Phillips (eds) (1999). *Case Studies in Latin American Political Economy* (Manchester: Manchester University Press).

Cafruny, A.W. and M.J. Ryner (2007). *Europe at Bay: In the Shadow of US Hegemony* (Boulder, CO.: Lynne Rienner).

Callinicos, A. (2010). *Bonfire of Illusions. The Twin Crises of the Liberal World* (Cambridge and Malden, MA: Polity Press).

Calomiris, C. (2000). *U.S. Bank Deregulation in Historical Perspective* (Cambridge: Cambridge University Press).

Cameron, Maxwell (2009). 'Latin America's Left Turns: beyond good and bad,' *Third World Quarterly* 30(2): 331–348.

Cameron, M. and E. Hershberg (eds) (2010). *Latin America's Left Turns: Politics, Policies, and Trajectories of Change* (Boulder: Lynne Rienner).

Cammack, P. (2009). 'Why are Some People Better Off than Others?' in J. Edkins and M. Zehfuss (eds) *Global Politics. A New Introduction* (London: Routledge).

Carchedi, G. (2001). *For Another Europe: A Class Analysis of European Economic Integration* (London: Verso).

Carroll W.K. (2009). 'Transnationalists and National Networkers in the Global Corporate Elite', *Global Networks* 9(2): 289–314.

Carroll W.K. (2010). *The Making of A Transnational Capitalist Class: Corporate Power in the 21st Century* (London and New York: Zed Books).

Carroll W.K. and C. Carson (2003). 'The Network of Global Corporations and Elite Policy Groups: a Structure for Transnational Capitalist Class Formation?', *Global Networks* 3(1): 29–57.

Carroll, W.K. and M. Fennema (2002). 'Is There a Transnational Business Community?', *International Sociology* 17(3): 393–419.

Carroll W.K., M. Fennema and E. Heemskerk (2010). 'Constituting Corporate Europe: A Study of Elite Social Organization', *Antipode* 42(4): 811–843.

Castañeda, J. (2006). 'Latin America's Left Turn', *Foreign Affairs* 85(3): 28–43.

Cerny, P. (1997). 'Paradoxes of the Competition State: The Dynamics of Political Globalisation', *Government and Opposition* 32(2) : 251–274.

CFR (2006). 'National Security Consequences of U.S. oil dependency', *Council of Foreign Relations, Independent Task Force Report No. 58*, John Deutch and James R. Schlesinger – Chairs, CFR, New York.

Chávez, F. (2010). 'Gasolinazo desata huelga indefinida de transporte'. *Inter Press Service*. 27 December. Available at: http://ipsnoticias.net/nota. asp?idnews=97211.

Cheney et al. (2001). 'Reliable, Affordable and Environmentally Sound Energy for America's Future', *Report of the National Energy Development Group* May 2001, Washington.

Chin, G. and E. Helleiner (2008). 'China as a Creditor: a Rising Financial Power?', *Journal of International Affairs* 62(1 Fall/Winter): 87–102.

ChinaStakes (2009). BRIC, SCO Discuss Super-Sovereignty Currency, *ChinaStakes* 26 October.

Chong, A. (2007). 'Singapore's Political Economy, 1997–2007: Strategizing Economic Assurance for Globalization', *Asian Survey* 67(6): 952–976.

Chu, Y. (ed.) (2010). *Chinese Capitalisms: Historical Emergence and Political Implications* (London: Palgrave).

CIEP (2004). *Study on Energy Supply Security and Geopolitics*, conducted by the Clingendael International Energy Programma, Institute for International Relations 'Clingendael', The Hague.

Clark, J. B. (1965 [1899]). *The Distribution of Wealth: A Theory of Wages, Interest and Profits* (New York, Augustus M Kelley).

Clarke, Simon (2001). 'The Globalization of Capital, Crisis and Class Struggle', *Capital and Class* 75: 93–101.

Clark, G.L. and A.H.B. Monk (2009). Nation-state Legitimacy, Trade, and the China Investment Corporation, http://ssrn.com/abstract=1582647.

Clarke, G.L. and A.H.B. Monk (2010). Rethinking the Sovereign in Sovereign Wealth Funds, http://ssrn.com.

Cleary, Matthew (2006). 'Explaining the Left's Resurgence', *Journal of Democracy* 17(4): 35–49.

Clifton, J., F. Comin and D. Diaz Fuentes. (2007). 'Transforming Network Services in Europe and the Americas: From Ugly Ducklings to Swans?', in Clifton, J., F. Comín. and D. Díaz Fuentes (eds) *Transforming Public Enterprise in Europe and North America: Networks, Integration and Transnationalization* (London/New York: Palgrave Macmillan), pp. 3–15.

Cline, W.R. (2010). Renminbi Undervaluation, China's Surplus, and the US Trade Deficit, *PIIE Policy Brief* PB10-20, August.

Clinton, W.J. (1999). *Remarks by the President on Foreign Policy*. Grand Hyatt Hotel, San Francisco, CA: Office of the Press Secretary (February 26). Available at: http://clinton6.nara.gov/1999/02/1999-02-26-foreign-policy-speech.html.

Coates, D. (2000). *Models of Capitalism: Growth and Stagnation in the Modern Era* (Cambridge: Polity).

Cognato, Michael H. (2008). 'China Investment Corporation: Threat or Opportunity?', *NBR Analysis* 19(1): 9–36.

Cohen, B. (2009). 'Sovereign Wealth Funds and National Security: The Great Tradeoff', *International Affairs* 85(4): 713–731.

Cohen, A. and Harcourt, G. (2003). 'Whatever Happened to the Cambridge Capital Theory Controversies?', *Journal of Economic Perspectives* 17(1): 199–214.

Colás, A. (2008). 'Open Doors and Closed Frontiers: The Limits of American Empire', *European Journal of International Relations* 14(4): 619–643.

Collier, D. and J. Mahon(1993). 'Conceptual "Stretching" Revisited: Adapting Categories in Comparative Analysis', *The American Political Science Review* 87(4) (December): 845–855.

Commodity Future Trading Commission (2008) Interagency Task Force on Commodity Markets, Interim Report on Crude Oil, Washington D.C.

Correljé A. and C. van der Linde (2006). 'Energy Supply Security and Geopolitics: A European Perspective', *Energy Policy* 34: 532–543.

Cox, Robert (1981). 'Social Forces, States, and World Orders: beyond International Relations Theory', *Millennium* 10(2). Reprinted in Robert Cox and Timothy Sinclair (1996) *Approaches to world order* (Cambridge: CUP).

Cox, R. (1987). *Production, Power and World Order. Social Forces in the Making of History* (New York: Columbia University Press).

Crabtree, J. (2009). 'Bolivia's Prospects for Transformation' in Geraldine Lievesley and Steve Ludlam (eds) *Reclaiming Latin America. Experiments in Radical Social Democracy* (London: Zed Books).

Crotty, J. (2002). The Effects of Increased Product Market Competition and Changes in Financial Markets on the Performance of Nonfinancial Corporations in the Neoliberal Era. *Working Paper of Political Economy Research Institute, University of Massachusetts, Amherst, USA.*

Crotty, J. (2009). 'Structural Causes of the Global Financial Crisis: a Critical Assessment of the "New Financial Architecture"', *Cambridge Journal of Economics* 33(4): 563–580.

Crouch, C. (2008). 'What Will Follow the Demise of Privatised Keynesianism?', *The Political Quarterly* 79(4): 476–487.

Da Silva, A.G. and Sansom, M. (2009). 'Antitrust Implications of the Financial Crisis: A UK and EU View', *Antitrust* 23(2): 24–31.

Dahlmann, C. J. and Frischtak, C. R. (1993). 'National Systems Supporting Technical Advance in Industry: The Brazilian Experience' in Nelson, R.R. (ed.) *National Innovation Systems: A Comparative Analysis* (Oxford: Oxford University Press), pp. 414–450.

Das, N. (2007). 'The Emergence of Indian Multinationals in the New Global Order', *International Journal of Indian Culture and Business Management* 1(1/2): 136–150.

Dasch, E. and N.D. Schwartz (2010). 'In a Final Push, Banking Lobbyists Make a Run at Reform Measures', *New York Times*, 21 June, p. B01.

Davies, K. (2010). Outward FDI from China and its policy context, *Columbia FDI Profiles*, 18 October.

De Graaff, N. (2011). 'A Global Energy Network? Expansion and Integration of non-triad National Oil Companies', *Global Networks* 11(2) : 262–283.

De Graaff, N. (forthcoming). 'Oil Elite Networks in a Transforming Oil Market' , *International Journal of Comparative Sociology.*

De Graaff, N., and B. van Apeldoorn (2011). 'Varieties of US Post-Cold War Imperialism: Anatomy of a Failed Hegemonic Project and the Future of US Geopolitics', *Critical Sociology* 37(4): 403–427.

De Ville, F. and Orbie, J. (2011). 'The European Union's Trade Policy Response to the Crisis: Paradigm Lost or Reinforced?', *European Integration online Papers. (EIoP)*, 15(2).

Development Assistance Committee (DAC) (1989). Note by the Secretariat. *Development co-operation in the 1990s: working with developing countries towards sustainable and equitable development*, DAC (89)5, 1st Revision, 22 May (Paris: or. English).

DeYoung, K. and G. Jaffe (2010). 'U.S. "Secret War" Expands Globally', *Washington Post* 4 June, p. A01.

Dixon, A. (2010). 'Variegated Capitalism and the Geography of Finance: Towards a Common Agenda', *Progress in Human Geography* 34 (online first): 1–18.

Dølvik, J. E. (1999). *An Emerging Island? – ETUC, Social Dialogue and the Europeanisation of Trade Unions in the 1990s* (Brussels: ETUI).

Domhoff, G. W. (1967). *Who Rules America?* (Englewood Cliffs, N.J: Prentice Hall).

Domhoff, G.W. (1979). *The Powers that Be. Processes of Ruling Class Domination in America* (New York: Vintage Books).

Domhoff, G. W. (2009). *Who Rules America?: Challenges to Corporate and Class Dominance*, 6th edn (McGraw-Hill: New York).

Dominguez, Francisco (2009). 'The Latin Americanization of the politics of emancipation' in Geraldine Lievesley and Steve Ludlam (eds) *Reclaiming Latin America. Experiments in Radical Social Democracy* (London: Zed Books).

Dorrien, G. (2004). *Imperial Designs. Neoconservatism and the New Pax Americana* (Routledge: New York, Oxfordshire).

Dowbor, L. (2009). ,Die Krise aus globaler Sicht und ihre Bedeutung für Brasilien', *Nueva Sociedad*, Sonderheft, 111–132.

Drahokoupil, J. (2009). 'After Transition: Varieties of Political-Economic Developments in Eastern Europe and the Former Soviet Union', *Comparative European Politics* 7(2), 279–298.

Drainville André (1994). 'International Political economy in the Age of Open Marxism' *Review of International Political Economy* 1(1): 105–132.

Drezner, D. W. (2009). 'Bad Debts: Assessing China's Financial Influence in Great Power Politics', *International Security* 34(2): 7–45.

Dueck, C. (2004). 'Ideas and Alternatives in American Grand Strategy, 2000–2004', *Review of International Studies* 30: 511–535.

Duffield, M. (2001). *Global Governance and the New Wars. The Merging of Development and Security* (London: Zed Books).

Dumbrell, J. (2002). 'Was there a Clinton Doctrine? President Clinton's Foreign Policy Reconsidered', *Diplomacy and Statecraft* 13(2): 43–56.

Duménil, G. and D. Lévy (2001). 'Costs and Benefits of Neoliberalism: A class analysis', *Review of International Political Economy* 8(4): 578–607.

Duménil, G. and D. Lévy (2004). 'Neoliberal Income Trends. Wealth, Class and Ownership in the USA', *New Left Review* 30: 105–33.

Duménil, G. and D. Lévy (2011). *The Crisis of Neoliberalism* (Harvard: Harvard University Press).

Duménil, G., M. Glick, and D. Lévy. (2001). 'Brenner on Competition', *Capital & Class* 74: 61–77.

Dunkerley, J. (2007). *Bolivia: revolution and the power of history in the present* (London: Institute for the Study of the Americas).

Eaton, S., and M. Zhang (2008). *Dragon on a Short Leash: An Inside-Out Analysis of China Investment Corporation* (Beijing: CASS).

Eaton, S., and Zhang Ming (2010). 'A Principal-Agent Analysis of China's Sovereign Wealth System: Byzantine by Design', *Review of International Political Economy* 17(3): 481–506.

ECLAC (2010). Foreign Direct Investment in Latin America and the Caribbean 2009 (Santiago: United Nations).

Economist Intelligence Unit (2010). Country Brief: Venezuela. Available at : http://www.economist.com/countries/venezuela/.

EFR (2009). 'EFR Input for the de Larosière Group', Brussels, 10 February 2009.

Ellner, S. (2008). *Rethinking Venezuelan Politics: Class, Conflict and the Chávez Phenomenon* (Boulder: Lynne Rienner).

Ellner, S. and T. M. Salas (2005). 'The Venezuelan Exceptionalism Thesis. Separating Myth from Reality', *Latin American Perspectives* 32(2): 5–19.

Elsenhans, H. (1996). *State Class and Development* (New Delhi: Radiant Books).

Energy Intelligence Group (2008, 2002, 1997). *The Energy Intelligence Top 100: Ranking The World's Oil Companies* (UK: Energy Intelligence Group, Inc.).

Engdahl, W. (2008). 'Perhaps 60% of today's oil price is pure speculation' *Center for Research on Globalisation*, http://www.globalresearch.ca/index.php?context=va&aid=8878, (visited 20 September 2008).

Engelen, E. (2008). 'The Case for Financialization', *Competition and Change* 12(2): 111–119.

Epstein, G. A. (ed.) (2005). *Financialization and the World Economy* (Cheltenham: Edward Elgar).

Epstein, G. and D. Power (2002). The Return of Finance and Finance's Returns: Recent Trends in Rentier Incomes in OECD Countries, 1960–2000. *Working*

Paper of Political Economy Research Institute, University of Massachusetts, Amherst, USA 2002(2).

Erne, R. (2008). *European Unions. Labor's Quest for a Transnational Democracy* (Cambridge: Cornell University Press).

ERT (1988). 'Press statement. Merger regulation', Brussels, 15 June.

ERT (2001). 'Response to the 'Green Paper on the Review of Council Regulation (EEC)', ERT, Competition Policy Task Force, Brussels.

ERT (2009). 'ERT Message to the Informal European Council Meeting (1 March 2009)', Brussels, 24 February.

ETUC (2003). *Modernising Company Law and Enhancing Corporate Governance in the European Union ETUC comments on the Commission Communication* (Com 284), November 2003.

ETUC (2005). *Executive Committee Resolution,* 15–16 March 2005, available at http://www.etuc.org/IMG/pdf/Resolutions_2005-EN-5-2.pdf (last accessed 10 January 2011).

ETUC (2006). *Corporate Governance at European level,* Resolution adopted by the ETUC Executive Committee in their meeting held in Brussels on 14–15 March 2006, available at http://www.etuc.org/a/2250 (last accessed 1 December 2011).

ETUC (2007). Strategy and Action Plan, 2007–2011. Seville 21–24 May 2007, available at http://www.etuc.org/IMG/pdf_Rapport_congress_EN.pdf (last accessed 10 January 2011).

ETUI (2011) *GOODCORP*, see project website http://www.etui.org/Networks/GoodCorp-the-research-network-on-Corporate-Governance (last accessed 12 December 2011).

Euromemorandum (2007). *Full Employment with Good Work, Strong Public Services, and International Cooperation. Democratic Alternatives to Poverty and Precariousness in Europe,* available at http://www.memo-europe.uni-bremen.de/downloads/EM07_final_version_19_Nov.pdf (last accessed 29 July 2011).

EuroMemo Group (2010). *Confronting the Crisis: Austerity or Solidarity.* EuroMemorandum 2010/2011.

European Commission (1975). *Employee representation and company structure in the European Community* COM (75) 570, 12 November 1975.

European Commission (1993). *Growth, Competitiveness, Employment: The Challenges and Ways Forward into the 21st Century* (White Paper, Brussels).

European Commission (2003a). *Modernising company law and enhancing corporate governance in the European Union – a plan to move forward,* COM (2003) 284, 21 May 2003.

European Commission (2003b). *Report of the high level group of independent experts, on cross-border obstacles to financial participation of employees for companies having a transnational dimension,* 18 December 2003.

European Commission (2004). *Industrial Relations in Europe 2004* (Luxembourg: Official Publications of the European Communities).

European Commission (2005). *The economic costs of non-Lisbon.* EC Directorate General for Economic and Financial Affairs, Brussels, March 2005.

European Commission (2007a). 'State Aid: Latest Scoreboard Analyses Harm Done By Illegal Aid', Press Release IP/07/955, Brussels, 28 June.

European Commission (2007b). 'An Energy Policy for Europe', Communication from the Commission to the European Council and the European Parliament, Brussels.

European Commission (2008). *A common European approach to Sovereign Wealth Funds*, Communication from the Commission to the European Parliament, the Council, the European Economic and Social Committee and the Committee of the Regions, Brussels, 27 February 2008, COM(2008) 115 final.

European Commission (2009a). '*State aid scoreboard, Spring 2009 Update. Special edition on state aid interventions in the current financial and economic crisis*', COM(2009) 164, Brussels.

European Commission (2009b). 'Temporary community framework for state aid measures to support access to finance in the current financial and economic crisis', 2009/C83/01.

European Commission (2009c). 'Competition and financial markets. Roundtable 3 on real economy: the challenges for competition policy in periods of retrenchment', OECD, DAF/COMP/WD(2009)12/ADD2, 10 February.

European Commission (2010a). *Europe 2020. A European strategy for smart, sustainable and inclusive growth*, Brussels.

European Commission (2010b). 'Cartel statistics. Situation as of 19 May 2010', http://ec.europa.eu/competition/cartels/statistics/statistics.pdf, date accessed 16 June 2010.

European Commission (2010c). 'Merger statistics. 21 September 1990 to 31 May 2010', http://ec.europa.eu/competition/mergers/statistics.pdf, date accessed 16 June 2010.

European Commission (2010d). Corporate governance in financial institutions and remuneration policies, Green Paper COM(2010) 284, Brussels, 2 June 2010.

European Commission (2011). 'State aid: recovery of illegal State aid gets faster as Commission tightens procedures', press release IP/11/201, 18 February.

European Council (2000). 'Presidency conclusions', Lisbon European Council, 23 and 24 March.

European Parliament (2006) Recent developments in and prospects for company law, INI/2006/2051, Brussels 4 July 2006.

Evans, P. (1979). *Dependent Development: The Alliance of Multinational, State and Local Capital in Brazil* (Princeton: Princeton University Press).

Evenett, S.J. (2003). 'The Cross Border Mergers and Acquisitions Wave of the Late 1990s', *NBER Working Paper,* W9655.

Fama, E.F. and French, K.R. (1997). 'Industry Costs of Equity', *Journal of Financial Economics* 43: 153–193.

Farrell, D., S. Lund, K. Sadan (July 2008). *The New Power Brokers: Gaining Clout in Turbulent Markets* McKinsey Global Institute (www.mckinsey.com/mgi).

Feenstra, R.C. and Hamilton, G.C. (2006). *Emergent Economies, Divergent Paths* (New York: Cambridge University Press).

Felder, R. (2008). 'From Bretton Woods to Neoliberal Reforms: the International Financial Institutions and American Power', in L. Pantich and M. Konings (eds) *American Empire and the Political Economy of Global Finance* (Basingstoke and New York: Palgrave Macmillan), pp. 175–197.

Fernandez, D. G., and B. Eschweiler (2008). *Sovereign Wealth Funds: A Bottom-up Primer* (JPMorgan Research Singapore: JPMorgan Chase Bank).

Financial Times (2006a). 'Welcome to the world of block-thy-neighbour', 4 March.

Financial Times (2006b). 'France in new moves to defend companies', 2 March.

Financial Times (23 September 2009). 'CIC makes food security a priority', p. 28.

Financial Times (28 May 2010). 'CIC "very concerned" over shaky eurozone', p. 1.

Financial Times (18 August 2010). 'China increases foreign access to interbank bond market', p. 2.

Financial Times (19 August 2010) 'China doubles haul of South Korean treasuries as it seeks to diversify', p. 1.

Financial Times (30 November 2010). 'China leads clean energy surge', p. 6.

Financial Times (29 December 2010). 'Beijing wage rises amid fears for the poor', p. 11.

Financial Times (12 January 2011). 'Failed equity plan dogs investment pilot', p. 4.

Financial Times (14 January 2011). 'Beijing edges closer to global role for renminbi', p. 6.

Financial Times (18 January 2011). 'An embarrassment of riches, albeit "unreal"', p. 7.

Financial Times (16 February 2011). 'China's rising wage bill poses risk of relocation', p. 3.

Financial Times (22 February 2011). 'Workers call the tune in China', p. 3.

Financial Times (9–10 April 2011). 'An inflated outlook', p. 5.

Financial Times (13 April 2011). 'Property groups spur rise in Chinese borrowing overseas', p. 15.

Financial Times (16–17 April 2011). 'Beijing poised to let renminbi rise to fight inflation', p. 3.

Financial Times (20 April 2011). 'Singapore aims to be renminbi trade hub', p. 1.

Financial Times (26 April 2011a) 'Chinese investment in Europe: Focus on deals high up value chain', p. 16.

Financial Times. (26 April 2011b). 'Beijing to boost sovereign fund by $200 bn.', p. 1.

Financial Times. (5 May 2011a). 'Chinese poised to amass over $ 1,000bn of foreign assets', p. 4.

Financial Times. (5 May 2011b). 'Mexico buys 100 tonnes of gold in shift from dollar', p. 15

Financial Times. (21 June 2011). 'Trades reveal China shift from dollar', p. 1.

Fisher, I.S.. (1930). *The Theory Of interest* (New York, Macmillan).

Flynn, M. (2007). 'Between Subimperialism and Globalization: A Case Study on the Internationalization of Brazilian Capital', *Latin American Perspectives* 34(6): 9–27.

Foster Carter, A. (1978). 'The Mode of Production Controversy', *New Left Review* 107 (January–February): 47–77.

Foster, J.B. (2010a). 'The Age of Monopoly-Finance Capital', *Monthly Review* 61(9): 1–13.

Foster, J.B. (2010b). 'The Financialization of Accumulation', *Monthly Review* 62(5): 1–17.

Foster, J.B. and H. Holleman (2010). 'The Financial Power Elite', *Monthly Review* 62(1): 1–19.

Foster, J.B. and F. Magdoff (2009). *The Great Financial Crisis: Causes and Consequences* New York: Monthly Review Press.

Foster, J.B. and R.W. McChesney (2010). 'Listen Keynesians, It's the System!', *Monthly Review* 61(11): 1–13.

Foxley, A. and L. Whitehead (1980). 'Economic Stabilization in Latin America: Political Dimensions – Editor's Introduction', *World Development* 8: 823–832.

Froud, J., Haslam, C., Johal, S. and Williams, K. (2000). 'Restructuring for Shareholder Value and Its Implications for Labour', *Cambridge Journal of Economics* 24: 771–797.

Froud, J., Haslam, C., Sukhdev, J. and Williams, K. (2000). 'Shareholder Value and Financialization. Consultancy Promises, Management Moves', *Economy and Society* 29(1): 80–110.

Froud, J., Johal, S., Leaver, A. and Williams, K. (2006). *Financialization and Strategy: Narrative and Numbers* (London: Routledge).

FSA (Financial Services Authority of the United Kingdom) (March 2009). *The Turner Review: A Regulatory Response to the Global Banking Crisis* (London: United Kingdom Financial Services Authority).

Fukuyama, F. (1992). *The End of History and the Last Man* (The Free Press, Avon Books Inc. New York).

Fukuyama, F. (2008). 'The Fall of America, Inc.' *Newsweek*, 13 October, pp. 31–36.

Gajewska, K. (2008). 'The Emergence of a Europan Labour Protest Movement?', *European Journal of Industrial Relations* 14(1): 104–121

Gamble, A. (1988). *The Free Economy and the Strong State. The Politics of Thatcherism* (London: Macmillan).

Gamble, A. (2009). *The Spectre at the Feast. Capitalist Crisis and the Politics of Recession* (Houndmills: Palgrave Macmillan).

García Linera, Á. (2006). 'State Crisis and Popular Power', *New Left Review* 37 (January–February): 73–85.

Gardels, N. (2008). 'Stiglitz: The Fall of Wall Street Is to Market Fundamentalism What the Fall of the Berlin Wall Was to Communism', *The Huffington Post* 16 September (available at: http://www.huffingtonpost.com/nathan-gardels/stiglitz-the-fall-of-wall_b_126911.html, accessed 24 January 2011).

Germain, R. (2010). *Global Politics and Financial Governance* (Houndmills: Palgrave Macmillan).

Gibbon, P., Bair, J. and Ponte, S. (2008). 'Governing Global Value Chains: An Introduction', *Economy and Society* 37(3): 315–338.

Gill, S. (1990). *American Hegemony and the Trilateral Commission* (Cambridge: Cambridge University Press).

Gill, S. (1995). 'Globalisation, Market Civilization and Disciplinary Neoliberalism', *Millennium: Journal of International Studies* 24(3): 299–423.

Gill, S. (2003). *Power and Resistance in the New World Order* (Basingstoke: Palgrave).

Gill, S. (2010). 'The Global Organic Crisis: Paradoxes, Dangers, and Opportunities', available at http://mrzine.monthlyreview.org/2010/gill150210.html.

Gill, S.R. and D. Law (1988). *The Global Political Economy: Perspectives, Problems and Policies* (London: Harvester-Wheatsheaf).

Girvan, N. (2008). 'ALBA, PetroCaribe and Caricom: Issues in a New Dynamic', available at http://www.normangirvan.info/girvan-alba-caricom-may0/ (accessed on 10 January 2010).

Gjerstad, S. and Smith, V.L. (2009). 'Monetary Policy, Credit Extension, and Housing Bubbles: 2008 and 1929', *Critical Review* 21(2–3): 269–300.

Glyn, A. (2006). *Capitalism Unleashed: Finance, Globalization and Welfare* (Oxford: Oxford University Press).

Glyn, A., Hughes, A., Lipietz, A. and Singh, A. (1990). 'The Rise and Fall of the Golden Age', in S.A. Marglin and J.B. Schor (eds) *The Golden Age of Capitalism. Reinterpreting the Postwar Experience* (Cambridge: Clarendon Press).

Goldstein, A. (2002). 'Embraer: From National Champion to Global Player', *CEPAL Review* 77: 97–115.

Goldstein, A. (2007). *Multinational Companies from Emerging Economies* (New York: Palgrave Macmillan).

Gorton, G.B. and A. Metrick (2009). 'Securitized Banking and the Run on the Repo', *Yale International Center for Finance Working Paper* No. 09–14.

Gourevitch, P. A. and Shinn, J. (2005). *Political Power and Corporate Control. The New Global Politics of Corporate Governance* (Princeton and Oxford: Princeton University Press).

Gowan, P. (1999). *Global Gamble – America's Faustian Bid for World Leadership* (London: Verso).

Gowan, P. (2009). 'Crisis in the Heartland: Consequences of the New Wall Street System', *New Left Review* 55: 5–29.

Gramsci, A. (1971). *Selections from the Prison Notebooks* (New York: International Publishers).

Gratius, S. and L. Tedesco (March 2009). 'Bolivia and Venezuela: different political paths', *FRIDE Policy Brief.*

Grebe, H. (1983). 'Excedente sin acumulación' in René Zavaleta (ed.) *Bolivia, Hoy* (Mexico: Siglo XXI Editores).

Greenspan, A. (2007). *The Age of Turbulence: Adventures in a New World* (New York: Penguin).

Gregory, A. and Michou, M. (2007). 'Industry Cost of Capital: UK Evidence', *Working paper of the University of Exeter Centre for Finance and Investment.*

Griffith-Jones, S., and J. Ocampo (2008). *Sovereign Wealth Funds: A Developing Country Perspective*, paper prepared for the workshop on Sovereign Wealth Funds organized by the Andean Development Corporation, London, 18 February 2008.

Grün, R. (2010). 'For a Brazilian Sociology of Finance', *Economic Sociology: The European Electronic Newsletter* 11(2): 10–15.

Gupta, A. (2006). 'Emergence of Indian Multinationals', *Technology Exports* 8(3): 1–12.

Gupta, A. and P.K. Dutta (2005). *Indian Innovation System*, paper prepared for Asia-Pacific Forum on National Systems for High Level Policy Makers.

Hager, S.B. (2010). *The Political Economy of American Investment Banking: From Golden Age to Crisis?*, paper presented at the 2010 Eastern Economic Association Conference 26–28 February, Philadelphia, USA.

Hall, W. (1986). 'Money Centre Banks Challenge Rules on Commercial Paper Business', *Financial Times*, 11 June: 34.

Hall, P. and Gingerich, D. W. (2004). *Varieties of Capitalism and Institutional Complementarities in the Macroeconomy: An Empirical Analysis*, MPIfG Discussion Paper 04/05 (Cologne: Max Planck Institute for the Study of Societies).

Hall, P. and Soskice, D. (eds) (2001a). *Varieties of Capitalism: The Institutional Foundations of Comparative Advantage* (Oxford: Oxford University Press).

Hall, P. and Soskice, D. (2001b). 'An Introduction to Varieties of Capitalism' in Hall, P. and Soskice, P. (eds) *Varieties of Capitalism: the Institutional Foundations of Comparative Advantage* (Oxford: Oxford University Press), pp. 1–68.

Halliday, F. (2002). 'The Pertinence of Imperialism' in Mark Rupert and Hazel Smith (eds) *Historical Materialism and globalization* (London: Routledge).

Halper, S. and Clark J. (2004). *America Alone. The Neo-Conservatives and the Global Order* (Cambridge University Press: Cambridge).

Hancké, B. M. Rhodes and Thatcher, M. (2007). 'Introduction: Beyond Varieties of Capitalism' in Hancké, B., Rhodes, M. and Thatcher, M. (eds) *Beyond Varieties of Capitalism: Conflict, Contradictions, and Complementarities in the European Economy* (Oxford: Oxford University Press).

Harmes, A. (2001). 'Institutional Investors and the Reproduction of Neoliberalism', *Review of International Political Economy* 5(1): 92–121.

Harris J (2009). 'Statist Globalization in China, Russia and the Gulf States', *Science and Society* 73(1): 6–33.

Harrod, J. and O'Brien, R. (eds) (2002). *Global Unions? Theory and Strategies of Organized Labour in The Globalpolitical Economy* (London: Routledge).

Harvey, D. (2003). *The New Imperialism* (Oxford University Press: Oxford and New York).

Harvey, D. (2005). *A Brief History of Neoliberalism* (Cambridge: Oxford University Press).

Harvey, D. (2006 [1982]) *The Limits to Capital* (London and New York: Verso) [First edition originally published by Basil Blackwell: Oxford, 1982]

Harvey, D. (2007). 'Neoliberalism as Creative Destruction', *The Annals of the American Academy of Political and Social Science* 610(1): 21–44.

Harvey, D. (2009). 'The Crisis and the Consolidation of Class Power: Is This Really the End of Neoliberalism?', *Counterpunch* 13–15 (March), available at: http://www.counterpunch.org/harvey03132009.html (accessed on 24 January 2011).

Harvey, D. (2010). *The Enigma of Capital and the Crises of Capitalism* (London: Profile Books).

Hay, C. (2011). 'Pathology Without Crisis? The Strange Demise of the Anglo-Liberal Growth Model', *Government and Opposition* 46(1): 1–31.

Hayes, S.L. and P.M. Hubbard (1990). *Investment Banking: A Tale of Three Cities* (Boston: Harvard Business School Press).

Heemskerk E.M. (2007). *Decline of the Corporate Community. Network Dynamics of the Dutch Business Elite* (Amsterdam: Amsterdam University Press).

Heilbrun, J. (2006). 'Return of the Liberal Hawks; Channelling Kennedy and Truman, Democratic Neocons Want to Beef up the Military and Won't Run from a Fight', *LA Times* 28 May, M.1.

Helleiner, E. (1993). 'When Finance was the Servant: International Capital Movements in the Bretton Woods Order' in Ph. G. Cerny (ed.) *Finance and World Politics* (Cheltenham: Edward Elgar).

Helleiner, E., (ed.) (2009). 'The Geopolitics of Sovereign Wealth Funds', special section in *Geopolitics* 14(2): 300–359.

Helleiner, E., S. Pagliari and H. Zimmermann (eds) (2010). *Global Finance in Crisis. The Politics of International Regulatory Change* (London and New York: Routledge).

Helleiner, E. and T. Lundblad (2008). 'States, Markets, and Sovereign Wealth Funds', *German Policy Studies* 4(3): 59–82.

Helm, D. (2005). 'The Assessment: The New Energy Paradigm', *Oxford Review of Economic Policy* 21(1): 1–18.

Henderson, J. (2008). 'China and Global Development: towards a Global-Asian Era?', *Contemporary Politics* 14(4): 375–392.

Henwood, D. (2010). 'Before and after Crisis: Wall Street Lives on', in Leo Panitch, Greg Albo and Vivek Chibber (eds) (2010) *The Crisis This Time*. Socialist Register 2011. (London: Merlin Press), pp. 83–97.

Hilferding, R. (1910). *Das Finanzkapital: Eine Studie über die jüngste Entwicklung des Kapitalismus* (Wien).

Hobsbawm, E. (1994). *Age of Extremes: The Short Twentieth Century 1914–91* (Cambridge: Michael Joseph).

Hodgson, G.M. (1997). 'The Fate of the Cambridge Capital Controversy', in Arestis, P., Palma, G. and Sawyer, M. (eds) *Capital Controversy, Post-Keynesian Economics and the History of Economics. Essays in Honour of Geoff Harcourt.* London, Routledge.

Hollingsworth, J. and Boyer, R. (1997). *Contemporary Capitalism: The Embeddedness of Institutions* (Cambridge: Cambridge University Press).

Holloway, John (2007). 'Against and beyond the state: an interview with John Holloway', available at www.upsidedownworld.org (accessed on 18 March 2008).

Hoover, K. (2005). '"Mayday" Move in 1975 Led to Low Commissions and New Era for Traders', Investor's Business Daily, 2 May, p. C01.

Höpner, M. (2003). 'Der organisierte Kapitalismus in Deutschland und sein Niedergang' in Czada, R. and Zintl, R. (eds) *Politik und Markt* PVS-Sonderheft 34. (Wiesbaden: VS Verlag für Sozialwissenschaften).

Höpner, M. (2005). 'What Connects Industrial Relations and Corprorate Governance? Explaining Institutional Complementarity', *Socio-Economic Review* 3: 331–358.

Horn, L. (2011). *Regulating Corporate Governance in the EU – Towards a Marketisation of Corporate Control* (Basingstoke: Palgrave Macmillan).

Horn, J., V. Singer and J. Woetzel (2010). A truer picture of China's export machine: China's growth depends less on exports than conventional wisdom suggests, *McKinsey Quarterly*, September 2010.

Howard, M.C. and J.E. King (1992). *A History of Marxian Economics: Volume II, 1929–1990* (Princeton: Princeton University Press).

Hung, H. (2009). 'America's Head Servant? The PRC's Dilemma in the Global Crisis', *New Left Review* 60(November—December): 5–25.

Huntington, S. (1990). *The Third Wave: Democratization in the Late Twentieth Century* (Norman: University of Oklahoma Press).

Hyman, R. (2004). 'The Future of Trade Unions' in Anil Verma and Thomas A. Kochan (eds) *Unions in the 21st Century* (Basingstoke: Macmillan).

Hyman, R. (2005). 'Trade Unions and the Politics of the European Social Model', *Economic and Industrial Democracy* 26(1): 9–40.

IFSL (March 2009). *Sovereign Wealth Funds 2009* (London: International Financial Services London) (www.ifsl.org.uk).

International Monetary Fund (IMF) (October 1998). 'Venezuela: Recent Economic Developments'. IMF Staff Country Report 98/117.

IMF (2007). Bolivia: 2007 Article IV Consultation – Staff Report July. Report No. 07/248.

IMF (October 2008a). *World Economic Outlook* (Washington DC).

IMF (2008b). *Sovereign Wealth Funds – A Work Agenda*, prepared by the Monetary and Capital Markets and Policy Development and Review Departments (Washington: IMF).

IMF (January 2009). Bolivia: Article IV Consultation – Staff Report. Report No. 09/27.

IMF (January 2011). *IMF Performance in the Run-Up to the Financial and Economic Crisis: IMF Surveillance in 2004–07* (Washington: International Monetary Fund).

International Bank for Reconstruction and Development (IBRD) (1993). *Progress Report on Private Sector Development*, 12 March. Prepared for Development Committee Meeting 1 May 1993.

Ivanova, M. N. (2010). Origins of the New Great Collapse: From Marx to Minsky and back to Marx, paper given to the International Studies Association, 16–20 February.

IWG (2008). *Sovereign Wealth Funds. Generally Accepted Principles and Practices 'Santiago Principles'*, International Working Group on Sovereign Wealth Funds (available at www.iwg-swf.org/pubs), last accessed 20 August 2009.

Jackson, G. (2001). 'Comparative Corporate Governance: Sociological Perspectives' in Gamble A. et al. (eds) *The Political Economy of the Company* (Hart Publishers Oxford), pp. 265–287.

Jackson, G. and Deeg, R. (2006). *How Many Varieties of Capitalism? Comparing the Comparative Institutional Analyses of Capitalist Diversity*, MPIfG Discussion Paper 06/02 (Cologne: Max Planck Institute for the Study of Societies).

Jackson, James K. (2008). The U.S. Financial Crisis: Lessons From Sweden. *Congressional Research Service (CRS) Report for Congress*, 29 September http://fpc.state.gov/documents/organization/110770.pdf (last accessed 10 May 2011).

Jácome, Luis (December 2001). 'Legal Central Bank Independence and inflation in Latin America during the 1990s'. *IMF Working Papers* WP 01/212.

Jacques, Martin (2009). *When China Rules the World. The Rise of the Middle Kingdom and the End of the Western World* (London: Allen Lane).

Jaffe et al (2007). The Changing Role of National Oil Companies in International Energy Markets. *Baker Institute Policy Report* 35. (Houston: Rice University, James A. Baker III Institute for Public Policy).

Jen, S. (2007). How Big Could Sovereign Wealth Funds Be by 2015? *Morgan Stanley Research Report* 3 May 2007.

Jessop, R. (1990). *State Theory: Putting the Capitalist State in its Place* (Cambridge: Polity).

Jessop, R. (2007). *State Power: A Strategic-Relational Approach* (Oxford: Polity).

Jessop, R. (2010). From Hegemony to Crisis? The Continuing Ecological Dominance of Neoliberalism, in Birch and Mykhnenko (eds), pp. 171–187.

Jessop, R. (2011). The World Market, Variegated Capitalism, and the Crisis of European Integration, paper presented to the workshop 'The Eurozone in Crisis', Goethe University Frankfurt, 18–19 February.

Jessop, R. (forthcoming). The World Market, Variegated Capitalism, and the Crisis of European Integration, in Petros Nousos, Henk Overbeek and Andreas Tsolakis (eds), *Globalisation and European Integration* (London: Routledge).

Jessop, B. and N.L. Sum (2006). *Beyond the Regulation Approach. Putting Capitalist Economies in their Place* (Cheltenham: Edward Elgar).

Jessop, B., K. Bonnett, S. Bromley and T. Ling (1988). *Thatcherism* (Cambridge: Polity Press).

Johnson, C. (2001). *Blowback: The Costs and Consequences of American Empire* (New York: Henry Holt and Company).

Johnson, S. and J. Kwak (2010). *13 Bankers: The Wall Street Takeover and the Next Financial Meltdown* (New York: Pantheon Books).

Johnson, S. (2009). 'The Quiet Coup', *The Atlantic Monthly* 303(4): 46–56.

Johnson, Simon (2010). *China's lending activities and the US debt, Testimony submitted to the US-China Economic and Security Review Commission Hearing on US Debt to China*, 25 February (www.piie.com/publications/papers/print. cfm?researchid–1502&doc=pub), last accessed 26 April 2011.

Kagan, R. and Kristol, W. (eds) (2000). *Present Dangers: Crisis and Opportunity in American Foreign and Defense Policy* (Encounter Books: San Francisco).

Kahn, Joseph (2006). 'A Sharp Debate Erupts in China Over Ideologies', *New York Times* 12 March.

Kaplinsky, R. and Morris, M. (2001). *A Handbook for Value Chain Research.*

Kaplinsky, R. (1998). Globalisation, Industrialisation and Sustainable Growth: The Pursuit of the nth Rent. *Ids - Institute of Development Studies Discussion Paper* 365.

Kaplinsky, R. (2001). 'Is globalization all it is cracked up to be?', *Review of International Political Economy* 8(1): 45–65.

Kaufman R.K. and B. Ullman (2009). 'Oil Prices, Speculation and Fundamentals: Interpreting Causal Relations among spot and future prices', *Energy Economics* 31: 550–558.

Kaufman, F. (2010). 'The Food Bubble', *Harper's Magazine* 321(1922): 27–34.

Kern, S. (2009). Sovereign wealth funds – state investments during the financial crisis, *Deutsche Bank Research* July 2009.

Kindleberger, C.P. (2000). *Manias, Panics and Crashes: A History of Financial Crises* (Basingstoke: Palgrave).

Kirshner J. (2009). 'Sovereign Wealth Funds and National Security: The Dog that Will Refuse to Bark', *Geopolitics* 14(2): 305–316.

Klare MT (2001). *Resource Wars. The New Landscape of Global Conflict* (New York: Metropolitan/Owl Book).

Klare M.T. (2004). *Blood and Oil. The Dangers and Consequences of America's Growing Dependency on Imported Petroleum* (New York: Metropolitan Books paperback, Owl Books, 2005).

Klein, N. (2008). 'The Fall of Wall Street Should Be for Neoliberalism What Fall of Berlin Wall Was for Communism' lecture to the University of Chicago October Broadcast 6 October 2008. http://www.democracynow.org/2008/10/6/naomi_klein.

Kohl, B. and L. Farthing (2005). *Impasse in Bolivia: Neoliberal Hegemony and Popular Resistance* (London: Zed Books).

Kok, W. (2004). Facing the Challenge – The Lisbon Strategy for Growth and Employment. Report from the High Level Group chaired by Wim Kok, November 2004.

Konings, M. (2008). 'American Finance and Empire in Historical Perspective', in L. Pantich and M. Konings (eds) *American Empire and the Political Economy of Global Finance* (Basingstoke and New York: Palgrave Macmillan), pp. 48–68.

Konings, M. (ed.) (2010). *The Great Credit Crash* (London and New York: Verso).

Kotz, D.M. (2010). 'Financialization and Neoliberalism', in G. Teeple and S. McBride (eds), *Relations of Global Power: Neoliberal Order and Disorder* (Toronto: University of Toronto Press).

Kregel, J. (2010). 'No Going Back: Why We Cannot Restore Glass-Steagall's Segregation of Banking and Finance', *Levy Institute Public Policy Brief Highlights* 107A.

Krippner, G.R. (2005). 'The Financialization of the American Economy', *Socio-Economic Review* 3(2): 173–208.

Kroes, N. (2005). 'Antitrust Reform in Europe: A Year in Practice' speech 05/157, 10 March, Brussels.

Kroes, N. (2007). 'European Competition Policy in a Changing World and Globalised Economy: Fundamentals, New Objectives And Challenges Ahead', speech 07/364, 5 June, Brussels.

Kroes, N. (2009). 'Competition Law in an Economic Crisis', Fiesole, 11 September.

Labaton, S. (2008). 'Agency's '04 Rule Let Banks Pile Up New Debt', *New York Times*, 3 October: 1.

Labban M. (2008). *Space, Oil and Capital* (London and New York: Routledge).

LaFeber, W. (1994) *The American Age: United States Foreign Policy at Home and Abroad 1750 to the Present*, 2nd edn (New York and London: W.W. Norton).

LaFeber, W. (1998 [1963]). *The New Empire: An Interpretation of American Expansion, 1860–1898* – 35th anniversary edn (Ithaca, NY: Cornell University Press).

LaFeber, W. (2002). 'The Bush Doctrine', *Diplomatic History* 26(4): 543–557.

Lardy, N. and P. Douglass (2011). 'Capital Account Liberalization and the Role of the Renminbi', *PIIE Working Paper* Series 11–16 (Washington: Peterson Institute for International Economics).

Larosière, J. De (2009). *Report of the High-Level Group on Financial Supervision in the EU* (Brussels, 25 February 2009).

Lavelle, K. (2008). 'The Business of Governments: Nationalism in the Context of Sovereign Wealth Funds and State-Owned Enterprises', *Journal of International Affairs* Fall/Winter 62(1): 131–147.

Layne, C. (2006). *The Peace of Illusions. American Grand Strategy from 1940s to the Present* (Cornell University Press: Ithaca and London).

Layne, C. (2009a). 'The Waning of U.S. Hegemony – Myth or Reality? A Review Essay', *International Security* 34(1): 147–172.

Layne, C. (2009b). 'America's Middle East Grand Strategy after Iraq: the Moment for Offshore Balancing Has Arrived', *Review of International Studies* 35: 5–25.

Lazonick, W. and M. O'Sullivan (2000). 'Maximizing Shareholder Value: A New Ideology for Corporate Governance?', *Economy and Society*, 29(1): 13–35.

Li Cheng (2007). 'China in the Year 2020: Three Political Scenarios', *Asia Policy* 4(July): 17–29.

Li Cheng (2008). 'China's Fifth Generation: Is Diversity a Source of Strength or Weakness?', *Asia Policy* 6 (July): 53–93.

Li Cheng (2009). 'One Party, Two Coalitions in China's Politics', *East Asia Forum*, 16 August.

Li Cheng (2010). 'China's Midterm Jockeying: Gearing up for 2012 (Part 1 Provincial Chiefs)', *China Leadership Monitor* 31 (February): 1–24.

Li Hong (2011). 'Depoliticization and Regulation of Sovereign Wealth Funds: A Chinese Perspective', *Asian Journal of International Law* 1: 403–422.

Li Minqi (April 2008). 'An Age of transition. The United States, China, Peak Oil, and the Demise of Neoliberalism', *Monthly Review* (www.monthlyreview.org/080401li.php).

Lievesley, G. (2009). 'Is Latin America Really Moving Leftwards? Problems and Prospects' in Geraldine Lievesley and Steve Ludlam (eds) *Reclaiming Latin America. Experiments in Radical Social Democracy* (London: Zed Books).

Lievesley, G. and S. Ludlam, (eds) (2009). *Reclaiming Latin America. Experiments in Radical Social Democracy* (London: Zed Books).

List, F. (1841). *Das nationale System der politischen Ökonomie* (Stuttgart/Tübingen).

Luce, E. (2010). 'A middle course', *Financial Times* 18 May, p. 11.

Lyons, G. (2007). *State Capitalism: The Rise of Sovereign Wealth Funds*, Standard Chartered Bank, Global Research (available at http://banking.senate.gov/public/_files/111407_Lyons.pdf, last accessed 17 August 2009).

Mabro R. (August 2000). 'Oil Markets and Prices', *Oxford Energy Comment*, Oxford Institute for Energy Studies: http://www.oxfordenergy.org/comment_prn.php?0008 (accessed on 11 April 2011).

Mabro R. (2005). 'The International Oil Price Regime. Origins, Rationale and Assessment', *The Journal of Energy Literature* 11(1): 3–20.

Mackinder H.J. (1904). 'The Geographical Pivot of History', *The Geographical Journal* 23: 421–437.

Madisson, A. (2003). *The World Economy: Historical Statistics* (Paris: OECD).

Magdoff, H. and P.M. Sweezy (1987). *Stagnation and the Financial Explosion* (New York: Monthly Review Press).

Magnus, G. (2011). China risks credit-fuelled Minsky moment, *Financial Times* 4 May, p. 8.

Mankiw, G. (2007). *Macroeconomics*, 6th edn (New York: Worth Publishers).

Marcel V. (2006). *Oil Titans; National Oil Companies in the Middle East* (Washington, DC: Brookings and Chatham House).

Markowitz, H. M. (1952). 'Portfolio Selection', *Journal of Finance* 7: 77–91.

Martin, M. F. (2008). *China's Sovereign Wealth Fund*, CRS Report for Congress (Washington, DC: Congressional Research Service).

Marx, K. (1965[1887]). *Capital, Vol. 1* (Moscow: Progress Publishers).

Marx, K. (1991[1894]). *Capital, Vol. 3* (London: Penguin).

Mayer-Ahuja, N. (2006). IT-Arbeitsverhältnisse unter Bedingungen globaler Wirtschaftsintegration. Eindrücke von Veränderungen des indischen Gesellschafts- und Produktionsmodells, in: *SOFI-Mitteilungen* 34: 43–51.

McCartney, H. (2011). *Variegated Neoliberalism. EU Varieties of Capitalism and International Political Economy* (London and New York: Routledge).

McDonough, T., M. Reich, and D.M. Kotz, (eds) (2010). *Contemporary Capitalism and Its Crises. Social Structure of Accumulation Theory for the 21st Century* (Cambridge and New York: Cambridge University Press).

McNally, C. (ed.) (2008). *China's Emergent Political Economy* (London: Routledge).

McNally, D. (2009). 'From Financial Crisis to World-Slump: Accumulation: Financialisation, and the Global Slowdown', *Historical Materialism* 17(2): 35–83.

Mendales, R. E. (2009). 'Collateralized Explosive Devices: Why Securities Regulation Failed to Prevent the CDO Meltdown, and How to Fix it', *University of Illinois Law Review* 5: 1359–1415.

Mendelson, M. (1967). 'Underwriting Compensation', in I. Friend et al. (eds) *Investment Banking and the New Issues Market* (New York: World Publishing Company).

Minsky, H. P. (1982). 'The Financial-Instability Hypothesis: Capitalist Processes and the Behaviour of the Economy' in C.P. Kindleberger and J.P. Laffargue (eds) *Financial Crises: Theory, History and Policy* (Cambridge, Cambridge University Press).

Mirowski, P. and D. Plewhe (eds) (2009). *The Road from Mont Pèlerin: The Making of the Neoliberal Thought* (Harvard: Harvard University Press).

Mishel, L. and J. Bernstein (2007). 'Economy's Gains Fail to Reach Most Workers' Paychecks', *Economic Policy Institute Briefing Paper* 195, available at http://www.epi.org/publications/entry/bp195/

Mommer, Bernhard (2002) *Global Oil and the Nation State* (Oxford University Press, for the Oxford).

Mongiovi, G. (2002). 'Symposium on Piero Sraffa's Legacy in Economics. Classics and Moderns: Sraffa's Legacy in Economics', *Metroeconomica* 53: 223–41.

Monitor Group / FEEM (2009), *Weathering the Storm. Sovereign Wealth Funds in the Global Economic Crisis of 2008*, Monitor Group / Fondazione ENI Enrico Mattei (available at http://www.monitor.com/Portals/0/MonitorContent/documents/Monitor-FEEM_SWF_Weathering_the_Storm_04_2009.pdf), last accessed 20 August 2009.

Monk, Ashby H. B. (2009). *Recasting the Sovereign Wealth Fund Debate: Organizational Legitimacy, Institutional Governance and Geopolitics*, http://ssrrn.com/abstract=1134862.

Monk, A.H.B. (2010). *Sovereignty in the Era of Global Capitalism: The Rise of Sovereign Wealth Funds and the Power of Finance*, http://papers.ssrn.com/sol3/papers.cfm?abstract_id=1587327 (10-04-2010).

Monks, J. (2008). Locusts versus Labour: *Handling the new capitalism*, speech at Harvard University, 16 April 2008.

Monten J. (2005). 'The Roots of the Bush Doctrine. Power, Nationalism, and Democracy Promotion in U.S. Strategy', *International Security* 29(4): 112–56.

Morgan, J. (2009). *Private Equity Finance: Rise and Repercussions* (Basingstoke: Palgrave Macmillan).

Morrison, A. and W. Wilhelm Jr. (2007). *Investment Banking: Institutions, Politics and Law* (Oxford: Oxford University Press).

Morton, A. (2007). *Unravelling Gramsci* (London: Pluto Press).

Mossin, J. (1966). 'Equilibrium in a Capital Asset Market', *Econometrica* 34: 768–83.

Murphy, C.N. (1994). *International Organization and Industrial Change: Global Governance since 1850* (Cambridge: Polity).

Murphy, M., and F. Guerrera (2011). 'Pay-outs bounce back in face of protests', *Financial Times* 10 January, p. 16.

Murray, A. (2004). *A Fair Referee? The European Commission and EU Competition Policy* (London: Centre for European Reform).

Naphtali, F. (1928/1966). *Wirtschaftsdemokratie. Ihr Wesen, Weg und Ziel* (Frankfurt: Europäische Verlagsanstalt).

Nederveen Pieterse, J. (2004). 'Neoliberal Empire', *Theory, Culture & Society* 21(3): 119–140.

New York Times (2008). 'Stopping a Financial Crisis, the Swedish Way', 22 September.

Newsweek (2009). 'The most popular politician on earth', 22 September.

Nitzan J. and S. Bichler (2002). *The Global Political Economy of Israel* (London and Sterling VA: Pluto Press).

Nitzan, J. and S. Bichler (2009). *Capital as Power: A Study of Order and Creorder* (London: Routledge).

Nolan, P. and J. Zhang (2010). 'Global competition after the financial crisis', *New Left Review* 64(July–August): 97–108.

Nölke, A. (2009). 'Finanzkrise, Finanzialisierung und die kapitalistische Vielfalt', *Zeitschrift für Internationale Beziehungen* 16(1): 123–139.

Nölke, A. (2011). 'Die BRIC-Variante des Kapitalismus und soziale Ungleichheit', in Burchardt, H.J. und Wehr, I. (eds), *Der verweigerte Sozialvertrag: Politische Partizipation und blockierte soziale Teilhabe in Lateinamerika* (Nomos: Baden-Baden).

Nölke, A. and Taylor, H. (2010). 'Non-Triad Multinationals and Global Governance. Still a North-South Conflict?' in Ougaard, M. and Leander, S. (eds), *Business and Global Governance* (London and New York: Routledge), pp. 156–177.

Nölke, A. and Vliegenthart, A. (2009). 'Enlarging the Varieties of Capitalism. The Emergence of Dependent Market Economies in East Central Europe', *World Politics* 61(4): 670–702.

NYMEX (2008). New York Mercantile Exchange: http://www.nymex.com/lsco_pre_agree.aspx (visited 20 Sepetember 2008).

Obama, B. (2007). 'Renewing American Leadership', *Foreign Affairs* July/August 86(4): 2–16.

Obama, B. (2008). *Change We Can Believe In: Barack Obama's Plan to Renew America's Promise* (Edinburgh: Cannongate Books).

Obama, B. (2011). 'Remarks by the President in Address to the Nation on Libya', National Defense University, Washington DC, 28 March (http://www.white-house.gov/the-press-office/2011/03/28/remarks-president-address-nation-libya, consulted 18 April 2011).

Odell, P.R. (2006). 'The Long-Term Evolution of the Global Energy Industry', *Geopolitics of Energy* September 28(9).

Organisation for Economic Cooperation and Development (OECD) (2004). *OECD Principles of Corporate Governance.* http://www.oecd.org/dataoecd/32/18/31557724.pdf.

OECD (2008a). *OECD Policy Brief May 2008: Making Trade Work for Developing Countries* (Paris: OECD).

OECD (2008b). *Sovereign Wealth Funds and Recipient Country Policies.* Report by the OECD Investment Committee (Paris: OECD).

OECD (2009). 'The Corporate Governance Lessons from the Financial Crisis', *Financial Market Trends* 01/2009.

OECD (2010). Factbook: *Special Focus: The Crisis and beyond – Financial Conditions – Debt and Securitisation*, Economic, Environmental and Social Statistics.

Oficina Internacional del Trabajo (OIT – *International Labour Organization*) (2008). 'Evolución de los salarios en América Latina 1995-2006', Santiago, October, available at http://oit.org.pe/WDMS/bib/publ/documentos/salarios-latinoamerica_1995-2006.pdf (accessed on 2 June 2010).

O'Sullivan, M.A. (2000). Contests for Corporate Control. Corporate Governance and Economic Performance in the United States and Germany (Oxford: Oxford University Press).

Ouchi, W.G. (1980). 'Markets, Bureaucracies and Clans', *Administrative Science Quarterly* 25: 129–141.

Overbeek, H. (1990). *Global Capitalism and National Decline. The Thatcher Decade in Perspective* (London: Unwin Hyman).

Overbeek, H. (ed.) (1993). *Restructuring Hegemony in the Global Political Economy. The rise of transnational neoliberalism in the 1980s* (London: Routledge).

Overbeek, H. (2000a). 'Globalisation and Britain's Decline', in Richard English and Michael Kenny (eds) *Rethinking British Decline* (Houndmills: Macmillan), pp. 231–256.

Overbeek, H. (2000b). 'Transnational Historical Materialism: Theories of Transnational Class Formation and World Order' in Ronen Palan (ed.) *Global Political Economy: Contemporary Theories* (London: Routledge).

Overbeek, H. (2004). 'Transnational Class Formation and Concepts of Control: Towards a Genealogy of the Amsterdam Project in International

Political Economy' in Bastiaan van Apeldoorn (ed.) Transnational Historical Materialism: The Amsterdam International Political Economy Project *Journal of International Relations and Development* 7(2): 113–141.

Overbeek, H. (2005). Class, Hegemony and Global Governance: A Historical Materialist Perspective, in M. Hoffmann and A. Ba (eds), *Contending Perspectives on Global Governance: Coherence, Contestation, and World Order* (London: Routledge).

Overbeek, H. (2010). 'Global Governance: From Radical Transformation to Neoliberal Management', *International Studies Review* 12(4): 697–702.

Overbeek, H. and K. van der Pijl (1993). 'Restructuring capital and restructuring hegemony: neoliberalism and the unmaking of the post-war order', in H. Overbeek (ed.) *Restructuring Hegemony in the Global Political Economy. The rise of transnational neoliberalism in the 1980s* (London: Routledge), pp. 1–27.

Palan, Ronen, (ed.) (2000). *Global Political Economy. Contemporary Theories* (London: Routledge).

Panitch, L. and Gindin, S. (2005). 'Superintending Global Capital', *New Left Review* 35 (September–October): 101–123.

Panitch, L. and S. Gindin (2008). 'American Finance and Empire in Historical Perspective' in L. Pantich and M. Konings (eds) *American Empire and the Political Economy of Global Finance* (Basingstoke and New York: Palgrave Macmillan), pp. 17–49.

Panitch, L. and S. Gindin (2009). 'The Current Crisis: A Socialist Perspective', *Studies in Political Economy* 83: 7–31.

Panitch, Leo, G. Albo and V. Chibber, (eds) (2010). *The Crisis This Time*. Socialist Register 2011 (London: Merlin Press).

Panizza, F. (1999). 'Brazil', in Julia Buxton and Nicola Phillips (eds) *Case Studies in Latin American Political Economy* (Manchester: Manchester University Press).

Panizza F. (2005). 'Unarmed Utopia Revisited: The Resurgence of Left-of-Centre Politics in Latin America', *Political Studies* 53: 716–734.

Parmar, I.S. (2005). 'Catalysing Events, Think Tanks and American Foreign Policy Shifts: A Comparative Analysis of the Impacts of Pearl Harbor 1941 and 11 September 2001', *Government and Opposition* 40(1): 1–25.

Partnoy, F. and Skeel, D.A.J. (2007). 'The Promise and Perils of Credit Derivatives', *University of Cincinnati Law Review* 75: 1119–1051.

Pastor, M. (1987). *The International Monetary Fund and Latin America. Economic Stabilization and Class Conflict* (Boulder: Westview Press).

Peck, Jamie (2010). *Constructions of Neoliberal Reason* (Oxford: Oxford University Press).

Peck, J. and N. Theodore (2007). 'Variegated Capitalism', in *Progress in Human Geography* 31(6): 731–772.

Peck, J., and A. Tickell (2002). 'Neoliberalizing Space', *Antipode* 34(3): 380–404.

Peck, J., N. Theodore, and N. Brenner (2010). 'Postneoliberalism and its Malcontents', *Antipode* 41(Supplement S1): 94–116.

Perez, C. (2009). 'The Double Bubble at the Turn of the Century: Technological Roots and Structural Implications', *Cambridge Journal of Economics* 32: 779–805.

PES (2007). *Hedge Funds and Private Equity: A Critical Analysis,* report available at http://www.nyrup.dk/cgi-bin/nyrup/uploads/media/Hedgefunds_web.pdf (last accessed 29 July 2011).

Petras, J. (1997). 'Latin America: the Resurgence of the Left', *New Left Review* 223.

Petras, J. and H. Veltmeyer (2009). *What's left in Latin America?: Regime Change in New Times* (Farnham: Ashgate).

Phillips, N. (2004). *The Southern Cone Model: The Political Economy of Regional Capitalist Development in Latin America* (London: Routledge).

Pistor, K. (2009a). Global Network Finance. Organizational Hedging in Times of Uncertainty, *Columbia Law and Economics Working Paper 339* 14 October 2008, available at http://ssrn.com/abstract=1284606, last accessed 3 August 2009.

Pistor, K. (2009b). 'Sovereign Wealth Funds, Banks and Governments in the Global Crisis: Towards a New Governance of Global Finance?', *European Business Organization Law Review* 10: 333–352.

Plehwe, D., B. Walpen, and G. Neunhöffer (eds) (2006). *Neoliberal Hegemony. A Global Critique* (London: Routledge).

PNAC (September 2000). Rebuilding Americas Defenses. Strategy, Forces and Resources For a New Century. *A Report of the Project for the New American Century.*

Polanyi, K. (1944/1978). *The Great Transformation: Politische und ökonomische Ursprünge von Gesellschaften und Wirtschaftssystemen* (Frankfurt: Suhrkamp).

Polanyi, K. (1957). *The Great Transformation. The Political and Economic Origins of Our Time* (Boston: Beacon Press [or. 1944]).

Poulantzas, N. (1978). *State, Power, Socialism* (London: NLB)..

Prins, N. (2004). *Other People's Money: The Corporate Mugging of America* (New York: The New Press).

Prins, N.(2009). *It Takes a Pillage: An Epic Tale of Power, Deceit and Untold Trillions* (Hoboken NJ: John Wiley & Sons).

Prodi, R. (2001). 'Looking towards Laeken', Speech by Romano Prodi to the plenary session of the European Parliament, SPEECH/01/590, Brussels, 28 November 2001.

Quaglia, L. (2011). 'The 'Old' and 'New' Politics of Financial Services Regulation in the European Union, paper presented at the Critical Political Economy Network Conference 18–19 February, Göthe Universität, Frankfurt.

Rachman, G. (2011). *Zero-Sum Future: American Power in an Age of Anxiety* (Simon & Schuster).

Rappaport, A. (1998). *Creating Shareholder Value: A Guide For managers and Investors* (New York and London: Free Press).

Rappaport, A. (2006). '10 Ways to Create Shareholder Value', *Harvard Business Review* 84: 66–77.

Reardon, J. (2011). 'Venezuelan President Increases University and Public Sector Wages by over 40%'. Venezuelanalysis.com. 28 April. Available at: http://venezuelanalysis.com/news/6158.

Reich, R. (2010). 'Why Obama must take on Wall Street', *Financial Times* January 13, p. 11.

Reinhart, C.M. and Rogoff, K.S. (2008). Banking Crises: An Equal Opportunity Menace. *NBER Working Paper Series* Working Paper 14587, pp. 1–82.

Reisen, H. (2008). *How to spend it: Commodity And non-commodity Sovereign Wealth Funds* Deutsche Bank Research, Research Note 28, 18 July 2008.

RGE Monitor (2009a). 'What Do We Know About the Strategy of the China Investment Corporation?', 17 August 2009.

RGE Monitor (2009b). 'How Significant Are Chinese Steps towards Internationalization of the Renminbi?', 24 October.

Ritholz, B. with A. Task (2009). *Bailout Nation: How Greed and Easy Money Corrupted Wall Street and Shook the World Economy* (Hoboken NJ: John Wiley & Sons).

Robinson, J. (1953). 'The Production Function and the Theory of Capital', *The Review of Economic Studies* 21(2): 81–106.

Robinson, W. (1996). *Promoting Polyarchy: Globalization, US Intervention, and Hegemony* (Cambridge: CUP).

Robinson, W. (2008). Latin America and Global Capitalism: A Critical Globalization Perspective (Baltimore: JHUP).

Robinson, W.I. (2004). *A Theory of Global Capitalism. Production, Class, and State in a Transnational World* (Baltimore and London: John Hopkins University Press).

Robinson, W.I. (2010). 'The Crisis of Global Capitalism', in Martin Konings (ed.) *The Great Credit Crash* (London: Verso).

Robinson W. and J. Harris (2000). 'Towards a global ruling class? Globalization and the Transnational Capitalist Class', *Science & Society* 64(1): 11–54

Rosenstein, Jay (1989). 'Greenspan Urges Expanded Powers to Help US Banks in Global Markets', *American Banker* 15 June, 154(116): 1.

Rowland, K. (2011). 'Business Community lauds Obama's new chief of staff; But Daley note a favourite of progressives', *The Washington Post* January 7, Section A, p. 3.

Roxburgh, C., et al. (July 2009). *The new power brokers: How oil, Asia, hedge funds and private equity are faring in the financial crisis* (McKinsey Global Institute) (www.mckinsey.com/mgi).

Roxburgh, C., S. Lund, T. Wimmer, E. Amar, C. Atkins, J. Kwek, R. Dobbs, and J. Manyika (2010). *Debt and Deleveraging: The Global Credit Bubble and its Economic Consequences* (London: McKinsey Global Institute).

Roy, William G. (1997) *Socializing Capital: The Rise of the Large Industrial Corporation in America* (Pinceton, NJ: Princeton University Press).

Ruggie, J.G. (1982). 'International Regimes, Transactions, and Change: Embedded Liberalism in the Postwar Economic Order', *International Organization* 36(2): 379–415.

Rupert, M. (1995). *Producing Hegemony: The Politics of Mass Production and American Global Power* (Cambridge: Cambridge University Press).

Saad-Filho, A. (2010). 'Crisis *in* neoliberalism or crisis *of* neoliberalism', in Leo Panitch, Greg Albo and Vivek Chibber (eds), pp. 242–259.

Sachs, J. (ed.) (1990). *Developing Country Debt and Economic Performance Vol.2: Country Studies: Argentina, Bolivia, Brazil, Mexico* (Chicago: University of Chicago Press).

Sader E. (2008). 'The Weakest Link? Neoliberalism in Latin America', *New Left Review* 52: 5–31.

Saich, T. (2011). *Governance and Politics of China*, 3rd edn (Houndmills: Palgrave Macmillan).

Salles-Filho, S., da Silveira, M., Luz, X, Bonacelli, M. B. (2009). *How to Build a Globally Competitive High-Tech Firm with No Internal R&D: Contractual Innovation in the Brazilian Aeronautics Industry*, paper for the SASE-Conference, Paris 2009.

Sarai, D. (2008). 'US Structural Power and the Internationalization of the US Treasury', in L, Pantich and M. Konings (eds) *American Empire and the Political*

Economy of Global Finance (Basingstoke and New York: Palgrave Macmillan), pp. 71–89.

Sauvant, K.P. and K. Davies (2010). What will an appreciation of China's currency do to inward and outward FDI? *Columbia FDI Perspectives* No. 30.

Schamis, H. (2006). 'Populism, Socialism, and Democratic Institutions', *Journal of Democracy* 17(4): 20–34.

Scharpf, F. (2008). 'Der einzige Weg ist, dem EuGH nicht zu folgen' *Mitbestimmung* 7(8).

Schepel, H. and Wesseling. R. (1997). 'The legal community: judges, lawyers, officials and clerks in the writing of Europe', *European Law Journal* 3(2): 165–188.

Schlesinger, J.M. (2002). 'Did Washington Set the Stage for Current Business Turmoil?', *Wall Street Journal* 17 October: A1.

Schmidt, V.A. (2003). 'French Capitalism Transformed. Yet Still a Third Variety of Capitalism', *Economy and Society* 32: 526–554.

Schneider, B. R. (2009). *Hierarchical Market Economies and Varieties of Capitalism in Latin America* (Boston: Massachusetts Institute of Technology).

Schneider, B. R. and Soskice, D. (2009). 'Inequality in Developed Countries and Latin America: Coordinated, Liberal and Hierarchical Systems', *Economy and Society* 30(1): 17–52.

Schrank, A. (2009). 'Understanding Latin American Political Economy: Varieties of Capitalism or Fiscal Sociology?', *Economy and Society* 30(1): 53–61.

Schwartz, H. M. (2000). *States versus Markets. The Emergence of a Global Economy*, 2nd edn (Houndmills: Palgrave Macmillan).

Schwartz, H. M. (2009). *Subprime Nation. American Power, Global Capital, and the Housing Bubble* (Ithaca, NY: Cornell University Press).

Schwartz, H. M. (2011). Sovereign Wealth Funds and Varieties of Hybridization, unpublished paper.

Scott, J. (1991). *Social Network Analysis. A Handbook* (London, Newbury Park, New Dehli: Sage Publications).

Scott, J. and P. J. Carrington (eds) (2011). *The Sage Handbook of Social Network Analysis* (Sage).

Seager, H. (1912). 'The Impatience Theory of Interest', *American Economic Review* 2: 835–7.

Servan-Schreiber, J.J. (1968). *The American Challenge* (London: Hamish Hamilton).

Setser, B., and R. Ziemba (2009). How Much Do the Major Sovereign Wealth Funds Manage? *RGE Monitor* 3 August 2009 (available at www.rgemonitor.com).

Sharma, A. (2006). 'Flexibility, Employment and Labour Market Reforms in India', *Economic and Political Weekly* 2078–2085.

Sharpe, W. F. (1964). 'Capital Asset Prices – A Theory of Market Equilibrium Under Conditions of Risk', *Journal of Finance* XIX: 425–42.

Shemirani, Manda (2011). *Sovereign Wealth Funds and International Political Economy* (Farnham: Ashgate).

Shih, V. (2008). *Factions and Finance in China. Elite Conflict and Inflation* (Cambridge: Cambridge University Press).

Shih, V. (2009). 'Tools of Survival: Sovereign Wealth Funds in Singapore and China', *Geopolitics* 14(20): 328–344.

Shleifer A. and Vishny, R.W. (1996 and 1997). 'A Survey of Corporate Governance' in *NBER Working Paper*, No. 5554 and *Journal of Finance* 52(2): 737–783.

Shonfield, A. (1965). *Modern Capitalism* (New York: Oxford University Press).

Shortgen, F. (2006). Protectionist Capitalists vs Capitalist Communists: CNOOC's Failed Unocal Bid in Perspective, *Asia Pacific Perspectives* VI (2), 2–10.

Shoup, L.H. and W. Minter (2004 [1977]). *Imperial Brain Trust: The Council on Foreign Relations and United States Foreign Policy* (Lincoln, NE: Authors Choice Press).

Silver, B.J. (2003). *Forces of Labour: Workers' Movements and Globalisation Since 1870* (Cambridge: Cambridge University Press).

Skidmore, D. (2005). 'Understanding the Unilateralist Turn in U.S. Foreign Policy', *Foreign Policy Analysis* 1(2): 207–28.

Sklair L (2001). *The Transnational Capitalist Class* (Oxford: Blackwell Publishers).

Skocpol, Theda (ed.) (1984). *Vision and method in historical sociology* (Cambridge: Cambridge University Press).

Soederberg, S. (2004). *The Politics of the New International Financial Architecture: Reimposing Neoliberal Dominance in the Global South* (London: Zed Books).

Soederberg, S. (2010). *Corporate Power and Ownership in Contemporary Capitalism. The Politics of Resistance and Domination* (London and New York: Routledge).

Sombart, W. (1932/1987). *Die Zukunft des Kapitalismus* (Berlin-Charlottenburg: Buchholz & Weisswange).

Sraffa, P. (1960). *Production of Commodities by Means of Commodities. Prelude to a Critique of Economic Theory* (Cambridge: Cambridge University Press).

Stanford, J. (2008). *Economics for Everyone. A Short Guide to the Economics of Capitalism* (London: Pluto Press).

Steil, B. (2010). *China, the dollar, and the return of the Triffin dilemma*, What Matters McKinsey&Company, 12 January (http://whatmatters.mckinseydigital.com, 30 August 2010).

Stelzer, I. (2004). *The Neocon Reader* (Grove Press: New York).

Stephens, P. (2010) 'Three Years On – And the Markets are Masters Again', *Financial Times* 30 July: 7.

Stevens P. (2008) 'National Oil Companies and International Oil Companies in the Middle East: Under the Shadow of Government and the Resource Nationalism Cycle', *Journal of World Energy Law & Business* 1(1): 5–30.

Stiglitz J. and Bilmes, L. (2008). *The Three Trillion Warfare* (W.W. Norton & Company Inc. New York: London).

Stockhammer, E. (2008). 'Some Stylized Facts on the Finance-dominated Accumulation Regime', *Competition and Change* 12(2): 184–202.

Stokes D (2007). 'Blood for oil? Global Capital, Counter-insurgency and the Dual Logic of American Energy Security', *Review of International Studies* 33(2): 245–264.

Strange, Susan (1996) *The Retreat of the State: the Diffusion of Power in the World Economy* (Cambridge: CUP).

Streeck, W. (1998). *The Internationalization of Industrial Relations in Europe: Prospects and Problems* MPIfG Discussion Paper 98/2 (Cologne).

Streeck, W. and Schmitter, P.C. (1991). 'From National Corporatism to Transnational Pluralism: Organized Interests in the Single European Market', *Politics and Society* 19(2): 133–164.

Sutcliffe, Bob (2002). 'How Many Capitalisms? Historical Materialism in the Debates about Imperialism and Globalisation' in Mark Rupert and Hazel Smith (eds) *Historical Materialism and globalization* (London: Routledge).

Sweezy, P.M. (1941). 'The Decline of the Investment Banker', *Antioch Review* 1(1): 63–8.

Sweezy, P.M. (1942). *The Theory of Capitalist Development: Principles of Marxian Political Economy* (New York: Monthly Review Press).

Sweezy, P.M. (1981). 'Investment Banking Revisited', *Antioch Review* 39(2): 241–251.

Sweezy, P.M. (1994). 'The Triumph of Financial Capital', *Monthly Review* 46(2): 1–11.

Taibbi, M. (2009). 'The Great American Bubble Machine', *Rolling Stone* 1082/1083: 52–62.

Taibbi, M. (2010). 'Wall Street's Big Win', *Rolling Stone* 1111: 57–62.

Taylor, H. and Nölke, A. (2010). 'Indian Multinationals and their Institutional Environment: A Varieties of Capitalism Perspective' in Egbert, H. and Esser, C. (eds) *Aspects in Varieties of Capitalism: Dynamics, Economic Crisis, New Players* (Saarbrücken: Lambert Academic Publishing), pp. 41–64.

Ten Brink, T. (2010). *Strukturmerkmale des chinesischen Kapitalismus* MPIfG Discussion Paper 10/01 (Cologne: Max Planck Institute for the Study of Societies).

Tett, G. (2009). *Fool's Gold – How Unrestrained Greed Corrupted a Dream, Shattered Global Markets and Unleashed a Catastrophe* (London, Little, Brown).

The Economist (1987). 'A survey of Wall Street: Bustle, Bustle', 11 July, pp. 1–18.

The Economist (2007). 'Black Boxes', 19 May, p. 11.

The Economist (2008). 'Capitalism at Bay' (Leader), 16 October, p. 12.

The Economist (2009a). 'Sinecures in peril', 29 October.

The Economist (2009b). 'Now for the long term' Matthew Bishop, 13 November.

The Economist (2010a). 'A different class. Would giving long-term shareholders more clout improve corporate governance?', 18 February.

The Economist (2010b). 'Falling in love again with the state', 31 March.

The Guardian (2009). 'Rio's deal with Chinalco collapses', 4 June.

The Guardian (2011). 'Bob Diamond stands firm against MPs' calls he forgo his bonus', http://www.guardian.co.uk/business/2011/jan/11/bob-diamond-stands-firm-mp-bonus, 11 January.

Tidow, S. (2003). 'The Emergence of European Employment Policy as a Transnational Political Arena' in Overbeek, H. (ed.) *The Political Economy of European Employment. European Integration and the Transnationalization of the (Un)employment Question* (London: Routledge), pp. 77–98.

Truman, E. M. (2007). *The Management of China's International Reserves: China and a SWF Scoreboard*, paper prepared for Conference on China's Exchange Rate Policy, Peterson Institute for International Economics, 19 October.

Truman, E. M. (2008). *Sovereign Wealth Funds: New Challenges from a Changing Landscape*, Testimony before the Subcommittee on Domestic and International Monetary Policy, Trade and Technology, Financial Services Committee, US House of Representatives, 10 September 2008.

Tsolakis, A. (2010a). 'Opening Up Open Marxist Theories of the State: A Historical Materialist Critique', *British Journal of Politics and International Relations* 12(3): 387–407.

Tsolakis, A. (2010b). *The Reform of the Bolivian State: Domestic Politics in the Context of Globalization* (Boulder: Lynne Rienner Publishers/First Forum Press).

Tsolakis, A. (2011). 'Defining neoliberalism and the 'left' in Latin America', Unpublished paper.

Turner, A. (2011). Reforming finance: are we being radical enough? 2011 Clare College Distinguished Lecture in Economics and Public Policy, 18 February 2011. Cambridge, UK.

Tyers, R. and Y. Zhang (2011). 'Appreciating the Renminbi', *The World Economy*, pp. 265–297.

UNICE (1974). 'Proposition d'un reglement (C.E.E.) du Conseil sur le controle des concentrations', January 1974.

UNICE (1987). 'Merger Control at Community Level', UNICE Declaration, November 1987.

US Chamber of Commerce (2002). *The State of American Business 2002* (United States Chamber of Commerce: Washington DC).

US Chamber of Commerce (2004). *The State of American Business 2004* (United States Chamber of Commerce: Washington DC).

Useem M. (1984). *The Inner Circle. Large Corporations and the Rise of Business Political Activity in the U.S. and the U.K.* (Oxford University Press: New York and Oxford).

Van Apeldoorn, B. (2002). *Transnational Capitalism and the Struggle Over European Integration* (London and New York: Routledge).

Van Apeldoorn, B. (2004). 'Theorizing the Transnational: A Historical Materialist Approach', *Journal of International Relations and Development* 7(2): 142–176.

Van Apeldoorn, B. and N. de Graaff (forthcoming). 'Corporate Elite Networks and US post-Cold War Grand Strategy from Clinton to Obama', *European Journal of International Relations*.

Van Apeldoorn B., and S. B. Hager (2010). 'The Social Purpose of New Governance: Lisbon and the Limits of Legitimacy', *Journal of International Relations and Development* 13 (3): 209–238.

Van Apeldoorn, B. and Horn, L. (2007a). 'The Marketisation of Corporate Control: A Critical Political Economy Perspective', *New Political Economy* 12(2): 211–235.

Van Apeldoorn, B., Drahokoupil, J. and L. Horn (eds) (2008). *Contradictions and Limits of Neoliberal European Governance: From Lisbon to Lisbon* (Basingstoke: Palgrave Macmillan).

Van der Linde, C. (2005). *Energy in a Changing World*, Inaugural Lecture, December 2005, Clingendael Energy Papers No. 11, CIEP 03/2005, The Hague: Clingendael International Energy Programma, Groningen: Energy Delta Institute.

Van der Pijl, K. (1984). *The Making of an Atlantic Ruling Class* (London: Verso).

Van der Pijl, K. (1998). *Transnational Classes and International Relations* (London: Routledge).

Van der Pijl, K. (2006). *Global Rivalries. From Cold War to Iraq* (Pluto Press: London, Ann Arbor, MI).

Van der Pijl, K. (2010). Will Asia Save Capitalism? Class Struggle and Contender State Development in Contemporary China. Unpublished manuscript.

Van Gennip, J. (2006). 'Energy and Security – A Key Variable in National Security Calculations', NATO Parliamentary Assembly, http://www.nato-pa. int/Default.asp?SHORTCUT=917 (visited 10 June 2007).

Veblen, T. (1923/1964). *Absentee Ownership and Business Enterprise in Recent Times*, Reprints of Economic Classics (New York: Augustus M. Kelly).

Villiers, C. (2006). 'The Directive on Employee Involvement in the European Company: Its Role in European Corporate Governance and Industrial Relations', *International Journal of Comparative Labour Law and Industrial Relations* 22(2): 183–211.

Vitols, S. and N. Kluge (eds) (2011). *The Sustainable Company* (Brussels: ETUI).

Vivoda V. (2009) 'Resource Nationalism, Bargaining and International Oil Companies: Challenges and Change in the New Millennium', *New Political Economy* 14(4): 517–534.

Voice of Russia (2010). 'Russia, China start yuan trade', December 13.

Wade, Robert (2008). 'Financial Regime Change?', *New Left Review* 53(September–October): 5–21.

Wälde, T. (2008). 'Renegotiating Acquired Rights in the Oil and Gas Industries: Industry and Political Cycles Meet the Rule of Law', *Journal of World Energy Law & Business* 1 (1): 55–97.

Wallerstein, I. (1984). 'Socialist States: Mercantilist Strategies and Revolutionary Objectives' in I. Wallerstein, *The Politics of the World-Economy. The States, the Movements and the Civilizations* (Cambridge: Cambridge University Press), pp. 86–96.

Wallerstein, I. (2000). 'A Left Politics for the 21st Century? Or, Theory and Praxis Once Again', *New Political Science* 22(2): 143–59.

Wasserman S. and K. Faust (1994). *Social Network Analysis: Methods and Applications* (Cambridge, New York, Melbourne: Cambridge University Press).

Webber, J. (2008). 'Rebellion to Reform in Bolivia, Part I: Domestic Class Structure, Latin American Trends and Capitalist Imperialism', *Historical Materialism* 16(2): 23–58.

Weiss, M. (2008). *Sovereign Wealth Funds: Background and Policy Issues for Congress* Washington DC, Congressional Research Service, CRS Report for Congress.

Wen J. (2011). How China is winning the fight against inflation, *Financial Times* 24 June, p. 9.

Westad, O. A. (2005). *The Global Cold War: Third World Interventions and the Making of Our Times* (Cambridge: Cambridge University Press).

White House (1995). *A National Security Strategy of Engagement and Enlargement* Washington: The White House (February).

White House (1998). *A National Security Strategy for a New Century* Washington: The White House (October).

White House (2002). *The National Security Strategy of the United States of America* Washington: The White House (September).

White House (2006). *The National Security Strategy of the United States of America* Washington: The White House (March).

White House (2010). *National Security Strategy* Washington: The White House (May).

Whitehead, L. (1997). 'Beyond Neo-Liberalism: Bolivia's Capitalization as a Route to Universal Entitlements and Substantive Citizenship Rights?', in Margaret Hollis Peirce (ed.) *Capitalization: A Bolivian Model of Social and Economic Reform* (Boulder: North South Centre Press).

Whitehead, L. (2002). 'The Viability of Democracy' in John Crabtree and Lawrence Whitehead (eds) *Towards Democratic Viability: The Bolivian Experience* (London: Palgrave).

Wicksell, K. (1911 [1934]). *Lectures on Political Economy, Volume 1* (London: Routledge & Kegan).

Wigger, A. (2007). 'Towards A Market-Based Approach: The Privatization and Micro-Economization of EU Antitrust Law Enforcement'. Chapter 6 in B. van

Apeldoorn, A. Nölke and H. Overbeek *The Transnational Politics of Corporate Governance Regulation* (London and New York: Routledge).

Wigger, A. (2009). 'The Political Role Of Transnational Experts In Shaping EU Competition Policy: Towards A Pan-European System Of Private Enforcement', *Legisprudence* 3(2): 251–75.

Wilks, S. (2005). 'Agency Escape: Decentralization or Dominance of the European Commission in the Modernization of Competition Policy?', *Governance* 18(3): 431–452.

Williams, K. (2000). 'From Shareholder Value to Present-day Capitalism', *Economy and Society* 29(1): 1–12.

Williams, W.A. (2009 [1959/72]). *The Tragedy of American Diplomacy*, 50th anniversary edn (W.W. Norton & Company: New York).

Wilmore, J. (2007). 'A broken stick: IMF conditionality in Latin America', presented at the 48th *Annual Congress of the International Studies Association*, Chicago.

Wilpert, G. (2007). *Changing Venezuela by Taking Power: The History and Policies of the Chávez Government* (London and New York: Verso).

Wilson III, E. J. (1987). 'World Politics and International Energy Markets', *International Organization* 41(1): 125–149.

Windolf, P. (2005). 'Was ist Finanzmarkt-Kapitalismus?', *Kölner Zeitschrift für Soziologie und Sozialpsychologie* Sonderheft 45: 20–57.

WIR (2007). 'Transnational Corporations in Extractive Industries', *The World Investment Report* UNCTAD, United Nations.

Wolf, C. (2008). 'Does ownership matter? The performance and efficiency of state oil vs. private oil (1987–2006)', Cambridge Working Paper in Economics, EPRG Working Paper no. 0831 (Cambridge: University of Cambridge).

Wolf, Martin (2009). 'Seeds of its own destruction', *Financial Times* 9 March, p. 7.

Wolf, Martin (2011). 'How China should rule the world', *Financial Times* 23 March, p. 11.

Wolfe, T. (1987) *Bonfire of the Vanities* (Toronto: Bantam Books).

Wood, E. M. (2003). *Empire of Capital* (London and New York: Verso).

World Bank (WB) (1997). Memorandum of the President of the IBRD to the Executive Directors on a Country Assistance Strategy for the Republic of Venezuela. April 8. Report No. 16471-VE.

WB (1998). *Bolivia Country Assistance Review* Operation Evaluation Department Report No. 17957, 5 June.

WB (2002). Memorandum of the President of the IBRD to the Executive Directors on an Interim Country Assistance Strategy for the Bolivarian Republic of Venezuela. November 18. Report No.25125-VE.

WB (2003). Memorandum of the President of the IBRD and the IFC to the Executive Directors on a Country Assistance Strategy 2003–2007 for the Federative Republic of Brazil in Support of a more Equitable, Sustainable and Competitive Brazil. 10 November. Report No. 27043-BR.

WB (2006a). *Poverty Reduction and Growth: From Vicious to Virtuous Circles* (Washington, DC: The World Bank Group).

WB (2006b). IBRD and IFC Country Partnership Strategy Progress Report for the Federative Republic of Brazil for the period FY2004-2007. 8 May. Report No. 36116-BR.

WB (2009). 'Bolivia Interim Strategy Note', 7 June, available at http://web.world-bank.org/WBSITE/EXTERNAL/COUNTRIES/LACEXT/BOLIVIAEXTN/0,,cont entMDK:20198460~pagePK:141137~piPK:141127~theSitePK:322279,00.html

WB (2010). IBRD and IFC Country Partnership Strategy Progress Report for the Federative Republic of Brazil for the period FY2008-2011. 11 March. Report No. 53356-BR.

WB (2011). *Global Development Horizons 2011. Multipolarity: The New Global Economy* (Washington, DC: World Bank).

World Trade Organization (WTO) (2007). *Ten Benefits of the WTO Trading System.* Geneva. Available at http://www.wto.org/English/res_e/doload_e/10b_e.pdf>

Wright, L. (2008). CIC and SAFE: Coordination or Bureaucratic Conflict? *China Stakes* June 24, available at http://www.chinastakes.com/2008/6/ (accessed on 25 January 2010).

Wu, F. and A. Seah (2008). 'Would China's Sovereign Wealth Fund Be a Menace to the USA?', *China & World Economy* 16(4): 33–47.

Wu, F. R. Pan, D. Wang (2010). 'Renminbi's Potential to Become a Global Currency', *China & World Economy* 18(1): 63–81.

Xiao Geng (2010). *China's exchange rate policy and what it means for the dollar* What Matters (McKinsey&Company), 13 January, available at http://what-matters.mckinseydigital.com (accessed on 30 August 2010).

Xu Y. and G. Bahgat (eds) (2010). *The Political Economy of Sovereign Wealth Funds* (Houndmills: Palgrave Macmillan).

Yergin, D. (1991). *The Prize. The Epic Quest For Oil, Money and Power* (New York, London, Toronto, Sydney: Free Press).

Yergin, Daniel (2006). 'Ensuring Energy Security', *Foreign Affairs* April/March 85(2): 69.

Zadeh-Hossein, I. (2008). 'Is There An Oil Shortage?', *Information Clearing House* http://www.informationclearinghouse.info/article20271.htm.

Zhang M. and F. He (2009). 'China's Sovereign Wealth Fund: Weaknesses and Challenges', *China & World Economy* 17(1): 101–116.

Zhou, S. (2009). 'BRIC, SVO Discuss "Super-Sovereignty" Currency, USD Alternatives', *ChinaStakes* 26 October.

Ziemba, R. (November 2007). 'Responses to Sovereign Wealth Funds: Are "Draconian" Measures on the Way?', *RGE Monitor.*

Ziemba, R. (2010). A Glimpse Inside the CIC's Portfolio, *RGE Economonitor* 7 February.

Zumbansen, P. (2006). *The Parallel Worlds of Corporate Governance and Labor Law* CLPE Research Paper No. 6/2006.

Index